11-28-73

Edited by Peter Haining
THE GENTLEWOMEN OF EVIL
THE SATANISTS
A CIRCLE OF WITCHES
THE WILD NIGHT COMPANY
THE HOLLYWOOD NIGHTMARE
THE CLANS OF DARKNESS
GOTHIC TALES OF TERROR
THE LUCIFER SOCIETY
THE MAGICIANS
NIGHTFRIGHTS

By Peter Haining
THE ANATOMY OF WITCHCRAFT

the magicians

the magicians
the occult in fact and fiction

edited by PETER HAINING

introduction by COLIN WILSON

New York | Taplinger Publishing Company

First published in the United States in 1973 by
TAPLINGER PUBLISHING CO., INC.
New York, New York

Library of Congress Catalog Card Number: 72-9806

ISBN 0-8008-5045-9

ACKNOWLEDGEMENTS

The editor wishes to acknowledge his gratitude to the following authors,
agents, and executors for permission to include copyright material in this
volume:

"Rosa Alchemica" by W. B. Yeats. From *Collected Short Stories*. Copy-
right 1926 by W. B. Yeats; copyright renewed 1954 by Macmillan & Co.,
Ltd., London, and reprinted with their permission.
"Strange Occurrence in Clerkenwell" by Arthur Machen. From *The
Three Imposters*. Copyright 1930 by Arthur Machen. Reprinted with
the permission of Methuen & Co. Ltd., London.
"Playing with Fire" by Sir Arthur Conan Doyle. Copyright 1926 by
Arthur Conan Doyle; copyright renewed 1958 by the Author's Execu-
tors, and reproduced with their permission.
"Breath of Allah" by Sax Rohmer. From *Tales of Secret Egypt*. Copyright
1918 by Sax Rohmer. Reprinted with the permission of Methuen & Co.
Ltd., London.
"Lucifer Over London" by Lewis Spence. Copyright 1951 by Hulton
Educational Publications Ltd., London, for *Mystery,* and reprinted
with their permission.
"The Witch Cult" by Gerald Gardner. From *High Magic's Aid,* published
by Michael Houghton Ltd. Copyright © 1956 by the Author's Executors, and reproduced by permission of the author's estate.

The editor also wishes to thank Colin Wilson for his Introduction and
John Symonds for his invaluable advice and assistance.

For Philippa, Richard and Sean - as always

1774126

Acknowledgement

The Editor is indebted to Colin Wilson for his Introduction and assistance in the selection of material.

Contents

'Let him who, in spite of the warnings of this volume, determines to work evil, be assured that the evil will recoil on himself and that he will be struck by the reflex current.'

S. L. MacGregor Mathers,
Founder Hermetic Order
of the Golden Dawn

First-hand experience of occult rituals and their power is something
denied to, and, perhaps equally, not sought by, the average person.
The fear of the unknown, be it based on superstitious grounds or
a dread of tampering with the ill-defined forces of evil, has empow-
ered these activities with an aura of great mystery and uncertainty.
Those, however, who have chosen to 'tread the secret paths', to
quote one authority, have in the main cloaked themselves in
anonymity, and sought to work and practise in the utmost privacy
far from the curious eyes of society. Yet for all this secrecy, the
last hundred years boast a formidable number of people whose
reputation as experimenters in the occult are known far and wide :
Aleister Crowley, dabbler in black magic and known grandiosely
as 'The Great Beast'; S. L. MacGregor Mathers, founder of the
famous Hermetic Order of the Golden Dawn and transcriber of
ancient rituals; Madame Blavatsky, propounder of a new occult
philosophy and perhaps more deeply versed in the mystic arts than
any other woman of modern times; Sir Arthur Conan Doyle,
creator of Sherlock Holmes and devotee of spiritualism; Gerald
Gardner, the motivating force behind the recent widespread resur-
gence of interest in the ancient religion of *Wica* or witchcraft; and
so on – the list is really quite extensive. Indeed, since the later part
of the last century there has taken place what W. B. Yeats described
as 'the revolt of soul against intellect' when certain people in a
society seemingly dedicated to materialism and the crushing of the
romantic feeling have determined to seek the old ways and a communion with the ancient spirits, a course which led them through
either 'white' (good) or 'black' (evil) magic, on to a goal of outer-
world satisfaction and fulfilment. These were the Magi or Master
Magicians.

For a number of years I have been closely involved in investigat-
ing and writing about the occult and during my researches I have
had the opportunity to study not only the factual writings of these
men, but in certain cases their excursions into fiction (some, indeed,
became particularly famous in this area). As I read I became increasingly aware of how often the stories and novels were merely the
medium in which the authors imparted further truths about what
they had learned of the mystic arts. Sometimes a man (or woman)

had found a tale of fiction the most convenient method of recounting an attitude or practice – reason for which, in most cases, one can only hazard a guess – with the result that as I built up a collection of these items a unique picture of the occult began to emerge. Hence, selecting still more closely from the writings of each of the most prominent author-magicians of the period I saw it was virtually possible to tell the story of magic through their work. The result is the present book.

In this volume, then, you will find stories and extracts which cover virtually every aspect of the occult and are truly remarkable in that in each case the author is a person with practical experience of his subject. No such collection has been attempted before and, apart from its inherent interest for all those who enjoy a good tale for its own sake, throws fresh and revealing light on the darkest corners of the supernatural. If you have ever shuddered over purely imaginary tales of magic and mystery, read now a group of stories that provide for even more surprises, yet are authentic in almost every detail. In a sentence, the world of the Occult is one of strange experience and the impossible becoming possible.

For myself, I conclude this task with the regret which all anthologists feel when their work is over, but also with some thankfulness for, as the master French magician Eliphas Levi wrote of himself, 'The author of this book has dared many things in his life and never has fear retained his thought a prisoner – *yet it is not at the same time without legitimate dread that he approaches the magical doctrine.*'

PETER HAINING

Introduction

COLIN WILSON

The last great 'magical revival' took place in France towards the end of the nineteenth century, and spread from there to Germany and England. When it petered out, round about 1900, it seemed a fair assumption that the western world had finally seen the last of magic. When I became interested in the subject – in 1950 – I would certainly have taken a bet on it. And now, as we enter the seventies, we suddenly find ourselves in the midst of another 'occult revival', as unexpected and as unexplainable as the ones that preceded it.

For this is the odd thing about these revivals – that they seem to be so weirdly unpredictable. The great age of witchcraft came to an end in the late 1600s, and the age of Newton and Leibniz and Priestley began. In 1750, any historian who predicted a magical revival would have been regarded as mad; but by 1770, Cagliostro and St Germain and Mesmer were on the scene, and astrologers and alchemists were as popular as two centuries earlier. With the death of Cagliostro in the papal prison in 1795, the 'revival' stopped as abruptly as it had begun. A new age of science and industry dawned; the dark Satanic mills roared day and night. (And Blake's 'Satanic mills' are not those of the industrial revolution, but of logic and science.) Surely the age of magic was at an end? Then the Fox sisters began their spirit rapping; Daniel Dunglas Home made tables float in the air; Eliphas Levi conjured up the spirit of Apollonius of Tyana; the sinister Abbé Boullan performed sexual rites with the aid of a nun; Mathers, Woodman and Westcott founded the Order of the Golden Dawn; Madame Blavatsky and Colonel Olcott founded the Theosophical Society. Occultism swept from America to Russia in the biggest revival so far.

It is true that interest in the occult is usually a romantic reaction against 'civilisation'; most of the great figures of occultism are *poètes manqués*. In a few cases – Crowley and A. E., for example –

the poetry was by no means bad; and this increases our suspicion that magic is basically a form of fantasy, of escape from the boredom of everyday living. But although there is some truth in this, it misses the real point. 'Magic' springs from man's recognition that he possesses powers that are inaccessible to everyday awareness. Man has spent thousands of years learning to master this physical world in which he lives; but in learning to deal with everyday reality, he has also become its slave. It is all very well for Milton to talk about 'thoughts that wander through eternity', but most people's thoughts never go much further than next year's Cup Tie or World Series. Like a deep-sea diver, man has put heavy weights on his spirit to hold him on the bottom, and he doesn't know how to take them off.

And yet all intelligent people *know* that the spirit can soar like a bird. 'Every man has an innate inclination to fly,' remarked Hoffmann, 'and I have known serious, respectable people who in the late evening fill themselves with champagne so as to rise like a balloon.' 'Flying' is obviously a part of human destiny, and this applies to businessmen as well as poets. You only have to set out on a holiday to experience something that can only be described as 'expansion of the senses' : your faculties seem to *stretch out*, as if your nerves had been extended like strands of a spider's web; everything strikes you as fresh and exciting and full of possibilities. And occasionally, these moods of 'expansion' become so intense that they might be described as 'cosmic consciousness'. One of the classic descriptions of such an experience occurs in *The Brothers Karamazov*, where Alyosha walks about into a starry night, and suddenly feels as if there are threads linking his soul with all the stars; he flings himself down, weeping and kissing the earth.

Now the rationalist would dismiss this by saying it is 'just a feeling'. There aren't *really* threads between Alyosha's soul and the stars. According to this view, mystical experiences have no more objective reality than the pink elephants of an alcoholic. And this is the very root of the argument. For an 'occultist' would reply that there are thousands of authenticated cases of telepathy, second sight, thaumaturgic cures ('miracles'), premonitions of danger or disaster. . . .

Take this example, which can be found in *Doubtful Schoolmaster*, the autobiography of an ex-headmaster, Hugh Heckstall Smith. He was standing by a piano, looking through some music. An Irish girl, sitting nearby, said : 'No, it isn't there'. 'What isn't?' 'What you're looking for – Beethoven's Appassionata.' She was right. I mention this case because Hugh is an old friend; he is a Quaker, not in the least interested in the occult – his real enthusiasm being for mathematical physics. In the same book, he tells a story of his schooldays. His father arrived at his school one day having bought him a cycling cape. His father started to say : 'You won't guess where I bought this. . . .' 'Don't tell me,' said Hugh, 'I'll tell you.' And he proceeded to describe the small second-hand shop, many miles away. I asked him how he could be so certain. 'I don't know. As he spoke, I suddenly got a clear picture of the second-hand shop.'

You will observe the jump in my argument – from Alyosha's moment of 'cosmic consciousness' to a case of ordinary telepathy. But this *is* the basic assumption of magic and occultism : that if we could 'free' our senses, at a moment's notice, and allow them to float and stretch out to the stars, we would become 'aware' of all kinds of things that we do not usually know. All animals possess a certain degree of 'psychic powers' – 'second sight', the homing instinct, sense of danger. Human beings do not *need* these powers – at least, not very often. In the long course of evolution, we have 'retracted our occult faculties, like a snail drawing in its horns'. We *had* to : we had to remain alert and concentrated on the present; we had to learn to do boring things like building houses and digging sewers. But we have now reached a point in evolution where this no longer applies. Western man has too much leisure. Most of his psychological problems today are due to boredom. He needs to 'expand' again, to re-activate the latent faculties.

This is not as difficult as it sounds. To begin with, it requires mainly a kind of relaxation. Here is an example. A couple of years ago, I took my family to Disneyland, near Los Angeles; it is basically a vast amusement park covering many acres. I left them there for the morning, while I went off to lecture at a nearby college. I arrived back around midday, and then remembered I had forgotten to arrange exactly where to meet them. In theory, I could have spent the afternoon wandering through the crowds. Instead, I deliberately relaxed and 'opened myself', then strolled wherever my feet wanted to take me. Within five minutes, I had found them. If I had remained 'tense', or tried searching systematically, it would probably have taken hours.

This makes another central point. There *are* other ways of 'opening up' : psychedelic drugs will do it; so, to a lesser extent, will alcohol. I suspect that if I had taken LSD, I might have found my family just as effectively. (The only time I have taken a psyche-delic – mescalin – I had a strong sense of acquiring powers of second sight and telepathy.) But it would have lasted for the rest of the day, and I shouldn't have been a very good guardian of my children in that state. We need to learn to 'expand' our faculties at a moment's notice, *but also to contract them again*. Cows and dogs do not possess our power of 'contraction'; it has taken us millions of years to acquire it. It would be stupid to throw it away. This is why I have always felt so strongly that drugs are *not* the answer to the problem of how to expand the senses.

I must try to be more precise about these 'inner powers'. In order to exercise them, it is necessary to use the imagination. A few months ago, I approached an occultist named Robert Leftwich, to ask for information on psycho-kinesis – the power to move physical objects by the mind alone. He obligingly sent me a kind of paper dart, made by folding a small square of paper across the middle, and also from corner to corner (so the folds look like the crosses on a Union Jack). When the folds are pinched inwards, this makes a paper dart with four fins. Leftwich told me to stick a needle in a cork, and to balance this dart on top of it – so the whole thing looks like a little roundabout. I should then tie a handkerchief across my nose and mouth – so as not to breathe on it – and try to *will* the roundabout to move. Well, I tried it until I was black in the face, and I couldn't make it budge. But I kept it beside my typewriter, and the next day, had another try. This time, to my surprise, it moved. I kept it there for several days, trying whenever I thought of it. Once I had got the knack, it seemed fairly easy to make it move. I would cup my hands around it, stare at one side, and will it to move. After a moment or so, it would start off slowly. Then I would try concentrating on the other side; the thing would come to a stop, then revolve the other way. Being a natural sceptic, I was inclined to suspect that the heat of my hands might have influenced it – like those lampshades in restaurants that turn in the heat of the bulb. Not long afterwards, I mentioned the phenom-enon to another student of the occult, Alun Hull Walton, who pointed out that the 'knack' involves using the imagination as well as the will. I immediately saw that this seemed to fit my own experience; after the first day, I *imagined* it turning as well as willing it to turn.

And this brings me to the central problem. The powers of the human imagination are so enormous that they are *dangerous*, like high-voltage electricity. It is just as well that we limit them so much. Think of what happens if you feel sick. If something distracts you – like rain pattering on the windows – you often find that the sickness has vanished. And if you can get the knack, you can learn to dissipate your sickness. It seems to depend on your *attitude*. If you use your imagination positively, not expecting to be sick, you cease to feel sick. If you feel gloomy and distracted, your imagination becomes negative and *amplifies* the nausea. People stutter and get stage-fright for the same reason. The human imagination is an enormous force. If a man can envisage something delightful or desirable, his mind stretches into the future and he becomes irresistible. As soon as he allows his imagination to become possessed by forebodings or self-pity, his strength ebbs away.

It is amazing that human beings have never recognised this. If you merely lift your hand, or wriggle your fingers, the 'trigger' is imagination. When a great pianist or violinist plays a concerto, the imaginative control is tighter, more precise. And, as Aleister Crowley points out in a passage of his autobiography, 'magic' is basically the use of this same faculty – this confident 'stretching out' of our hidden powers to produce a certain result. Most people, for example, possess the power of the 'evil eye'. Bernard Shaw, who might be assumed to be an arch sceptic, wrote in a letter of 1885 : 'All the people I ever hated died. A deadly but horrible emanation comes from the hater to his victim.' In 1925, he experienced this at first hand. He was making a speech, urging the dramatist Granville Barker to return to the theatre; suddenly he experienced an agonising pain down his back, 'as if my spine had become a bar of rusty iron'. For precisely a month he was unable to lean forward. Someone later told him that throughout his speech, Granville Barker's wife had been glaring at his back with a look of concentrated fury. I am inclined to believe that anyone with any power of concentration can exercise this power. I am equally certain that anyone who does so deliberately ruins their chance of 'expanding' the senses; for some law of reciprocity says that hatred does equal damage to both parties.

The imagination is dangerous because we do not yet know how to control it. It is rather like carrying a large, flat bowl of water across a room; if you tilt it ever so slightly, the water rushes from one side to the other, and you spill it. Imaginative people have the same trouble. When they are happy, or have something to look forward to, imagination transforms their world into a foretaste of paradise; when they are miserable or frightened, it wrecks their vitality, tears the bottom out of their self-confidence like a ship crashing into rocks. This also explains why psychedelic 'trips' often drive people insane. The mind is opened to a wider range of experience – the great stimulant of imagination. If the imagination is focused on the pleasant aspects, the experience is delightful; but if imagination is negative, the result is 'nausea' magnified many times over.

In short, we possess inner mechanisms that can flood us with ecstasy or plunge us into a horrible sense of meaninglessness. And unlike the simple mechanisms by which we start the washing machine or flush the lavatory, these are at once simple and extremely subtle. This was the subject of Proust's enormous novel : the taste of a biscuit dipped in tea suddenly brings back his childhood as though it were yesterday, but he spends years trying to repeat the trick and even then only succeeds briefly, by accident, in the twelfth volume. The mind is a vast world in itself; and, like the external world, its 'natural resources' are enormous. The romantic poets caught glimpses of gigantic inner vistas, mountain ranges and oceans; then the clouds covered the scene, and they were again trapped in the boring world of everydayness.

All this is so mysterious that I have become increasingly convinced that the legend of the 'Fall' is basically true. At some time in his remote history, man must have been godlike. Otherwise, how can we explain these powers that he glimpses in flashes? For example, the powers of mathematical prodigies, who, at the age of ten, can multiply together two eighteen-figure numbers *in the head* and produce the answer in half a minute? It is true that these prodigies normally lose their powers as they approach manhood; but they are obviously *there*, lying latent inside them, waiting to be called upon. So is the power that Proust glimpsed – to recall one's *whole* past with total reality, as if it were happening at the moment.

I do not know why man 'fell'. Perhaps just laziness; I define the problem in a novel called *The Man Without a Shadow** in a single

* Which contains a full-length portrait of Crowley. It is also called *The Sex Diary of Gerard Sorme.*

sentence : Human beings are like grandfather clocks driven by watchsprings. That is, we *have* the machinery, but not enough 'electricity' to drive it, any more than you could run an electric fire off a torch battery. We live in a kind of dream or delirium, with only brief glimpses of reality. But we possess the power to 'focus' reality – as Proust did for a moment. That power I have labelled 'Faculty X'.

And how does all this connect up with the kind of magic you will find described in this volume?

All magic springs from man's instinctive recognition that he was once a god, that there is a sleeping superman inside him, if only he could 'raise' it. Otherwise, why would the witches of the past have offered to sell their souls to the devil? Would anyone *choose* eternal damnation – which they took for granted – unless some strange power inside them stirred and said : 'I am sick of being *merely* human. I want to ride on the wind and conjure storms and feel myself the equal of the lightning.' Magic is an obscure striving towards the realisation of Faculty X. In this volume, you will learn nothing about its lengthy initiation ceremonies – starting with the necessity to copy out a whole *grimoire* (book of ritual magic) by hand, and sometimes involving months of rigorous preparation. These ceremonies are an attempt to *stir* the depths of the spirit – you might almost say, to blast them with a depth-charge. Sometimes, the ceremonies are deliberately disgusting – as can be seen in the Crowley story – because disgust also stirs the depths of the mind. I personally dislike this aspect of Crowley – crucifying cats, and so on – because I feel that it reflects a kind of immaturity, an inability to feel, a juvenile egoism, rather than any real understanding of a basic principle of magic. But there can be no doubt that Crowley was a real magician; he *could* control certain inner powers; and moral judgements must be left to the individual reader.

There are one or two stories in this volume which must be regarded as pure entertainment. I find it difficult to agree with Peter Haining that Arthur Machen, Conan Doyle and Sax Rohmer were real 'occultists', rather than literary men who dabbled in the subject. But their stories are worth reading because they catch something of the atmosphere of the 'occult revival' of the late nineteenth century. Others, I think, deserve to be taken altogether more seriously. Yeats's 'magic' was not all wishful thinking (like the fairyland of his early poems); he definitely understood something about it, something basic, as can be seen from his essay on magic in *Essays and Introductions*. Madame Blavatsky *was* an old charlatan; but she was another who knew about magic, and possessed a high degree of mediumistic powers. (I must emphasise that charlatanism and genuine powers often go together; just as, in Rasputin, charlatanism and religious mysticism went together; magical powers are often *accidental*, something that certain people are born with, and their personality and moral character may be on an altogether lower level.) Dion Fortune was an important and greatly underrated occultist, who was unfortunately born in the wrong half of the century – after the decline of magic; otherwise she would have achieved wider fame; her time is to come. Eliphas Levi was also something of a fake, and his natural powers were weaker than Madame Blavatsky's or Crowley's. (Crowley believed he was a reincarnation of Levi.) But his lifelong obsession with magic led him to understand something of its true nature, and the story of his raising of Apollonius of Tyana could well be more than 50 per cent true. As to Huysmans' description of the Black Mass, this can be taken as largely factual, the kind of thing that really was performed in Paris in the 1880s. It is interesting to note, by the way, that until this volume no full and complete translation of this Black Mass scene existed in English, various details having always been omitted.*

But what of such matters as raising the devil, or projecting the astral body (as described in Dion Fortune's story)? How seriously can these be taken?

Several years ago, an American publisher commissioned me to write a book, *The Occult*. I had always been interested in 'magic' – but in rather the same way as Yeats : that is, as a symbol of that 'other world' that the romantic poets strive to create. My attitude was basically scientific and sceptical. I suppose it still is. But as I went through the enormous amount of research required, I became increasingly impressed. Science and mathematics convince us by their *universality*; if I read a book on physics or astronomy by a Russian scientist, it sounds exactly like a book on physics or astronomy by an American or English scientist. There are no political or racial differences in this world; it is like an inner country whose landmarks looks exactly the same to *all* observers, and would prob-

---

* The Editor would like to record here his gratitude to Colin Wilson for his help in restoring these missing passages.

ably look the same to a man from Mars. In the world of magic, you expect the divergences to be enormous, because each nation has its own magical traditions, and each individual has his own temperamental peculiarities that determine the direction of his interest. What is so astonishing is that there seems to be so little contradiction or disagreement on fundamental points; the Tibetan Milarepa is likely to say something you remember from some mediaeval alchemist; an Ancient Egyptian description of 'astral travel' corresponds closely to something you found in the War Memoirs of a retired general who found himself floating over the battlefield after being blown up by a shell. It soon became apparent to me that certain basic 'psychic' or occult experiences seem to be common to all people at all times. When I started my book, I was inclined to be agnostic about 'life after death' for it seemed to me very likely that even highly trained observers may allow their secret wishes to influence their observation. I ended by concluding that there is as much evidence for life after death as for the existence of the planets. I was also surprised to find that there is so much solid evidence for reincarnation. (Amusingly enough, most 'spiritualists' do not accept this.) I was surprised by the extent to which astrology really works – at least, in the hands of a skilled astrologer. (They are as rare as mediums.) And I was extremely surprised to find that the 'astral body' seems to be more than a myth – for this seems to be an obvious example of superstition : the notion that we possess a 'body' made of finer material than our physical body, which can, under certain circumstances, float away. To put it simply, I had expected to be dealing with masses of old wives' tales, with a small core of inner truth, and I ended by finding that many of the old wives were more truthful than I would have thought possible.

This leads to the final point, the real stumbling block for the rationalist. Anyone who has read Freud or Jung may accept that the mind is a bigger and more mysterious place than our great grandfathers realised; and it seems arguable that the 'magical tradition' has always understood this instinctively. But these powers and forces are *inside* the mind. What about the belief in 'evil' as an external force?

Without wishing to sound too dogmatic – for my interest lies in philosophy rather than occultism – I would say that there appears to be evidence of 'forces' outside us, intelligent forces.

Suppose that some highly intelligent savages found a radio set, and discovered that it made strange noises when switched on. Their first assumption is that it contains demons. Then some of the cooler-headed suggest that a human being is hidden inside it. And after a much longer interval of time, a few of the more brilliant minds make the suggestion that these strange noises are purely natural forces at work, that these valves and wires are the digestive organs of the radio, which make the same grumbling noises as an empty stomach. This explanation satisfies everyone – no demons, no hidden manikins or elves. But then, one day, they accidentally tune in to a broadcast from a ship. And there can be no doubt that these are real voices issuing from the loudspeaker. How can they understand this phenomenon? The dogmatic rationalists will still assert that the voices were somehow 'natural' like the crackles and whines, while the more superstitious will fall back on the old explanation of demons. And it is hard to see how they can ever hit upon the true explanation, unless somebody is kind enough to explain.

In John Keir Cross's Introduction to the Faber volume *Black Magic Stories*, there is an anecdote that may help to make my point. Mr Cross tells how a BBC team once tried summoning the Devil on a Hallowe'en programme broadcast from Scotland. At the end of the programme – in which Mr Cross took part – a magic circle was drawn around the microphone, a mediaeval incantation was read aloud, then everyone tiptoed out of the studio, turning off the lights, but leaving the microphone 'live', just in case the Devil chose to utter a few words. Nothing happened. But when Mr Cross got home to his flat, and was warmly tucked up in bed, his six-month-old son began to scream. They found his face and hands bleeding, and something growling and scrabbling inside the window sill. They later killed the huge rat that had attacked the child. But they never discovered how it had got into a sealed room, with no fireplace, no hidden rat-holes, or why a rat had come all the way from the docks to a respectable Glasgow suburb. Mr Cross firmly believes – and I am inclined to agree – that the invitation to the Devil was basically responsible. Whether it was *the* Devil or not, some external force, probably evil, decided to show that such matters were not to be joked about.

The universe is full of forces and energies. Our 'radio set' can tune in to many of these – all the wavelengths of light between red and violet, sounds up to a certain pitch, and so on. Animals can tune in to a wider range – hence the homing instinct, sense of danger, 'second sight'. (Robins may navigate by picking up some electromagnetic vibration from the Milky Way.) But there must be thousands of forms of energy to which we cannot 'tune in', even with instruments (at least, with our present crude instruments). Surrounded by all this, how can we state dogmatically that there are no 'other intelligences' beyond the limited range of our senses? Dr David Foster, a cybernetician, has tried to explain the 'coding' of the genes by assuming that certain high-frequency energies (such as cosmic rays) may be carrying 'coded messages'; he originally called his book on the subject *The Cybernetic Universe*, but ended by deciding to call it boldly *The Intelligent Universe*. Anyone who wants to explore the meeting place of science and occultism should read it. Whether or not he ends by agreeing with Dr Foster, he should at least come to recognise that it is a kind of madness for human beings to assume that we are the only forms of intelligent consciousness in our universe. This may not 'prove' the existence of ghosts or the Devil, but it may jar us out of the narrow state of mind in which they appear to be an absurdity.

I

The general public's awareness of the extent of modern 'magical practices' – both 'black' and 'white' magic – virtually began with the publication of a single book, *Là-Bas*, in 1891. The work of an extraordinary French civil servant, the novel recounted in fictional form the actual experiences of the author who had involved himself in the occult rituals and ceremonies then being performed in Paris. Like so many before him, he was intrigued by the idea of adepts secretly trying to make contact with the forces of the unknown and plunged himself into an exhaustive enquiry which was to lead him through simple white magic, seances and spiritualism, to the very heart of black magic and that most profane of ceremonies, the Black Mass.

Georges Charles Huysmans (1848-1907) known as Joris-Karl, was born in Paris of Dutch ancestry and worked for much of his life in the Ministry of the Interior. Behind this somewhat traditional façade lurked the soul of a mystic, a mind deeply interested in all the forms of supernaturalism. His first literary endeavours found their inspiration from the work of Baudelaire and, like his mentor, he chose to depict life in all its harshest colours. In 1876 he published *Marthe*, an uncompromising novel of prostitution which brought a storm of protest from French readers who had grown sympathetic towards the 'fallen' through the novels of Émile Zola. But in Huysmans' eyes there could be no love for the sordid or the ugly, and it was through his own continued experimentation with the occult and his enquiries into the mystic circles of the French capital that he was led to writing his masterpiece *Là-Bas*. On its publication, the book created a sensation of the kind few other works have aroused. Both critics and the general populace were stunned that such an 'underworld' of magic and devil-worship could exist unknown in their very midst. Those who challenged its validity were met by an author willing to admit his own close involvement

with Satanism and to having actually witnessed everything he
had written about, including the Black Mass. 'At the present
moment,' he said, 'it is very evident that the Good Deity is
underdog, that the Evil One rules the world as master.'
Huysmans claimed that the followers of the Devil came from
all walks of society and included 'Superintendents of
Missions, Confessors of Religious Communities, Prelates,
Abbesses, and from the laity, recruits come from the wealthy –
all of which account for these scandals being hushed up.' He
mentioned, too, that the cult was not restricted to France, but
had followers throughout Europe, in Britain and even in
America. The book's success was not restricted to France,
either; in England it was widely praised by Arthur Symons
and Oscar Wilde, while in it Aubrey Beardsley found much
inspiration for his macabre talents.

Despite its popularity at the time, *Là-Bas* is now almost
forgotten and certainly few people today can claim to have
read it in its entirety. So great is its importance, though, that
in a collection such as this devoted to the work of modern
adepts of the occult, an extract from it must precede all else.
Here I have selected a climactic scene in which the hero –
Durtal (Huysmans himself) who is enquiring into Satanism
learns that his mistress Hyacinthe Chantelouve is herself a
devil-worshipper (for a time Huysmans had a mistress deeply
versed in sorcery) and that she is a disciple of the most notorious practitioner in Paris, Canon Docre. (This man is based
on Canon Roca, a Belgian priest who had once been a chaplain
in Bruges and had taken to practising black magic.) Durtal per-
suades her to take him secretly to one of their meetings. Such
is the horror and morbidity of the scene (indeed of the whole
book) that one can understand why in later life Huysmans
himself became increasingly depressed and introspective
through his absorption with the occult, and eventually sought
sanctuary and complete seclusion in a Benedictine monastery.

* * *

The Black Mass

Joris-Karl Huysmans

They were in a cab jolting along the Rue de Vaugirard. Mme Chantelouve had drawn herself into one corner, where she sat without breathing a syllable. Durtal scrutinised her face when, on passing a street-lamp, a fleeting gleam of light fell momentarily across her veil. She seemed to him agitated and nervous under her quiet exterior. He took her hand and she did not draw it away, but he could feel its coldness through her glove, and her hair this evening looked disordered, and less fine and glossy than usual.

'We are nearly there, dear?' he asked. But in a low, strained voice she bade him : 'Please, don't talk!' – and embarrassed by her silent, almost hostile attitude, he occupied himself by observing from the windows the route they were following.

The street stretched in endless perspective, almost deserted and so ill paved that the springs of their conveyance creaked at every yard; the pavement too was dimly lighted, the lamp-posts getting more and more widely spaced the nearer they approached the fortifications.

'What an odd caprice!' he muttered to himself, vexed at the woman's cold, reserved bearing.

At last the vehicle turned sharply down a dark side street, swung round a corner and stopped.

Hyacinthe got out. While waiting for the change the driver had to give him, Durtal glanced about him, examining his surroundings, to discover he was in a sort of blind alley. Low, dreary-looking houses lined a roadway cobbled and without sidewalks; turning round when the cabman took his departure, he found himself in front of a long, high wall, over which the rustle of shadowy trees could be heard. A small door, pierced by a wicket, was sunk in the thickness of the gloomy wall, which had been mended with streaks of plaster stopping up cracks and plugging holes. Suddenly further off, a light shone out from a shopfront, and attracted no doubt by the rumbling of wheels, a man wearing a wine-dealer's apron peered from a doorway, and spat on the doorstep.

'This is the place,' announced Mme Chantelouve.

She rang and the wicket opened; she raised her veil and the light

BLACK MAGIC CIRCLE, AFTER J. K. HUYSMANS

of a lantern fell on her face; the door fell back noiselessly and they walked on into a garden.

'Good evening, Madame.'

'Good evening, Marie. It is in the Chapel?'

'Yes, shall I show Madame the way?'

'No, thank you.'

The woman carrying the lantern stared hard at Durtal, who saw under her frilled cap grey locks coiled untidily above an old wrinkled visage; however, she gave him no time for further scrutiny as she at once retired into an outbuilding near the wall that served her as porter's lodge.

He followed Hyacinthe, who advanced along dark paths smelling dankly, up to the steps of a detached building. She seemed quite at home, pushing open the doors, and whilst her heels sounded over the gravel path.

'Take care,' she cried, after crossing an outer lobby, 'there are three steps.'

They emerged into a courtyard, and halted before the door of an old house, where she rang the bell. A short slight young man appeared and drew to one side, asking her how she did in an affected, sing-song voice. She passed on with a bow, and Durtal was confronted with a pale unhealthy countenance, watery, gummy eyes, cheeks plastered with rouge and painted lips.

'I have stumbled into a den of sodomites. You never told me

I should be mixing with such company,' he said to Hyacinthe, whom he came up with at the bend of a corridor lighted by a lamp.

'Were you expecting to meet Saints here?' – and she shrugged her shoulders, as she pulled open a door. They were in a Chapel, a room with a low ceiling crossed by beams daubed with tar, windows hidden behind heavy curtains, and cracked and discoloured walls. Durtal recoiled the instant he was inside. From overheated radiators came a blast of stifling air, while an abominable stench of mingled damp, mildew and a smelly stove, intensified by the acrid odour of saltwort, resin, and burning herbs, almost choked him and made his temples throb.

He groped his way forward, his eyes exploring the Chapel by the light of sanctuary lamps in bowls of gilt bronze and rose-coloured glass which were suspended from the roof. Hyacinthe signalled to him to be seated, and moved away towards a group of persons lounging on divans in a corner among the shadows. Somewhat embarrassed to find himself thus left alone, he noticed how these included very few men and a good many women; but it was in vain that he strove to distinguish their features. Here and there, however, when a lamp flared up for a moment, he caught a glimpse of the Juno-like figure of a big dark woman, then of a man's clean-shaven and grave face. He watched them, and observed that the women were not chatting together, but talked in frightened, serious tones; not a laugh, not an exclamation was to be heard, only a vague, furtive whispering, unpunctuated by a single gesture.

'Upon my soul!' he said to himself, 'Satan does not appear to make his flock very cheerful!'

An acolyte, robed in red, advanced to the upper end of the Chapel and lit a row of wax candles. The altar became visible, an ordinary church altar, surmounted by a tabernacle, and above it a Crucifix with a grotesque, squalid figure. The head was carried high on an absurdly elongated neck, while lines daubed on the cheeks transformed the suffering face into a mask twisted in an ignoble grin. Before the tabernacle was placed a chalice covered with the veil; the acolyte was smoothing out the altar linen with his hands, raising himself tiptoe on one foot, under pretence of reaching up to the black candles whose reek of bitumen and pitch was now added to the other suffocating effluvia of the place.

Durtal recognised under his red cassock the pouf who was in

charge of the door at his entrance, and understood the rôle reserved for the wretch, whose vile filthiness was a mockery in place of the purity the church requires from servers at her altars.

Then another, uglier than his comrade, stepped forward. Emaciated, hollow-chested, racked with coughing, his face made up with rouge and white grease-paint, he limped in, intoning a chant. He went up to the tripods standing on either side the altar, stirred the embers smouldering in the ashes, and threw on lumps of resin and handfuls of dry leaves.

Durtal was beginning to feel bored when Hyacinthe rejoined him; she excused herself for having left him so long alone, urged him to move his seat and led him to a spot behind all the rows of chairs, right at the back.

'So we are in a real Chapel?' he asked.

'Yes, this house, the church and the garden we came through are the remains of a Convent of Ursulines, now suppressed. For a long time the Chapel was used to store fodder in; the house belonged to a livery-stable keeper, who sold it to that lady over there,' and she indicated a big dark woman, the same Durtal had had a glimpse of before.

'And is she married, this lady?'

'No, she was once a nun, who was debauched by Canon Docre.'

'Oh! And those gentlemen who seem so anxious to remain in obscurity?'

'They are Satanists . . . there is one of them who was a Professor at the Ecole de Médicine; he has an oratory in his house, where he prays before a statue of Venus Astarte set up on an altar.'

'Nonsense!'

'It is a fact; he is getting old and his supplications to demons invigorate him. He spends his time and money on creatures of that sort' – and she pointed to the acolytes.

'You vouch for the truth of this story?'

'I am so far from inventing it that you will find it all told at full length in a religious periodical, *Les Annales de la Sainteté.* Well, though he was plainly pointed to in the article, he has never dared to proceed against the paper! Why, what is the matter with you?' she asked, staring at him.

'The matter is . . . I am suffocating; the smell of these perfuming pans is insufferable.'

'You will get used to it in a few moments.'

'But what is it they burn to stink like that?'

'Rue, henbane and thorn-apple leaves, dried nightshade and myrtle; they are perfumes beloved of Satan, our master!'

She said this in the gutteral, unnatural voice that on certain emotional occasions characterised her.

He looked hard at her; her face was pale, her teeth clenched, the lids flickering over her stormy eyes.

'Here he is!' she cried suddenly, while the women hurried across to kneel at the chairs in front.

Preceded by two acolytes and wearing a scarlet biretta decorated with a pair of bison's horns of red material, the Canon entered.

Durtal watched him as he advanced to the altar. He was tall, but ill proportioned, all head and shoulders; a bald forehead ran down in one unbroken line to a straight nose; lips and cheeks showed the harsh, dry stubble common to ecclesiastics who have shaved for years; the features were irregular and coarse; the eyes, like apple-pips, small, black, and close together either side the nose, had a phosphorescent glitter. Taken all together, the expression was thoroughly bad and untrustworthy, but full of fire and energy, and those hard, steady eyes had none of the sly, shifty look Durtal had expected to see.

He bowed solemnly before the altar, mounted the steps and began his mass.

Durtal then saw that, under his sacrificial robes, he was naked. The chasuble was of the usual shape, but of a dark blood-red colour, and in the middle, within a triangle, surrounded by a tangled growth of meadow-saffron, sorrel-apple and spurge, a black he-goat stood, butting with its horns.

Docre made the genuflexions and bowings, less or more profound, as specified in the ritual; the servers kneeling intoned the Latin responses in clear, ringing voices, dwelling long on the final syllables of the words.

'Why, it is just an ordinary low mass,' Durtal observed to Mme Chantelouve.

She shook her head. In fact, at that moment the two servers passed behind the altar and brought back with them, the one copper chafing dishes, the other small censers, which they distributed among the congregation. Soon all the women were wrapped in clouds of smoke; some of them dropped their heads over the chafing dishes and eagerly inhaled the fumes, emitting hoarse gasps.

At this point the office was suspended. The priest descended the altar steps backwards and in a quavering high-pitched voice cried :

'Lord of evil, thou who dost reward sins and heinous vices, Satan, it is thou whom we adore, God of Reason, God of Justice!

'Suzerain of the scornful, Defence of the down-trodden. Depositary of cherished hatreds, thou only dost make fertile the brain of the man crushed by injustice; thou dost whisper in his ear ideas of long-meditated vengeance and sure retaliation! thou dost incite him to murder and give him the exuberant joy of reprisals inflicted, the glorious intoxication of punishments he has accomplished and tears he has caused to flow!

'Master, thy faithful servants implore thee on their knees. They beseech thee grant them assurance of those sweet sins Justice takes no heed of; they beseech thee assist the spells whose unrecognised traces baffle human reason. Fame, fortune, power they ask of thee, King of the disinherited whom the inexorable Father drove forth from heaven!'

Then Docre got to his feet and, with outstretched arms, in a ringing voice of hate vociferated :

'And Thou, Thou, whom by right of my priesthood I force to come down and enter into this host and become transubstantiated in this bread. . . .'

Then followed a litany of insults, of invective that was almost insane in its vileness and its hate.

'Amen,' shrilled the clear voice of the acolytes.

Durtal, listening to this torrent of blasphemies and abuse, was astounded at the foul profanity of the priest. A silence ensued after his ravings; the Chapel was misty with the smoke of censers. The women, hitherto silent, stirred restlessly when, mounting again to the altar, the Canon turned towards them and blessed them with a sweeping gesture of the left hand.

And suddenly the servers tinkled little bells. This seemed to be a signal; women fell to the floor and rolled on the carpets. One, her eyes suddenly convulsed in a horrible squint, clucked like a hen, then, fallen dumb, gaped with wide open jaws, the tongue retracted till its tip touched the palate high up; another, her face puffed and livid, pupils dilated, lolled back her head on her shoulders, then stiffened in a sudden spasm and tore at her bosom with her nails; another, sprawling on her back, undid her skirts, revealing a huge and swollen belly; then her face twisted into a horrible grimace, and her tongue, which she could not draw in, stuck out, bitten at the edges, harrowed by red teeth, from a bloody mouth.

Suddenly Durtal rose, and he could see and hear the Canon distinctly. 1774126

Docre contemplated the Christ surmounting the tabernacle, and with arms spread wide apart, he spewed forth frightful insults, and, at the end of his strength, muttered the foul imprecations of a drunken cabman. One of the choirboys knelt in front of him, with his back to the altar. A shudder ran along the priest's spine. In a solemn but jerky voice he said *'Hoc est enim corpus meum'*, then, instead of kneeling after the consecration before the precious Body, he faced the congregation with an erect penis, haggard and dripping with sweat. He staggered between the two choirboys who, raising his chasuble, displayed his naked belly. Docre made a few jerky movements with his hand, and then the host sailed, tainted and slimy, over the steps.

Then Durtal felt a shudder run through him, for a wind of madness shook the assemblage. The breath of high hysteria succeeded the profane outrage and bowed the women's heads; they fell upon the Eucharistic bread, clawed at it and tearing off fragments, ate this filth.

One woman burst out in a strident laugh and insanely yelled : 'Father, Father!' An old beldam wrenched out handfuls of her hair, leapt high in the air, spun round on her heels, stood on one leg and collapsed beside a girl who, crouching against one wall, was writhing in convulsions, slavering at the mouth, weeping as she spat out hideous blasphemies. And Durtal, appalled, saw through the smoke as in a fog the red horns on Docre's head.

Then at the back of the Chapel in the shadows a little girl, who had not stirred till that moment, reeled forward and began to howl like a rabid bitch !

Overwhelmed with disgust and almost stifled, Durtal longed to escape. He looked for Hyacinthe, but she was not there. At last he saw her beside the Canon; stepping over the bodies on the carpets, he approached her. With quivering nostrils she was inhaling the odours of the perfumes.

'The savour of the Witches' Sabbath!' she said to him in a low voice through clenched teeth.

'Are you coming?' he said sharply.

She seemed to awake from a dream, hesitated a moment, then without a word she followed him.

He plied his elbows, forcing a way through the women, who with teeth bare seemed ready to snap and bite; he pushed Mme Chantelouve towards the door and the porter's lodge being open, pulled the cord and found himself in the street.

There he halted and drew in deep breaths of fresh air; Hyacinthe, eyes fixed on vacancy, stood motionless, leaning against the wall.

He looked at her. 'Do you wish to go back home?' he asked in a tone that betrayed a touch of scorn.

'No,' she brought out with an effort, 'but these scenes overcome me. I feel dizzy, I want a glass of water to put me right,' and she set off up the street making straight for a wine-shop where the light streamed from the open door.

It was a disreputable hole, a small hall with wooden tables and chairs, a zinc-covered counter, a zanzibar board, some blue jars, and hanging from the ceiling a gas-bracket in the shape of a U; two rather rough-looking navvies sat playing cards; they turned round and laughed, while the landlord took a short pipe from his mouth and expectorated on the sanded floor. He showed no surprise at seeing this elegantly attired woman in his den of a place. Durtal, who was eyeing him, even fancied he caught a wink exchanged between the fellow and Mme Chantelouve.

The man lit a candle, and said under his breath :

'You can't drink, without attracting attention, along with these chaps. I'm going to take you to a room you will have to yourselves.'

'Well, well,' grumbled Durtal to his companion, who was already mounting a spiral staircase, 'here's a fine how-d'ye-do for a simple glass of water.'

But she had already entered a bedroom with a tattered paper peeling off the damp walls, which were adorned with pictures cut from the illustrated papers and stuck up with drawing-pins; the floor was paved with cracked tiles gaping in holes and hollows, and it was barely furnished with a pole-bedstead without curtains, a table, a wash-hand basin and a couple of chairs.

Their host fetched a small decanter of brandy, sugar, a water-jug and glasses, then returned downstairs. Thereupon, with wild, sombre eyes, she threw her arms about Durtal's neck.

'No, no!' he cried, furious at having fallen into this trap, 'I have had enough of all that! And besides, it is getting late and your husband is expecting you; it is high time for you to go back to him!'

She did not even hear him.

'I want you,' she said, and grabbed him treacherously, obliging him to desire her. She undressed, threw her skirts on the floor, opened wide the abominable couch. A look of swooning ecstasy was in her eyes, and a smile of joy on her lips.

She seized him, and, with ghoulish fury, dragged him into obscenities of whose existence he had never dreamed. Suddenly, when he was able to escape, he shuddered, for he saw the bed was covered with fragments of hosts.

'Oh! you horrify me!' he told her, 'come, let us go!'

The foulness of the room sickened him. He was not absolutely certain about Transubstantiation. 'But supposing it to be true,' he said to himself, 'supposing the Presence to be real, as Hyacinthe and that scurvy priest avouch it is! No, decidedly I am more than fed up with filth and foulness; this is the end; here is a good opportunity to finish with this creature, whom after all, since our first meeting, I have only tolerated – and I am going to do it!'

Downstairs in the bar as he quickly passed through he had to put up with the sniggering of the navvies; he paid, and without bothering to wait for his change, made off as quickly as he could. They reached the Rue de Vaugirard, where he hailed a conveyance. They were driven along without once glancing at each other, absorbed in their own thoughts.

'I shall see you again soon!' whispered Mme Chantelouve almost timidly when she was put down at her door.

'No,' he answered her aloud, in a firm tone; 'there is really and truly no chance of our coming to an understanding; you want everything, and I want nothing. Far better to break off our relations, which will only drag on and on, to end in quarrels and mutual recriminations. Oh! and then, after what happened this evening, no! I say, no!' – and he gave his address to the cabman, flinging himself into the furthermost corner of the cab.

2

At the time of the publication of Huysmans' *Là-Bas* another Frenchman, Eliphas Levi, had become accepted in occult circles as the first great magician of the modern age. A grandiloquent and vital figure, Levi in his writings and teachings had brought the practice of ritual magic out of the mists of the Middle Ages and the unreasoning terrors of the Inquisition. His study of both witchcraft and the dark arts (including black magic) produced a series of textbooks which are still today the basis of many works and reports on the Occult – despite their undoubted elements of high fantasy and occasional wicked distortions of the truth.

Eliphas Levi (1810-75) – his real name was Alphonse Louis Constant – was the son of a humble shoemaker. He was educated at Saint-Sulpice seminary after which he entered the Roman Catholic priesthood. A strange catharsis brought on by his quiet upbringing and the gentle devotions of the priesthood produced a wildly rebellious streak in him, and apart from causing him to focus his intellect on the dark worlds of the Anti-Christ so bitterly opposed by his Church, it also threw him into a 'profane' love-affair with a sixteen-year-old girl, who bore him two children.

He wrestled for a time with his conscience, one of his biographers tells us, and then abandoned the cloth to devote himself whole-heartedly to the study of magical lore. He researched exhaustively through the well-stocked but untouched shelves of occult literature in the Paris libraries and immersed himself in the cabbala of the Jews, the gnostic sects of the East, the alchemists and the old orders of witches and sorcerers. He carried his enquiries to the very limits of experience and we have good reason to believe that a number of his rituals to evoke spirits actually succeeded. He records in 1854 how he summoned two spirits, one of whom revealed future events, while the other gave him instruction in the making of a secret pentacle. He also tells us he raised the spirit of the ancient mystic Apollonius, but was so overcome by fear at the sight of the shade before him that he fainted. 'I do not explain,' he wrote afterwards, 'the physical laws by which I saw and touched. I affirm solely that I did see and that I did touch.'

Apart from his own experiments, Levi was aware of much of the occult activity in France and, indeed, much of it can be said to have stemmed from him. He was also involved for a time with an English occult society led by Edward Bulwer, Lord Lytton. It is also fairly safe to assume that Levi was frequently approached by people of all mystical tendencies from white to the deepest shades of black for advice and guidance. His total commitment to magic makes it more than likely that he helped one and all and he may well have played a part in the shaping of several rituals and ceremonies still used today by adepts. His influence on magic as a whole, however, is undoubted and his part in the renaissance of its actual *practice* supreme. Virtually all Levi's writings are presented by him as fact (dubious though this is in several parts) and few of his stories meet the requirements of this collection. None the less, in 'The Magus' we have an item which serves admirably, for the central character is evidently Levi himself thinly disguised, while the renegade priest who approaches him for magical aid is clearly based on one of his 'clients'. The story follows most appropriately after the Huysmans extract because it examines further the cancer which had attacked priests of the Catholic faith and also reveals the developing climate for occult experiment. On a lesser plain it exposes Levi's own rebellion against the Church, and more than one commentator has attributed certain of its most violent statements as being those held by the author himself.

Here, then, is the man of whom A. E. Waite, the noted writer on the supernatural, said : 'No modern expositor of occult claims can bear any comparison with Eliphas Levi, for he is actually the spirit of modern thought forcing an answer for the times from the old oracles. Hence there are greater names, but there has been no influence so great : no fascination in occult literature exceeds that of the French Magus.'

* * *

The Magus

ELIPHAS LEVI

One winter's day a message reached the Magus that an ecclesiastic was looking for his address and demonstrating a great desire to see him urgently. The practitioner of magic immediately felt a lack of confidence about a meeting with this stranger, but decided to go ahead, taking the precaution of seeing him in the house of a friend, Madame A——, and in the company of one of his faithful disciples, Desbarrolles. So at the hour and date appointed, they went to the duly selected house and found on their arrival that the priest had been waiting for them for some moments.

He was a young, slim man; he had an arched and pointed nose, with dull blue eyes. His bony and projecting forehead was rather broad than high, his head was dolichocephalic, his hair flat and short, parted on one side, of a greyish blond with just a tinge of chestnut of a rather curious and disagreeable shade. His mouth was sensual and quarrelsome; his manners were affable, his voice soft, and his speech sometimes a little embarrassed. Questioned by the Magus concerning the object of his visit, he replied that he was on the look-out for the *grimoire* of Honorius, and he had come to learn from the Professor of Occult Science how to obtain that little black book, nowadays almost impossible to find.

'I would gladly give a hundred francs for a copy of that *grimoire*,' said he.

'The work in itself is valueless,' said the magician. 'It is a pretended constitution of Honorius II, which you will find perhaps quoted by some erudite collector of apocryphal constitutions. You can find it in the library.'

'I will do so, for I pass almost all my time in Paris in the public libraries.'

'You are not occupied in the ministry in Paris?'

'No, not now; I was for some little while employed in the parish of St-Germain-l'Auxerrois.'

'And now you spend your time, I understand, in curious researches in occult science.'

'Not precisely, but I am seeking the realisation of a thought. . . . I have something to do.'

THE SYMBOL OF LUCIFER
BY ELIPHAS LEVI

'I do not suppose that this something can be an operation of black magic? You know as well as I do, reverend sir, that the Church has always condemned, and still condemns, severely, everything which relates to these forbidden practices.'

A pale smile, imprinted with a sort of sarcastic irony, was all the answer that the Abbé gave, and the conversation ceased.

However, the cheiromancer Desbarrolles was attentively looking at the hand of the priest; he perceived it, a quite natural explanation followed, the Abbé offered graciously and of his own accord his hand to the experimenter. Desbarrolles knit his brows, and appeared embarrassed. The hand was damp and cold, the fingers smooth and spatulated; the mount of Venus, or part of the palm of the hand which corresponds to the thumb, was of noteworthy development, the line of life was short and broken, there were crosses in the centre of the hand and stars upon the mount of the moon.

'Reverend sir,' said Desbarrolles, 'if you had not a very solid religious education you would easily have become a dangerous sectary, for you are led on the one hand towards the most exalted mysticism, and on the other to the most concentrated obstinacy combined with the greatest secretiveness that can possibly be. You want much, but you imagine more, and as you confide your imaginations to nobody, they might attain proportions which would make them veritable enemies for yourself. Your habits are contemplative and rather easy-going, but it is a somnolence whose awakenings are perhaps to be dreaded. You are carried away by a passion which your state of life – but pardon, reverend sir, I fear that I am over-stepping the boundaries of discretion.'

'Say everything, sir, I am willing to hear all, I wish to know everything.'

'Oh, well! If, as I do not doubt to be the case, you turn to the profit of charity all the restless activities with which the passions of your heart furnish you, you must often be blessed for your good works.'

The Abbé once more smiled that dubious and fatal smile which gave so singular an expression to his pallid countenance. He rose and took his leave without having given his name, and without any one having thought to ask him for it.

The Magus and Desbarrolles conducted him as far as the staircase, in token of respect for his dignity as a priest.

Near the staircase he turned and said slowly :

'Before long, you will hear something. . . . You will hear me spoken of,' he added, emphasising each word. Then he saluted with head and hand, turned without adding a single word, and descended the staircase.

The two friends returned to Mme A——'s room.

'There is a singular personage,' said the professor of magic. 'What he said to us on his departure seemed to me very much like a threat.'

'You frightened him,' said Mme A——. 'Before your arrival, he was beginning to open his whole mind, but you spoke to him of conscience and of the laws of the Church, and he no longer dared to tell you what he wished.'

'Bah! What did he wish then?'

'To see the Devil.'

'Perhaps he thought I had him in my pocket?'

'No, but he knows that you give lessons in the cabbala, and in magic, and so he hoped that you would help him in his enterprise. He told my daughter and myself that in his vicarage in the country, he had already made one night an evocation of the Devil by the help of a popular *grimoire*. "Then," said he, "a whirlwind seemed to shake the vicarage; the rafts groaned, the wainscoting cracked, the doors shook, the windows opened with a crash, and whistlings were heard in every corner of the house." He then expected that formidable vision to follow but he saw nothing; no monster presented itself; in a word the Devil would not appear. That is why he is looking for the *grimoire* of Honorius, for he hopes to find in it stronger conjurations, and more efficacious rites.'

'Really! But the man is then a monster, or a madman!'

'I think he is simply in love,' said Desbarrolles. 'He is gnawed by some absurd passion, and hopes for absolutely nothing unless he can get the Devil to interfere.'

'But how then – what does he mean when he says that we shall hear him spoken of?'

'Who knows? Perhaps he thinks to carry off the Queen of England, or the Sultana Valide.'

The conversation dropped, and a whole year passed without Mme A——, or Desbarrolles, or the Magus hearing the unknown priest spoken of.

In the course of the night between 1st and 2nd of January 18– however, the professor of magic was awakened suddenly by the emotions of a bizarre and dismal dream. It seemed to him that he was in a dilapidated room of gothic architecture, rather like the abandoned chapel of an old castle. A door hidden by a black drapery opened on to this room; behind the drapery one guessed the hidden light of tapers, and it seemed to the Magus that, driven by a curiosity full of terror, he was approaching the black drapery. . . . Then the drapery was parted, and a hand was stretched forth and seized his arm. He saw no one, but he heard a low voice which said in his ear :

'Come and see your father, who is about to die.'

The Magus awoke, his heart palpitating, and his forehead bathed in sweat.

'What can this dream mean?' he thought. 'It is long since my father died; why am I told that he is going to die, and why has this warning upset me?'

The following night, the same dream recurred with the same circumstances; once more, he awoke, hearing a voice in his ear repeat :

'Come and see your father, who is about to die.'

This repeated nightmare made a painful impression upon the Magus. He had accepted, for 3rd of January, an invitation to dinner in pleasant company, but he wrote and excused himself, feeling himself little inclined for the gaiety of a banquet of artists. He remained, then, in his study; the weather was cloudy; at midday he received a visit from one of his magical pupils, Viscount M——. When he left, the rain was falling in such abundance that the professor offered his umbrella to the Viscount, who refused it. There followed a contest of politeness, of which the result was that the Magus went out to see the Viscount home. While they were in the street, the rain stopped, the Viscount found a carriage, and the Magus, instead of returning to his house, mechanically crossed the Luxembourg, went out by the gate which opens on the Rue d'Enfer, and found himself opposite the Panthéon.

A double row of booths, improvised for the Festival of St Geneviève, indicated to pilgrims the road to St Étienne-du-Mont. The Magus, whose heart was sad, and consequently disposed to prayer, followed that way and entered the church. It might have been at that time about four o'clock in the afternoon.

The church was full of the faithful, and the office was performed with great concentration, and extraordinary solemnity. The banners of the parishes of the city, and of the suburbs, bore witness to the public veneration for the virgin who saved Paris from famine and invasion. At the bottom of the church, the tomb of St Geneviève shone gloriously with light. They were chanting the litanies, and the procession was coming out of the choir.

After the Cross, accompanied by its acolytes, and followed by the choirboys, came the banner of St Geneviève; then, walking in double file, came the lady devotees of St Geneviève, clothed in black, with a white veil on the head, a blue ribbon around the neck with the medal of the legend, a taper in the hand, surmounted by the little gothic lantern that tradition gives to the images of the saint. For, in the old books, St Geneviève is always represented with a medal on her neck, that which St Germain d'Auxerre gave her, and holding a taper, which the Devil tries to extinguish, but which is protected from the breath of the unclean spirit by a miraculous little tabernacle.

After the lady devotees came the clergy; then finally appeared the venerable Archbishop of Paris, mitred with a white mitre, wearing a cope which was supported on each side by his two vicars; the prelate, leaning on his cross, walked slowly and blessed to right and left the crowd which knelt about his path. The Magus saw the Archbishop for the first time, and noticed the features of his countenance. They expressed kindliness and gentleness; but one might observe the expression of a great fatigue, and even of a nervous suffering painfully dissimulated.

The procession descended to the foot of the church, traversing the nave, went up again by the aisle at the left of the door, and came to the station of the tomb of St Geneviève; then it returned by the right-hand aisle, chanting the litanies as it went. A group of the faithful followed the procession, and walked immediately behind the Archbishop.

The professor of magic mingled in this group, in order more easily to get through the crowd which was about to reform, so that he might regain the door of the church. He was lost in reverie, softened by this pious solemnity.

The head of the procession has already returned to the choir, the Archbishop was arriving at the railing of the nave : there the passage was too narrow for three people to walk in file; the Archbishop was in front, and the two grand-vicars behind him, always holding the edges of his cope, which was thus thrown off, and drawn backwards, in such a manner that the prelate presented his breast uncovered, and protected only by the crossed embroideries of his stole.

Then those who were behind the Archbishop saw him tremble, and heard an interruption in a loud and clear voice; but without shouting, or clamour. What had been said? It seemed that it was 'Down with the goddesses!' However, the exclamation was repeated two or three times and then someone cried : 'Save the Archbishop!' Other voices replied : 'To arms!' The crowd, overturning the chairs and the barriers, scattered, and rushed towards the door shrieking. Amidst the wails of the children, and the screams of the women, the Magus, carried away by the crowd, found himself, somehow or other, out of the church; but the last look that he was able to cast upon it was smitten with a terrible and unforgettable picture!

In the midst of a circle made large by the fear of all those who surrounded him, the prelate was standing alone, leaning on his cross, and held up by the stiffness of his cope, which the grand-vicars had let go, and which accordingly hung down to the ground. The head of the Archbishop was a little thrown back, his eyes and his free hand raised to Heaven. There was in his gesture the whole epic of marytrdom; it was an acceptance and an offering; a prayer for his people, and a pardon for his murderer.

Before the Archbishop, a lifted arm, sketched in shadow like an infernal silhouette, held and brandished a knife. Policemen, sword in hand, were running up.

And while all this tumult was going on at the bottom of the church, the singing of the litanies continued in the choir, as the harmony of the orbs of Heaven goes on for ever, careless of our revolutions and of our anguish.

The Magus, as we said, had been swept out of the church by the crowd. He had come out by the right-hand door. Almost at the same moment the left-hand door was flung violently open, and a furious group of men rushed out of the church.

This group was swirling around a man whom fifty arms seemed to hold, whom a hundred shaken fists sought to strike.

Women were running after him shrieking: 'Kill him!'

'But what has he done?' cried other voices.

'The wretch! He struck the Archbishop with his fist!' said the women.

Then others came out of the church, and contradictory accounts were flying to and fro.

'The Archbishop was frightened, and has fainted,' said some.

'He is dead!' replied others.

'Did you see the knife?' added a third comer. 'It is as long as a sabre, and the blood was streaming on the blade.'

'It is nothing! It is nothing!' then cried a woman who rented chairs. 'You can come back to the church: Monseigneur is not hurt; they have just said so from the pulpit.'

The crowd made a movement to return to the church.

'Go! Go!' said at that very moment the very grave and anguished voice of a priest. 'The office cannot be continued: we are going to close the church: it is profaned.'

'How is the Archbishop?' said a man.

'Sir,' replied the priest, 'the Archbishop is dying; perhaps even at this very moment he is dead!'

The crowd dispersed in consternation to spread the mournful news over Paris.

A bizarre incident then happened to the professor of magic, and made a kind of diversion for his deep sorrow at what had just passed.

At the moment of the uproar, an aged woman of the most respectable appearance had taken his arm, and claimed his protection.

He made it a duty to reply to this appeal, and got her safely out of the crowd. 'How happy I am,' she then said, 'to have met a man who weeps for this great crime, for which at the moment, so many wretches rejoice!'

'What are you saying, madam? How is it possible that there should exist beings so depraved as to rejoice at so great a misfortune?'

'Silence!' said the old lady; 'perhaps we are overheard. . . . Yes,' she added, lowering her voice; 'there are people who are exceeding pleased at what has happened. And look there, just now, there was a man of sinister mien, who said to the anxious crowd, when they asked him what had happened: "Oh, it is nothing! It is a spider which has fallen." '

'No, madam, you must have misunderstood. The crowd would not have suffered so abominable a remark, and the man would have been immediately arrested.'

'Would to God that all the world thought as you do!' said the lady.

Then she added: 'I recommend myself to your prayers, for I see clearly that you are a man of God.'

'Perhaps every one does not think so,' replied the Magus with a pale smile as he turned and walked quickly on his way.

The trial of the assassin began, and the Magus reading in the newspapers that the man was a priest, that he had belonged to the clergy of St-Germain-l'Auxerrois, that he had been a country vicar, and that he seemed exalted to the point of madness, recalled the pale priest who, a year earlier, had been looking for the *grimoire* of Honorius. But the description which the public sheets gave of the criminal disagreed with the recollection of the professor of magic. In fact, the majority of the papers said that he had black hair. . . . 'It is not he, then,' thought the professor. 'However, I still keep in my ear and in my memory the words which would now be explained for me by this great crime: "You will soon learn something. Before long, you will hear me spoken of." '

The trial took place with all the frightful vicissitudes one might expect in such a case, and the accused was condemned to death.

The next day, the Magus read in a legal newspaper the account of this unheard-of scene in the annals of justice, but a cloud came over his eyes when he came to the description of the accused: 'He is blond.'

'It must be he,' said the professor of magic.

Some days afterwards, a person who had been able to sketch the convict during the trial, showed it to the Magus.

'Let me copy this drawing,' said he, all trembling with fear.

He made the copy, and took it to his friend Desbarrolles, of whom he asked, without other explanation:

'Do you know this head?'

'Yes,' said Desbarrolles energetically. 'Wait a moment: yes, it is the mysterious priest whom we saw at Mme A——'s, and who wanted to make magical evocations.'

'Oh, well, my friend, you confirm me in my sad conviction. The man we saw, we shall never see again; the hand which you examined has become a bloody hand. We have heard speak of him, as he told us we should – the pale priest!'

'Oh, my God!' said Desbarrolles, changing colour.

Some weeks after what we have just recorded, the Magus was talking with a bookseller whose speciality was in old books concerning the occult sciences. They were talking of Honorius.

'Nowadays, it is impossible to find it,' said the merchant. 'The last that I had in my hands I sold to a priest for a hundred francs.'

'A young priest? And do you remember what he looked like?'

'Oh, perfectly, but you ought to know him well yourself, for he told me he had heard of you, and it is I who sent him to you.'

No more doubt, then; the unhappy priest had found the fatal *grimoire*, he had done the evocation, and prepared himself for the murder by a series of sacrileges. For this is what the infernal evocation consists of according to the *grimoire* of Honorius:

Choose a black cock, and give him the name of the spirit of darkness which one wishes to evoke.

Kill the cock, and keep its heart, its tongue, and the first feather of its left wing.

Dry the tongue and the heart, and reduce them to powder.

Eat no meat and drink no wine, that day.

On Tuesday, at dawn, say a mass of the angels.

Trace upon the altar itself, with the feather of the cock dipped in the consecrated wine, certain diabolical signatures (those of the bloody hosts of Vintras).

On Wednesday, prepare a taper of yellow wax; rise at midnight, and alone, in the church, begin the office of the dead.

Mingle with this office infernal evocations.

Finish the office by the light of a single taper, extinguish it immediately, and remain without light in the church thus profaned until sunrise.

On Thursday, mingle with the consecrated water the powder of the tongue and heart of the black cock and let the whole be swallowed by a male lamb of nine days old.

Then are you ready for any action.

Having performed the ritual the wretch thought himself sure not to die. The Emperor, thought he, would be obliged to pardon him; an honourable exile awaited him; his crime would give him an enormous celebrity; his reveries would be bought for their weight in gold by the booksellers. He would become immensely rich, attract the notice of a great lady, and in time marry. It is by such promises that the phantom of the devil, long ago, lured Gilles de Laval, Seigneur of Retz, and made him wade from crime to crime. A man capable of evoking the devil, according to the rites of the *grimoire* of Honorius, has gone so far upon the road of evil that he is disposed to all kinds of hallucinations, and all lies. So, the priest slept in blood, and he awoke upon the scaffold.

One knows what desperate resistance he made to his executioners. 'It is treason,' said he; 'I cannot die so! Only one hour, an hour to write to the Emperor! The Emperor is bound to save me.'

Who, then, was betraying him?

Who, then, had promised him life?

Who, then, had assured him beforehand of a clemency which was impossible, because it would revolt the conscience of the public?

Ask all that of the *grimoire* of Honorius!

3

The focus of our attention at this point in time now switches from Europe to America and the activities of a certain Madame Blavatsky, founder of the Theosophical Society and in the forefront of the interest in the Occult which was burgeoning across the nation. Ever since the middle of the nineteenth century there had been an increasing interest in spirits and spiritualism – the country was going 'ghost crazy', to quote one contemporary writer – and seances were a frequent occurrence in any city from New York to the West Coast and far into the reaches of the steamy South. On the surface these appeared harmless enough, even if the occasional old lady was taken in by a little fakery and voice projection. But there were also sinister goings-on in back rooms in certain of the larger cities, and we have reports of the activities of more than one group of avowedly black magic practitioners, the most influential of these being probably those led by the Boston Satanist, Albert Pike, and a Scottish immigrant, Alexander Longfellow (no relation of the poet!). Other cults dabbled in ritual magic and the strange philosophies of the ancients, but all were untouched by international attention until the arrival of Madame Blavatsky.

Born in Russia, Helena Petrovna Blavatsky (1831-91) was the daughter of a renowned novelist Helena von Hahn (she wrote as 'Zenaida R'), while her father was a dedicated travel-ler who enjoyed showing the world to his young child, and fostered the same passion in her. In 1849 she married Nikifor Blavatsky, an elderly and senior state official, but left him shortly afterwards and travelled extensively throughout Europe, South America, India, Tibet and Burma. Her inhe-rent interest in the occult which had first flowered when she was a young girl, was increased by her travels in the East and finally resulted in, as one authority has put it, 'her moment of severe physical and psychic crisis'. At this time she declared herself under the guidance of a group of 'Secret

Masters' of the occult arts, 'half human and half divine', who lived in Tibet. In 1874, after unsuccessful attempts to form an organization to support her beliefs and practices in India (where she allegedly materialized objects out of the air) and Egypt, she received 'the call' to go to America, where in 1875 she formed the Theosophical Society. (She became an American citizen in 1878, the first Russian woman to be so allowed.)

The magnetism of her personality undoubtedly contributed to the almost immediate success of her group : she was a large dominating woman who chain-smoked cigarettes, carried a knife in her pocket, wore red shirts and an animal skin – complete with head – around her shoulders. Her knowledge of the occult, mostly gained at first hand on her travels, was prodigious, and this she poured into a series of books and pamphlets (most of which are still kept in print by the present members of her society). Spiritualism she attacked as fraudulent – but her campaign rebounded on her, and in 1884 charges that she herself used trickery forced her to leave for England. The remainder of her life was devoted to writing and to warning all who would take notice of the danger in dabbling carelessly with the occult. 'It is the motive,' she wrote, 'and the motive alone, which makes any exercise of power become Black, malignant, or White, beneficent, Magic. It is impossible to employ spiritual forces if there is the slightest tinge of selfishness remaining in the operator. For unless the intention is entirely unalloyed, the spiritual will transform itself into the psychic, will act on the astral plane, and dire results may be produced by it.'

In the body of Madame Blavatsky's work it is possible to find the occasional piece of fiction such as the following, which she wrote in 1875 and published under a pseudonym. In introducing the story – which was subtitled 'Vengeance Marvellously Wrought by Occult Methods' – she stressed that 'the events herein actually occurred' and that it was a tale which showed 'the enormous potential of the human will upon mesmeric subjects'. Madame Blavatsky was undoubtedly the most accomplished female Magus of modern times and the depth of her involvement with the occult practices she experienced during her wanderings around the world will probably never, despite her voluminous writings, be fully known.

* * *

A Story of the Mystical

Madame Blavatsky

One morning in 18— Eastern Europe was startled by news of the most horrifying description. Michael Obrenovitch, reigning Prince of Serbia, his aunt, the Princess Catherine, or Katinka, and her daughter, had been murdered in broad daylight, near Belgrade, in their own garden, the assassin or assassins remaining unknown. The Prince had received several bullet shots and stabs, and his body was actually butchered; the Princess was killed on the spot, her head smashed, and her young daughter, though still alive, was not expected to survive. The circumstances are too recent to have been forgotten, but in that part of the world, at that time, the case created a delirium of excitement.

In the Austrian dominions and in those under the doubtful protectorate of Turkey, from Bucharest down to Trieste, no high family felt secure. In those half-oriental countries every Montecchi has its Capuletti, and it was rumoured that the bloody deed was perpetrated by the Prince Kara-Georgevitch, an old pretender to the modest throne of Serbia, whose father had been wronged by the first Obrenovitch. The Jaggos of this family were known to nourish the bitterest hatred toward one whom they called a usurper, and 'the shepherd's grandson'. For a time, the official papers of Austria were filled with indignant denials of the charge that the treacherous deed had been done or procured by Kara-Georgevitch, or 'Czerno-Georgiy', as he is usually called in those parts. Several persons, innocent of the act, were, as is usual in such cases, imprisoned, and the real murderers escaped justice. A young relative of the victim, greatly beloved by his people, a mere child, taken for the purpose from a school in Paris, was brought over in ceremony to Belgrade and proclaimed Hospodar of Serbia. In the turmoil of political excitement the tragedy of Belgrade was forgotten by all but an old Serbian matron, who had been attached to the Obrenovitch family, and who, like Rachel, would not be consoled for the death of her children. After the proclamation of the young Obrenovitch, the nephew of the murdered man, she had sold out her property and disappeared; but not before taking a solemn vow on the tombs of the victims to avenge their deaths.

THE THEOSOPHICAL SOCIETY SYMBOL

The writer of this truthful narrative had passed a few days at Belgrade, about three months before the horrid deed was perpetrated, and knew the Princess Katinka. She was a kind, gentle and lazy creature at home; abroad she seemed a Parisian in manners and education. As nearly all the personages who will figure in this true story are still living, it is but decent that I should withhold their names, and give only initials.

The old Serbian lady seldom left her house, going out but to see the Princess occasionally. Crouched on a pile of pillows, and carpeting, clad in the picturesque national dress, she looked like the Cumaean Sibyl in her days of calm repose. Strange stories were whispered about her occult knowledge, and thrilling accounts circulated sometimes among the guests assembled round the fireside of my modest inn. Our fat landlord's maiden aunt's cousin had been troubled for some time past by a wandering vampire, and had been bled nearly to death by the nocturnal visitor; and while the efforts and exorcisms of the parish priest had been of no avail, the victim was luckily delivered by Gospoja P——, who had put to flight the disturbing ghost by merely shaking her fist at him, and shaming him in his own language. It was in Belgrade that I learned for the first time this highly interesting fact for philology, namely, that spooks have a language of their own. The old lady, whom I will call Gospoja P——, was generally attended by another personage destined to be the principal actress in our tale of horror. It was a young gypsy girl, from some part of Rumania, about fourteen years of age. Where she was born, and who she was, she seemed to know as little as anyone else. I was told she had been brought one day by a party of strolling gypsies, and left in the yard of the old lady; from which moment she became an inmate of the house. She was nicknamed 'the sleeping girl', as she was said to be gifted with the faculty of apparently dropping asleep wherever she stood, and speaking her dreams aloud. The girl's heathen name was Frosya.

About eighteen months after the news of the murder had reached Italy, where I was at the time, I was travelling over the Banat, in a small wagon of my own, hiring a horse whenever I needed it, after the fashion of this primitive, trusting country. I met on my way an old Frenchman, a scientist, travelling alone after my own fashion, but with the difference that while he was a pedestrian I dominated the road from the eminence of a throne of dry hay, in a jolting wagon. I discovered him one fine morning, slumbering in a wilderness of shrubs and flowers, and had nearly passed over him, absorbed as I was, in the contemplation of the surrounding glorious scenery. The acquaintance was soon made, no great ceremony of mutual introduction being needed. I had heard his name mentioned in circles interested in mesmerism, and knew him to be a powerful adept of the school of Du Potet.

'I have found,' he remarked in the course of the conversation, after I had made him share my seat of hay, 'one of the most wonderful subjects in this lovely Thebaide. I have an appointment tonight with the family. They are seeking to unravel the mystery of a murder by means of the clairvoyance of the girl. . . . She is wonderful; very, very wonderful!'

'Who is she?' I asked.

'A Rumanian gypsy. She was brought up, it appears, in the family of the Serbian reigning Prince, who reigns no more, for he was very mysteriously mur——. Holoah, take care! *Diable*, you will upset us over the precipice!' he hurriedly exclaimed, unceremoniously snatching from me the reins, and giving the horse a violent pull.

'You do not mean Prince Obrenovitch?' I asked, aghast.

'Yes, I do; and him precisely. Tonight I have to be there, hoping to close a series of seances by finally developing a most marvellous manifestation of the hidden power of human spirit, and you may come with me. I will introduce you; and, besides, you can help me as an interpreter, for they do not speak French.'

As I was pretty sure that if the somnambulist was Frosya, the rest of the family must be Gospoja P——, I readily accepted. At sunset we were at the foot of the mountain, leading to the old castle, as the Frenchman called the place. It fully deserved the poetical name given it. There was a rough bench in the depths of one of the shadowy retreats, and as we stopped at the entrance of this poetical place, and the Frenchman was gallantly busying himself with my horse on the suspicious-looking bridge which led across the water to the entrance gate, I saw a tall figure slowly rise from the bench and come toward us. It was my old friend, Gospoja P——, looking more pale and more mysterious than ever. She exhibited no surprise at seeing me, but simply greeting me after the Serbian fashion, with a triple kiss on both cheeks, she took hold of my hand and led me straight to the nest of ivy. Half reclining on a small carpet spread on the tall grass with her back leaning against the wall, I recognised our Frosya.

She was dressed in the national costume of the Valachian women, a sort of gauze turban intermingled with various gilt medals and bands on her head, white shirt with opened sleeves, and petticoats of variegated colours. Her face looked deadly pale, her eyes were closed, and her countenance presented that stony, sphinx-like look which characterises in such a peculiar way the entranced clairvoyant somnambulist. If it were not for the heaving motion of her chest and bosom, ornamented by rows of medals and bead necklaces which feebly tinkled at every breath, one might have thought her dead, so lifeless and corpse-like was her face. The Frenchman informed me that he had sent her to sleep just as we were approaching the house, and that she now was as he had left her the previous night : he then began busying himself with the *sujet*, as he called Frosya. Paying no further attention to us, he shook her by the hand, and then making a few rapid passes, stretched out her arm and stiffened it. The arm, as rigid as iron, remained in that position. He then closed all her fingers but one – the middle finger – which he caused to point at the evening star, which twinkled in the deep blue sky. Then he turned round and went over from right to left, throwing on some of his fluids here, again discharging them at another place; busying himself with his invisible but potent fluids, like a painter with his brush when giving the last touches to a picture.

The old lady, who had silently watched him, with her chin in her hand the while, put out her thin, skeleton-looking hand on his arm and arrested it, as he was preparing himself to begin the regular mesmeric passes.

'Wait,' she whispered, 'till the star is set, and the ninth hour completed. The Vourdalaki are hovering around; they may spoil the influence.'

'What does she say?' inquired the mesmeriser, annoyed at her interference.

I explained to him that the old lady feared the pernicious influences of the Vourdalaki.

'Vourdalaki? What's that, the Vourdalaki?' exclaimed the Frenchman. 'Let us be satisfied with Christian spirits, if they honour us tonight with a visit, and lose no time for the Vourdalaki.'

I glanced at the Gospoja. She had become deathly pale, and her brow was sternly knitted over her flashing black eyes.

'Tell him not to jest at this hour of the night!' she cried. 'He does not know the country. Even the Holy Church may fail to protect us, once the Vourdalaki are aroused. What's this?' pushing with her foot a bundle of herbs the botanising mesmeriser had laid near on the grass. She bent over the collection and anxiously examined the contents of the bundle, after which she flung the whole in the water.

'It must not be left here,' she firmly added; 'these are the St John's plants, and they might attract the wandering ones.'

Meanwhile the night had come, and the moon illuminated the landscape with a pale, ghostly light. The nights in the Banat are nearly as beautiful as in the East, and the Frenchman had to go on with his experiments in the open air as the priest of the Church had prohibited such in his tower, which was used as the parsonage, for fear of filling the holy precincts with the heretical devils of the mesmeriser, which, he remarked, he would be unable to exorcise on account of their being foreigners.

The old gentleman had thrown off his travelling blouse, rolled up his shirt sleeves, and now striking a theatrical attitude began a regular process of mesmerisation. Under his quivering fingers the odile fluid actually seemed to flash in the twilight. Frosya was placed with her figure facing the moon, and every motion of the entranced girl was discernible as in daylight. In a few minutes large drops of perspiration appeared on her brow and slowly rolled down her pale face, glittering in the moonbeams. Then she moved uneasily about and began chanting a low melody, to the words of which the Gospoja, anxiously bent over the unconscious girl, was listening with avidity and trying to catch every syllable. With her thin finger on her lips, her eyes nearly starting from their sockets, her frame motionless, the old lady seemed herself transfixed into a statue of attention. The group was a remarkable one, and I regretted that I was not a painter. What followed was a scene worthy to figure in *Macbeth*. At one side the slender girl, pale and corpse-like, writhing under the invisible fluid of him who for the hour was her omnipotent master; at the other the old matron, who, burning with her unquenched desire of revenge, stood like the picture of Nemesis, waiting for the long-expected name of the Prince's murderer to be at last pronounced. The Frenchman himself seemed transfigured, his grey hair standing on end; his bulky, clumsy form seemed to have grown in a few minutes. All theatrical pretence was now gone; there remained but the mesmeriser, aware of his responsibility, unconscious himself of the possible results, studying and anxiously expecting. Suddenly Frosya, as if lifted by some supernatural force, rose from her reclining posture and stood erect before us, motionless and still again, waiting for the magnetic fluid to direct her. The Frenchman, silently taking the old lady's hand, placed it in that of the somnambulist, and ordered her to put herself *en rapport* with the Gospoja.

'What seest thou, my daughter?' softly murmured the Serbian lady. 'Can your spirit seek out the murderers?'

'Search and behold!' sternly commanded the mesmeriser, fixing his gaze upon the face of the subject.

'I am – on my way – I go,' faintly whispered Frosya, her voice seeming not to come from herself, but from the surrounding atmosphere.

At this moment something so extraordinary took place that I doubt my ability to describe it. A luminous shadow, vapour-like, appeared closely surrounding the girl's body. At first about an inch in thickness, it gradually expanded, and, gathering itself, suddenly seemed to break off from the body altogether, and condense itself into a kind of semi-solid vapour, which very soon assumed the likeness of the somnambulist herself. Flickering about the surface of the earth, the form vacillated for two or three seconds, then glided noiselessly toward the river. It disappeared like a mist dissolved in the moonbeams, which seemed to absorb and imbibe it altogether.

I had followed the scene with intense attention. The mysterious operation, known in the East as the evocation of the *scîn-lâc*,* was taking place before my own eyes. To doubt was impossible, and Du Potet was right in saying that mesmerism is the conscious magic of the ancients, and spiritualism the unconscious effect of the same magic upon certain organisms.

As soon as the vaporous double had soaked itself through the pores of the girl, the Gospoja had, by a rapid motion of the hand which was left free, drawn from under her pelisse something which looked to us suspiciously like a small stiletto, and placed it as rapidly in the girl's bosom. The action was so quick that the mesmeriser, absorbed in his work, had not noticed it, as he afterwards told me. A few minutes elapsed in a dead silence. We seemed a group of petrified persons. Suddenly a thrilling and transpiercing cry burst from the entranced girl's lips. She bent forward, and snatching the stiletto from her bosom, plunged it furiously around her in the air, as if pursuing imaginary foes. Her mouth foamed, and incoherent, wild exclamations broke from her lips, among which discordant sounds I discerned several times two familiar Christian names of men. The mesmeriser was so terrified that he lost all control over himself, and instead of withdrawing the fluid, he loaded the girl with it still more.

'Take care!' exclaimed I. 'Stop! You will kill her or she will kill you!'

But the Frenchman had unwittingly raised subtle potencies of nature, over which he had no control. Furiously turning round, the girl struck at him a blow which would have killed him, had he not avoided it by jumping aside, receiving but a severe scratch on the right arm. The poor man was panic-stricken. Climbing with an

---

* *Scîn-lâc* means magic, necromancy and sorcery as well as a magical appearance, a spectral form, a deceptive appearance or a phantom (phantasma). *Scîn-lâeca* is a magician or sorcerer, and *Scîn-lâece*, a sorceress. – P.H.

extraordinary agility for a man of his bulky form on the wall over her, he fixed himself on it astride, and gathering the remnants of his will power, sent in her direction a series of passes. At the second, the girl dropped the weapon and remained motionless.

'What are you about?' hoarsely shouted the mesmeriser in French, seated like some monstrous night goblin on the wall. 'Answer me : I command you!'

'I did – but what she – whom you ordered me to obey – commanded me do,' answered the girl in French, to my amazement.

'What did the old witch command you?' irreverently asked he.

'To find them – who murdered – kill them – I did so – and they are no more! Avenged – avenged! They are . . .'

An exclamation of triumph, a loud shout of infernal joy rang loud in the air, and awakening the dogs of the neighbouring villages a responsive howl of barking began from that moment like a ceaseless echo of the Gospoja's cry.

'I am avenged. I feel it, I know it. My warning heart tells me that the fiends are no more.' And she fell panting on the ground, dragging down in her fall the girl, who allowed herself to be pulled down as if she were a bag of wool.

'I hope my subject did no further mischief tonight. She is a dangerous as well as a very wonderful subject!' said the Frenchman.

We parted. Three days after that I was at T——, and as I was sitting in the dining-room of a restaurant waiting for my lunch I happened to pick up a newspaper, and the first lines I read ran thus :

'VIENNA, 18—. Two Mysterious Deaths. Last evening, at 9.45, as P—— was about to retire, two of the gentlemen in waiting suddenly exhibited great terror, as though they had seen a dreadful apparition. They screamed, staggered, and ran about the room holding up their hands as if to ward off the blows of an unseen weapon. They paid no attention to the eager questions of the Prince and suite, but presently fell writhing upon the floor, and expired in great agony. Their bodies exhibited no appearance of apoplexy, nor any external marks of wounds; but wonderful to relate, there were numerous dark spots and long marks upon the skin, as though they were stabs and slashes made without puncturing the cuticle. The autopsy revealed the fact that beneath each of these mysterious discolourations there was a deposit of coagulated blood. The greatest excitement prevails, and the faculty are unable to solve the mystery.'

4

It is perhaps appropriate that the first modern Magus in England should also still be the most renowned. In Aleister Crowley we have the archetypal magician – a man with a craving for mystical discovery, self-driven through drugs, perversion, ancient rituals, strange ceremonies and the border-lands of hallucination and nightmare; a man who lived with, and indeed gloried in, the public epithet of 'The Wickedest Man in the World', and the personal designation of 'The Great Beast'. For all his gross flamboyance, his flaunting of society and its standards, and his almost maniacal search for the inner-most secrets of the black arts, Crowley was a magician of no mean ability and in his writings, beneath the extravagance and boasting, lies a rich vein of mystic exploration and discovery.

As in Europe and America, the great upsurge of interest in occultism in Britain came about in the last quarter of the nineteenth century, but in perhaps a less dramatic and dis-turbing manner. A number of occultists of like mind had come together in 1887 to form a society in which they could prac-tise esoteric rites and pursue the search for hidden truths – it was called the Hermetic Order of the Golden Dawn. Among these people were the writers W. B. Yeats, Arthur Machen, and Dion Fortune (all of whom we shall encounter later in this book), the Astronomer Royal of Scotland, the actress Florence Farr, a strange elderly clergyman who claimed to have discovered the elixir of life – and then lost it when he needed it – and the leader, a weird figure named S. L. MacGregor Mathers. Mathers was undoubtedly the main-spring of the new Order and indeed brought to it vast occult knowledge culled while studying ancient ritual magic in Paris. He also introduced to the Order his protégé, Aleister Crowley, who was later to surpass him in skill and appropriate many of his rituals.

Edward Alexander Crowley (1875-1947) was born in the year of Eliphas Levi's death and indeed later claimed to be the reincarnation of the French Magus. The son of strict Plymouth Brethren parents, Crowley at first embraced the Church enthusiastically, but then began to resent its rigours and demands and by the time he was a teenager was seeking darker pleasures through study of 'Satan and Scarlet Women'. At Cambridge University he distinguished himself as a mountaineer and chess player and revealed his undoubted literary talents by writing a series of exotic and erotic poems. His obsession with sex was also beginning to dominate his life and with his discovery of the Occult through reading a privately printed work, *The Book of Black Magic and Pacts*, he at once found a way of fusing his passion for the flesh with magical rites. This, in time, was to lead him to a meeting with MacGregor Mathers and his admission to the Golden Dawn.

Next, settling in London, Crowley built two 'temples' in his rooms in Chancery Lane – one for the performance of 'white magic' (it contained several large looking-glasses, to 'throw back the forces of the evocations') and one for 'black magic'. In the latter was an altar, a magic circle and a human skeleton 'to which he offered blood, small birds and beef tea', according to one biographer. Not surprisingly Crowley soon grew tired of the staid (by his standards) activities of the Golden Dawn and also of being in the shadow of Mathers. He decided to continue his experimentation elsewhere and moved to a Scottish mansion near Loch Ness. By now an impressive, bulky figure complete with shaven head, hypnotic eyes and beringed hands, he quickly threw the superstitious local populace into a state of terror and rumours proliferated about hideous rites being performed in the new laird's house. Crowley himself claimed that he had at last succeeded in raising demons as described in the old *grimoires* and that his occult power was such that he could now kill or punish at will – and certainly there were some strange and inexplicable deaths in the vicinity during his residence in the mansion.

In 1909, Crowley decided to travel abroad again and during this journey he announced that he had finally reached the highest realms of the occult and was now one of its 'Secret Chiefs'. He also propounded his philosophy of life in the simple statement, 'There is no law beyond Do what thou wilt.' In 1921 he settled in an old Abbey at Cefalu, off the coast of Sicily, with his two mistresses, several children and a number of followers. Already addicted to heroin, he used drugs in his further searches after the 'dark secrets' until word of his abominable behaviour (including the suggestion that he had sacrificed a child at a Black Mass) reached the ears of the authorities and he was ordered out of the country.

The final years of his life were spent wandering in Europe where he published his *Magick in Theory and Practice* (certainly one of the very best of all works on the occult) and completed *The Book of the Law*, a collection of reflections on magical experiments which remains in manuscript to this day. Crowley wrote of it : 'The study of this book is forbidden. . . . Those who discuss [its] contents are to be shunned by all as centres of pestilence.' One man who was said to have ignored this warning died in terrible agony.

The years of excess finally wore Crowley out and in 1947, while the press and public were still decrying him as 'the Wickedest Man in the World', he died in Hastings. He was buried by his followers in the local cemetery, and the special occult rites observed were described predictably and sensationally by reporters as a Black Mass.

There is no doubt that Crowley's life was a great deal more varied than it has been possible to describe here, and his biographer and literary executor, John Symonds, probably summed it up best in *The Confessions of Aleister Crowley* when he wrote : 'He spent his whole existence in struggling through the Abyss, or if you will, in explaining the Unconscious with the aid of every known stimulant and magic ritual.' To represent him here in fictional form I have chosen a somewhat gruesome episode about necromancy (the attempted raising of the spirits of the dead and a great passion of Crowley's) which is clearly based on certain rituals the master had himself performed. It will provide a stark contrast to the writings of some of Crowley's other colleagues in English occult circles which we shall come to later.

* * *

An Experiment in Necromancy

ALEISTER CROWLEY

The Neapolitan winter is one of uncommon clemency at most times, but in the year in which our story occurs even this state of affairs had been surpassed; indeed save for a touch of frost, kindly and wholesome, on a few nights, it had no frown or rigour. Day after day the sun enkindled the still air, and life danced with love upon the hills.

But on the night of her fullness, the moon was suddenly tawny and obscure, with a reddish vapour about her, as if she had wrapped herself in a mantle of anger; and the next dawn broke grey with storm, the wind tearing its way across the mountain spine of Italy, as if some horde of demon bandits were raiding the peasantry of the plains.

On one ridge particularly subjected to the senseless madness of the blast stood the villa of a certain occultist, one Dr Vesquit, who had come especially to this isolated region for the performance of a most terrible and dangerous experiment in necromancy — the operation for making contact with the spirits of the dead.

As the day passed, the violence of the storm increased and the Doctor began to fear somewhat for the safety of his plans. Then, dramatically, about an hour after noon the speed of the hurricane abated and the sky was visible, through the earth-vapours, as a wrack of wrathful clouds.

Though the gale was yet fierce, its heart broke in a torrent of sleet mixed with hail; for two hours more it drove almost horizontally against the hillside, and then, steadying and steepening, fell as a flood, a cataract of icy rain.

The slopes of Posilippo roared with their foaming load; gardens were washed clear of soil; walls broke down before the impetuosity of the waves they strove to dam; and the streets of lower Naples stood in water to the height of a man's thigh.

The hour for the beginning of the work of the Doctor was that of sunset; and at that moment, much to his relief, the rain, after a last burst of vehemence, ceased entirely; nightfall, though black and bitter, was silent as the grave.

In a little chapel behind Dr Vesquit's villa where the ritual was

ONE OF ALEISTER CROWLEY'S
NUMEROUS SYMBOLS

to take place a portion of the marble floor had been torn up; for it was desired to touch the naked earth with the bare feet, and draw her powers directly up from their volcanic stratum.

This raw earth had been smeared with mire brought from the swamps of the Maremma; and upon this sulphur had been sprinkled until it formed a thick layer. In this sulphur the magic circle had been drawn with a two-pointed stick, and the grooves thus made had been filled with charcoal powder.

It was not a true circle; no figure of sanctity and perfection might enter into that accursed rite; it had been made somewhat in the shape of an old-fashioned keyhole, a combination of circle and triangle.

In the centre of this shape lay the body of a man which had been secured for the rites by trusted and well-paid functionaries, its head towards the north; beside it stood the first of the Doctor's assistants, a tall, thin fellow named Arthwait, who held the mystical *grimoire* in one hand, and a lighted taper of black wax in the other. On the opposite side was a second man, a Turk, Abdul Bey, holding a goat in leash, and bearing the sickle which the Doctor was to use as the principal magical weapon of the ceremony.

Dr Vesquit was himself the last to enter the circle. In a basket he had four black cats; and, when he had lighted the nine small candles about the circle, he pinned the four cats, at the four quarters, with black arrows of iron. He was careful not to kill them; it was important that their agony should frighten away any undesirable spirits.

All being now ready, the necromancers fell upon their knees, for this servile position is pleasing to the enemies of mankind.

The forces which made man, alone of all animals, erect, love to see him thank them for that independence by refusing to surrender it.

The main plan of Dr Vesquit's ceremony was simple; it was to invoke the spirit of a demon into the goat, and slaying the animal at that moment of possession upon the corpse, to endow that corpse with the demoniac power, in a kind of hideous marriage.

The object was then identical with that of spiritism, or 'spiritualism', as it is commonly and illiterately called; but Dr Vesquit was a serious student, determined to obtain results, and not to be duped; his methods were consequently more efficient than those of the common or parlour medium.

The assistant, Arthwait, opened the *grimoire* and began his conjurations. It would be impossible to reproduce the hideous confusion and complexity of the manner, and undesirable to indicate the abomination of the matter. But every name of opposition to light was invoked in its own rite; the fearful deities of man's dawn, when nature was supposed to be a personal power of cruelty, delighting in murder, rape, and pillage, were called by their most secret names, and commemoration made of their deeds of infamy.

Such was the recital of horror that, cloaked even as it was in Arthwait's unintelligible style, the meaning was salient by virtue of the tone of the enchanter, and the gestures with which Vesquit accompanied him, going in dumb show through all the gamut of infernal discord, the music of the pit. He showed how children were cast into the fire, or thrown to bears, or offered up in sacrifice on bloody altars; how peaceful nations were uprooted by savage tribes in the name of their demon, their men slain or mutilated and enslaved, their women butchered, their virgins ravished; how miracle testified to the power of the evil ones, the earth opening to swallow heretic priests, the sun stopped in the sky that the hours of massacre might be prolonged.

It was in short one interminable recital of treachery and murder and revenge; never a thought of pity or of kindliness, of common decency or common humanity, struck a false note in that record of vileness; and it culminated in the ghastliest atrocity of human history, when the one man in all that cut-throat race who now and then showed gleams of a nobler mind was chosen for torture and death as a final offering to the blood-lust of the fiend.

With a sort of hellish laughter, the second conjuration continued the recital; how the demon had brought the corpse of his victim to life, and mocked and profaned his humanity by concealing himself in that man-shape, thence to continue his reign, and extend his empire, under the cloak of hypocrisy. The crimes that had been done openly in the fiend's name, were now to be carried on with fresh device of shame and horror, by those who called themselves the priests of his victim.

By this commemoration was concluded the first part of the ceremony; the atmosphere of the fiend, so to speak, was brought into the circle; in the second part the demon was to be identified with the goat; in the third part the two first were joined, and the goat as he died was to repeat the miracle wrought in long ages upon that other victim, by coming to life again humanised by the contact of the ghost of the sorcerer.

It is not permissible to describe the ritual in detail; it is too execrably efficient; but the Turk, brought up in a merciful and cleanly religion, with but few stains of savagery upon it, faltered and nigh fainted and indeed the brains of them all were awhirl. As Eliphas Levi says, evil ceremonies are a true intellectual poison; they do invoke the powers of hallucination and madness as surely as does hashish. And who dare call the phantoms of delirium 'unreal'? They are real enough to kill a man, to ruin a life, to push a soul to every kind of crime; and there are not many 'real' 'material' things that have such weight in work.

Phantoms, then, were apparent to the necromancers; and there was no doubt in any of their minds that they were dealing with actual and malignant entities.

The hideous cries of the tortured cats mingled with the triumphant bleating of the goat and the nasal monotone of Arthwait as he mouthed the words of the *grimoire*. And it seemed to all of them as though the air grew thick and greasy; that of that slime were bred innumerable creeping things, monsters misshapen, abortions of dead paths of evolution, creatures which had not been found fit to live upon the earth and so had been cast off by her as excrement. It seemed as if the goat were conscious of the phantoms; as if he understood himself as demon king of those regions; for he bounded under the manipulations of Vesquit with such rage and pride that Abdul Bey was forced to use all his strength to hold him. It was taken as a sign of success by all the necromancers; and as Vesquit made the final gesture, Arthwait turned his page, and Abdul struck home with a great knife to the brute's heart.

Now, as the blood stained their grave-clothes, the hearts of the three sorcerers beat heavily. A foul sweat broke out upon them. The sudden change – psychological or magical? – from the turgid drone of Arthwait to the grimness of that silence in which the howls of the agonising cats rose hideous, struck them with a deadly fear. Or was it that they realised for the first time on what a ship they had embarked?

Suppose the corpse did move? Suppose it rose in the power of the devil, and strangled them? Their sweat ran down, and mingled with the blood. The stench of the slain goat was horrible, and the corpse had begun decomposition. The sulphur, burning in little patches here and there, where a candle had fallen and kindled it, added the reek of hell to that of death. Abdul Bey of a sudden was taken deathly sick; at the end he pitched forward, prone upon the corpse. Vesquit pulled him roughly back, and administered a violent stimulant, which made him master of himself.

Now Arthwait started the final conjuration. It can hardly be called language; it was like the jabber of a monkey-house, and like the yells of a thousand savages, and like the moaning of damned souls.

Meanwhile Vesquit proceeded to the last stage of his task. With his knife he hacked off the goat's head, and thrust it into a cavity slashed in the abdomen of the other body. Other parts of the goat he thrust into the mouth of the corpse, while the obscene clamour of the cats mingled with the maniac howls of his colleague.

And then one thing happened which none of them expected. Abdul Bey flung himself down upon the carcasses, and began to tear them with his teeth, and lap the blood with his tongue. Arthwait shrieked out in terror that the Turk had gone mad; but Vesquit understood the truth. Abdul was the most sensitive of the party, and the least developed; it was in him that the spirit of the body, demon-inspired, would manifest.

A few minutes of that scene, and then the Turk sat up. His face expressed the most extreme pleasure. It was the release of a soul from agony that showed itself. But he must have known that his time was short, for he spoke rapidly and earnestly, with febrile energy. And his words were commanding and convincing : Vesquit had no doubt that they were in the presence of knowledge vastly superior to anything that he had yet found.

He wrote down the speech upon the tablets that he had prepared for this purpose.

> Hecate will come to help you !
> All the powers are at your service; but they are stronger !
> Treachery shall save you !
> Quick ! Conceal yourselves awhile. Even so, you are nigh to death !
> Oh haste ! Look yonder who is standing ready to smite !

The voice dropped. Well was it for Vesquit that he kept his presence of mind. The necromancers looked over their shoulders, and in the east was a blue mist shaped like an egg. In the midst of it, standing upon two crocodiles, was the image of a demon of the underworld, smiling, with his finger upon his lips. Vesquit realised that he was in contact with a force a thousand times greater than any at his disposal. He obeyed instantly the command spoken through Abdul Bey. 'I swear,' he cried, raising his right hand to heaven, 'I swear that we intend you no manner of hurt.' He flushed inwardly, knowing it for a lie, and therefore useless to avert the blow which he felt poised above him. He sought a new form of words. 'I swear that we will not seek to break through your defences.' Abdul Bey gasped out that it was well and fell backwards, as one dead.

In another moment Arthwait, with a yell, a last invocation of that fiend whom he really believed to be omnipotent, entered into spasmodic convulsions, like a man poisoned with strychnine, or dying of tetanus. Vesquit appalled at the fate of his companions, gazed on the figure of the Demon in an agony of fear and horror. It retained the smile, and Vesquit reached his arms towards it. 'Mercy !' he cried, 'oh, my lord, mercy !'

Arthwait was writhing upon the corpses, horribly twisting, foaming black blood from his lungs.

And the old Doctor saw in that instant that his life had been an imbecility, that he had taken the wrong path.

The Demon still smiled. 'Oh my lord!' cried Vesquit, rising to his feet, ' 'twere better I should die.'

The formula of humanity is the willing acceptance of death; and as love, in the male, is itself of the nature of a voluntary death, and therefore a sacrament, so that he who loves slays himself, therefore he who slays himself that life may live becomes a lover. Vesquit stretched out his arms in the sign of the Cross, the symbol of Him who gives life through his own death, or of the instrument of that life and of that death, of the Holy One appointed from the foundation of the world as its redeemer.

It was as if there had come to him a flash of that most secret Word of all initiated knowledge, so secret and so simple that it may be declared openly in the market-place, and no man hear it. At last he realised himself as a silly old man, whose weakness and pliability in the hands of evil had made him its accomplice. And he saw that death, grasped now, might save him.

The Demon still smiled.

'I invoke the return of the current!' cried Vesquit aloud; and thus, uniting justice with self-sacrifice, he died the death of the righteous.

The image faded away.

The great operation of necromancy had come to naught.

Yet the writing remained; and nearly a day later, when Abdul Bey came to himself, it was the first thing that caught his eye. He thrust it into his shroud, automatically; then stumbled to his feet, and sought his colleagues. At his feet the old Doctor lay dead; Arthwait, his convulsion terminated by exhaustion approximating coma, lay with his head upon the carrion, his tongue lolling from his mouth, chewed to a bloody pulp.

The Turk carried him from the chapel to the villa. His high connections made it easy for him to secure a silent doctor to certify the death of Vesquit, and to attend to Arthwait, who passed from one convulsion to another at frequent intervals. It was almost a month before he could be considered out of danger, and a week after that he was his own man again. The two men then repaired immediately to Paris and vowed never again to speak of, or undertake, another *Experiment in Necromancy*.

5

A contemporary of Aleister Crowley's, his erstwhile colleague, and – perhaps most surprisingly – an adept almost his equal in the ranks of magic, was the Irish poet and dramatist, W. B. Yeats. Today Yeats's reputation as one of Ireland's greatest sons – and certainly her most distinguished Nobel Prizewinner – has virtually obscured the details of his vast occult learning and great proficiency in the mystic sciences. He played a major part in the formation of the Hermetic Order of the Golden Dawn when Crowley was no more than a willing initiate and indeed largely composed the group's rituals with MacGregor Mathers. Certainly his enquiries into the secret arts were never to lead him to the same black depths as Crowley, but unquestionably he deserves a place as one of the great adepts of the modern era.

The public life of William Butler Yeats (1865-1939) and his work in bringing about a renaissance of interest in Irish folklore and culture has already been so well recorded as to need no mention here. Rather, it is of his private life and that part of it devoted to occultism that we should direct ourselves. Like Aleister Crowley he appears to have 'discovered' magic while a student, but his writings indicate he was aware of the secret practice of sorcery in Ireland from his childhood days.* Yeats met MacGregor Mathers in 1887 and when the poet found they shared an interest in what he called 'the dark side of the mind' he agreed to be one of the first members of the new Hermetic Order. After his initiation, he progressed swiftly through the minor grades of knowledge and in 1890 took the name of *Frater Daemon est Deus Inversus*, meaning the Devil is the reverse side of God. (Yeats took this title from Eliphas Levi and it underlined his particular interest in Diabolism, an interest also shared by, and much discussed with, Aubrey Beardsley.) The new adept was responsible, as we have noted,

* See W. B. Yeats, 'The Sorcerers' in *The Necromancers,* ed. Peter Haining (London Hodder & Stoughton, 1971; New York: William Morrow, 1972).

for the compiling of the Order's rituals and also introduced several new members, including the actress Florence Farr and Miss Horniman who later financed the Abbey Theatre in Dublin. Yeats's deep involvement with magic continued unabated until the arrival in the Order of Aleister Crowley. Both men being poets, they frequently discussed their work, but when the newcomer airily boasted of his 'superior talent' in this field, Yeats realised the Order could not long hold them both. Widespread internal dissent followed shortly thereafter, mainly through the somewhat tyrannical leadership of MacGregor Mathers – and although Yeats was anxious to remain in the group for the sake of his experiments, in 1905 he finally severed his connections. He was never again to involve himself in organised magic, but he continued his enquiries into the occult and in 1927 published his remarkable book of magical theories and practices, *The Trembling of the Veil*. In it he gave his summation of the working of magic : 'My friends believed that the dark portion of the mind (the subconscious) had an incalculable power, and even over events. To influence events and one's mind, one had to draw the attention of that dark portion, to turn it as it were into a new direction. One repeated certain names and drew or imagined certain symbolic forms which had acquired a precise meaning, not only to the dark portion of one's own mind but to the mind of the race.'

'Rosa Alchemica', which here represents W. B. Yeats, gives us a splendid insight into his views on the occult, and in its telling of the experiences of a young man becoming involved with dabblers in the unknown surely parallels some of his own experiences.

* * *

Rosa Alchemica

W. B. Yeats

I

It is now more than ten years since I met, for the last time, Michael Robartes, and for the first time and the last time his friends and fellow students; and witnessed his and their tragic end, and endured those strange experiences, which have changed me so that my writings have grown less popular and less intelligible, and driven me almost to the verge of taking the habit of St Dominic. I had just published *Rosa Alchemica*, a little work on the Alchemists, somewhat in the manner of Sir Thomas Browne, and had received many letters from believers in the arcane sciences, upbraiding what they called my timidity, for they could not believe so evident sympathy but the sympathy of the artist, which is half pity, for everything which has moved men's hearts in any age. I had discovered, early in my researches, that their doctrine was no merely chemical phantasy, but a philosophy they applied to the world, to the elements and to man himself; and that they sought to fashion gold out of common metals merely as part of an universal transmutation of all things into some divine and imperishable substance; and this enabled me to make my little book a fanciful reverie over the transmutation of life into art, and a cry of measureless desire for a world made wholly of essences.

I was sitting dreaming of what I had written, in my house in one of the old parts of Dublin; a house my ancestors had made almost famous through their part in the politics of the city and their friendships with the famous men of their generations; and was feeling an unwonted happiness at having at last accomplished a long-cherished design, and made my rooms an expression of this favourite doctrine. The portraits, of more historical than artistic interest, had gone; and tapestry, full of the blue and bronze of peacocks, fell over the doors, and shut out all history and activity untouched with beauty and peace; and now when I looked at my Crevelli and pondered on the rose in the hand of the Virgin, wherein the form was so delicate and precise that it seemed more

'THE TRUE AND OFFICIAL
ROSICRUCIAN CROSS'

like a thought than a flower, or at the grey dawn and rapturous
faces of my Francesca, I knew all a Christian's ecstasy without his
slavery to rule and custom; when I pondered over the antique
bronze gods and goddesses, which I had mortgaged my house to
buy, I had all a pagan's delight in various beauty and without his
terror at sleepless destiny and his labour with many sacrifices; and
I had only to go to my bookshelf, where every book was bound in
leather, stamped with intricate ornament, and of a carefully chosen
colour : Shakespeare in the orange of the glory of the world, Dante
in the dull red of his anger, Milton in the blue-grey of his formal
calm; and I could experience what I would of human passions
without their bitterness and without satiety. I had gathered about
me all gods because I believed in none, and experienced every
pleasure because I gave myself to none, but held myself apart,
individual, indissoluble, a mirror of polished steel : I looked in the
triumph of this imagination at the birds of Hera, glowing in the
firelight as though they were wrought of jewels; and to my mind,
for which symbolism was a necessity, they seemed the doorkeepers
of my world, shutting out all that was not of as affluent a beauty
as their own; and for a moment I thought as I had thought in so
many other moments, that it was possible to rob life of every
bitterness except the bitterness of death; and then a thought which
had followed this thought, time after time, filled me with a passion-

ate sorrow. All those forms: that Madonna with her brooding purity, those rapturous faces singing in the morning light, those bronze divinities with their passionless dignity, those wild shapes rushing from despair to despair, belonged to a divine world wherein I had no part; and every experience, however profound, every perception, however exquisite, would bring me the bitter dream of a limitless energy I could never know, and even in my most perfect moment I would be two selves, the one watching with heavy eyes the other's moment of content. I had heaped about me the gold born in the crucibles of others; but the supreme dream of the alchemist, the transmutation of the weary heart into a weariless spirit, was as far from me as, I doubted not, it had been from him also. I turned to my last purchase, a set of alchemical apparatus which, the dealer in the Rue le Peletier had assured me, once belonged to Raymond Lully, and as I joined the *alembic* to the *athanor* and laid the *lavacrum maris* at their side, I understood the alchemical doctrine, that all beings, divided from the great deep where spirits wander, one and yet a multitude, are weary; and sympathised, in the pride of my connoisseurship, with the consuming thirst for destruction which made the alchemist veil under his symbols of lions and dragons, of eagles and ravens, of dew and of nitre, a search for an essence which would dissolve all mortal things. I repeated to myself the ninth key of Basilius Valentinus, in which he compares the fire of the last day to the fire of the alchemist, and the world to the alchemist's furnace, and would have us know that all must be dissolved before the divine substance, material gold or immaterial ecstasy, awake. I had dissolved indeed the mortal world and lived amid immortal essences, but had obtained no miraculous ecstasy. As I thought of these things, I drew aside the curtains and looked out into the darkness, and it seemed to my troubled fancy that all those little points of light filling the sky were the furnaces of innumerable divine alchemists, who labour continually, turning lead into gold, weariness into ecstasy, bodies into souls, the darkness into God; and at their perfect labour my mortality grew heavy, and I cried out, as so many dreamers and men of letters in our age have cried, for the birth of that elaborate spiritual beauty which could alone uplift souls weighted with so many dreams.

II

My reverie was broken by a loud knocking at the door, and I wondered the more at this because I had no visitors, and had bid my servants do all things silently, lest they broke the dream of my inner life. Feeling a little curious, I resolved to go to the door myself, and, taking one of the silver candlesticks from the mantel piece, began to descend the stairs. The servants appeared to be out, for though the sound poured through every corner and crevice of the house there was no stir in the lower rooms. I remembered that because my needs were so few, my part in life so little, they had begun to come and go as they would, often leaving me alone for hours. The emptiness and silence of a world from which I had driven everything but dreams suddenly overwhelmed me, and I shuddered as I drew the bolt. I found before me Michael Robartes, whom I had not seen for years, and whose wild red hair, fierce eyes, sensitive, tremulous lips and rough clothes made him look now just as they used to do fifteen years before, something between debauchee, a saint, and a peasant. He had recently come to Ireland, he said, and wished to see me on a matter of importance, indeed, the only matter of importance for him and for me. His voice brought up before me our student years in Paris, and remembering the magnetic power he had once possessed over me, a little fear mingled with much annoyance at this irrelevant intrusion, as I led the way up the wide staircase, where Swift had passed joking and railing, and Curran telling stories and quoting Greek, in simpler days, before men's minds, subtilised and complicated by the romantic movement in art and literature, began to tremble on the verge of some unimagined revelation. I felt that my hand shook, and saw that the light of the candle wavered and quivered more than it need have upon the Maenads on the old French panel, making them look like the first beings slowly shaping in the formless and void darkness. When the door had closed, and the peacock curtain, glimmering like many-coloured flame, fell between us and the world, I felt, in a way I could not understand, that some singular and unexpected thing was about to happen. I went over the mantelpiece, and finding that a little chainless bronze censer, upon the outside, with pieces of painted china by Oraz

Fontana, which I had filled with antique amulets, had fallen upon its side and poured out its contents, I began to gather the amulets into the bowl, partly to collect my thoughts and partly with that habitual reverence which seemed to me the due of things so long connected with secret hopes and fears. 'I see,' said Michael Robartes, 'that you are still fond of incense, and I can show you an incense more precious than any you have ever seen,' and as he spoke he took the censer out of my hand and put the amulets in a little heap between the *athanor* and the *alembic*. I sat down, and he sat down at the side of the fire, and sat there for a while looking into the fire, and holding the censer in his hand. 'I have come to ask you something,' he said, 'and the incense will fill the room, and our thoughts, with its sweet odour while we are talking. I got it from an old man in Syria, who said it was made from flowers, of one kind with the flowers that laid their heavy purple petals upon the hands and upon the hair and upon the feet of Christ in the Garden of Gethsemane, and folded Him in their heavy breath, until He cried against the cross and his destiny.' He shook some dust into the censer out of a small silk bag, and set the censer upon the floor and lit the dust which sent up a blue stream of smoke, that spread out over the ceiling, and flowed downwards again until it was like Milton's banyan tree. It filled me, as incense often does, with a faint sleepiness, so that I started when he said, 'I have come to ask you that question which I asked you in Paris, and which you left Paris rather than answer.'

He had turned his eyes towards me, and I saw them glitter in the firelight, and through the incense, as I replied : 'You mean, will I become an initiate of your Order of the Alchemical Rose? I would not consent in Paris, when I was full of unsatisfied desire, and now that I have at last fashioned my life according to my desire, am I likely to consent?'

'You have changed greatly since then,' he answered. 'I have read your books, and now I see you among all these images, and I understand you better than you do yourself, for I have been with many and many dreamers at the same cross-ways. You have shut away the world and gathered the gods about you, and if you do not throw yourself at their feet, you will be always full of lassitude, and of wavering purpose, for a man must forget he is miserable in the bustle and noise of the multitude in this world and in time; or seek a mystical union with the multitude who govern this world

and time.' And then he murmured something I could not hear, and
as though to someone I could not see.

For a moment the room appeared to darken, as it used to do
when he was about to perform some singular experiment, and in
the darkness the peacocks upon the doors seemed to glow with a
more intense colour. I cast off the illusion, which was, I believe
merely caused by memory, and by the twilight of incense, for I
would not acknowledge that he could overcome my now mature
intellect; and I said : 'Even if I grant that I need a spiritual belief
and some form of worship, why should I go to Eleusis and not to
Calvary?' He leaned forward and began speaking with a slightl
rhythmical intonation, and as he spoke I had to struggle again
with the shadow, as of some older night than the night of the sun
which began to dim the light of the candles and to blot out the
little gleams upon the corner of picture-frames and on the bronz
divinities, and to turn the blue of the incense to a heavy purple
while it left the peacocks to glimmer and glow as though each
separate colour were a living spirit. I had fallen into a profoun
dream-like reverie in which I heard him speaking as at a distanc
'And yet there is no one who communes with only one god,' he was
saying, 'and the more a man lives in imagination and in a refined
understanding, the more gods does he meet with and talk with, an
the more does he come under the power of Roland, who sounde
in the Valley of Roncesvalles the last trumpet of the body's will an
pleasure; and of Hamlet, who saw them perishing away, an
sighed; and of Faust, who looked for them up and down the
world and could not find them; and under the power of all tho
countless divinities who have taken upon themselves spiritual bodi
in the minds of the modern poets and romance writers, and und
the power of the old divinities, who since the Renaissance have wc
everything of their ancient worship except the sacrifice of bir
and fishes, the fragrance of garlands and the smoke of incense. Th
many think humanity made these divinities, and that it can unma
them again; but we who have seen them pass in rattling harne
and in soft robes, and heard them speak with articulate voices wh
we lay in deathlike trance, know that they are always making an
unmaking humanity, which is indeed but the trembling of the
lips.'

He had stood up and begun to walk to and fro, and had becom
in my waking dream a shuttle weaving an immense purple w

whose folds had begun to fill the room. The room seemed to have become inexplicably silent, as though all but the web and the weaving were at an end in the world. 'They have come to us; they have come to us,' the voice began again; 'all that have ever been in your reverie, all that you have met with in books. There is Lear, his head still wet with the thunder-storm, and he laughs because you thought yourself an existence who are but a shadow, and him a shadow who is an eternal god; and there is Beatrice, with her lips half parted in a smile, as though all the stars were about to pass away in a sigh of love; and there is the mother of the God of humility who cast so great a spell over men that they have tried to un-people their hearts that he might reign alone, but she holds in her hand the rose whose every petal is a god; and there, O swiftly she comes! is Aphrodite under a twilight falling from the wings of numberless sparrows, and about her feet are the grey and white doves.' In the midst of my dream I saw him hold out his left arm and pass his right hand over it as though he stroked the wings of doves. I made a violent effort which seemed almost to tear me in two, and said with forced determination : 'You would sweep me away into an indefinite world which fills me with terror; and yet a man is a great man just in so far as he can make his mind reflect everything with indifferent precision like a mirror.' I seemed to be perfectly master of myself, and went on, but more rapidly : 'I command you to leave me at once, for your ideas and phantasies are but the illusions that creep like maggots into civilisations when they begin to decline, and into minds when they begin to decay.' I had grown suddenly angry, and seizing the *alembic* from the table, was about to rise and strike him with it, when the peacocks on the door behind him appeared to grow immense; and then the *alembic* fell from my fingers and I was drowned in a tide of green and blue and bronze feathers, and as I struggled hopelessly I heard a distant voice saying : 'Our master Avicenna has written that all life proceeds out of corruption.' The glittering feathers had now covered me completely, and I knew that I had struggled for hundreds of years, and I was conquered at last. I was sinking into the depth when the green and blue and bronze that seemed to fill the world became a sea of flame and swept me away, and as I was swirled along I heard a voice over my head cry, 'The mirror is broken in two pieces,' and another voice answer, 'The mirror is broken in four pieces,' and a more distant voice cry with an exultant cry, 'The mirror is broken into numberless pieces'; and then a multitude of pale hands were reaching towards me, and strange gentle faces bending above me, and half wailing and half caressing voices uttering words that were forgotten the moment they were spoken. I was being lifted out of the tide of flame, and felt my memories, my hopes, my thoughts, my will, everything I held to be myself, melting away; then I seemed to rise through numberless companies of beings who were, I understood, in some way more certain than thought, each wrapped in his eternal moment, in the perfect lifting of an arm, in a little circlet of rhythmical words, in dreaming with dim eyes and half-closed eyelids. And then I passed beyond these forms, which were so beautiful they had almost ceased to be, and, having endured strange moods, melancholy, as it seemed, with the weight of many worlds, I passed into that Death which is Beauty herself, and into that Loneliness which all the multitudes desire without ceasing. All things that had ever lived seemed to come and dwell in my heart, and I in theirs; and I had never again known mortality or tears, had I not suddenly fallen from the certainty of vision into the uncertainty of dream, and become a drop of molten gold falling with immense rapidity, through a night elaborate with stars, and all about me a melancholy exultant wailing. I fell and fell and fell, and then the wailing was but the wailing of the wind in the chimney, and I awoke to find myself leaning upon the table and supporting my head with my hands. I saw the *alembic* swaying from side to side in the distant corner it had rolled to, and Michael Robartes watching me and waiting. 'I will go wherever you will,' I said, 'and do whatever you bid me, for I have been with eternal things.' 'I knew,' he replied, 'you must need answer as you have answered, when I heard the storm begin. You must come to a great distance, for we were commanded to build our temple between the pure multitude by the waves and the impure multitude of men.'

III

I did not speak as we drove through the deserted streets, for my mind was curiously empty of familiar thoughts and experiences; it seemed to have been plucked out of the definite world and cast

naked upon a shoreless sea. There were moments when the vision
appeared on the point of returning, and I would half-remember,
with an ecstasy of joy or sorrow, crimes and heroisms, fortunes and
misfortunes; or begin to contemplate, with a sudden leaping of the
heart, hopes and terrors, desires and ambitions, alien to my orderly
and careful life; and then I would awake shuddering at the thought
that some great imponderable being had swept through my mind.
It was indeed days before this feeling passed perfectly away, and
even now, when I have sought refuge in the only definite faith, I
feel a great tolerance for those people with incoherent personalities,
who gather in the chapels and meeting-places of certain obscure
sects, because I also have felt fixed habits and principles dissolving
before a power, which was *hysterica passio* or sheer madness, if you
will, but was so powerful in its melancholy exultation that I tremble
lest it wake again and drive me from my new-found peace.

When we came in the grey light to the great half-empty term-
inus, it seemed to me I was so changed that I was no more, as man
is, a moment shuddering at eternity, but eternity weeping and
laughing over a moment; and when we had started and Michael
Robartes had fallen asleep, as he soon did, his sleeping face, in
which there was no sign of all that had so shaken me and that
now kept me wakeful, was to my excited mind more like a mask
than a face. The fancy possessed me that the man behind it had
dissolved away like salt in water, and that it laughed and sighed,
appealed and denounced at the bidding of beings greater or less
than man. 'This is not Michael Robartes at all : Michael Robartes
is dead; dead for ten, for twenty years perhaps,' I kept repeating
to myself. I fell at last into a feverish sleep, waking up from time
to time when we rushed past some little town, its slated roofs
shining with wet, or still lake gleaming in the cold morning light.
I had been too preoccupied to ask where we were going, or to notice
what tickets Michael Robartes had taken, but I knew now from
the direction of the sun that we were going westward; and presently
I knew also, by the way in which the trees had grown into the
semblance of tattered beggars flying with bent heads towards the
east, that we were approaching the western coast. Then immediately I saw the sea between the low hills upon the left, its dull
grey broken into white patches and lines.

When we left the train we had still, I found, some way to go,
and set out, buttoning our coats about us, for the wind was bitter

and violent. Michael Robartes was silent, seeming anxious to leave me to my thoughts; and as we walked between the sea and the rocky side of a great promontory, I realised with a new perfection what a shock had been given to all my habits of thought and of feelings, if indeed some mysterious change had not taken place in the substance of my mind, for the grey waves, plumed with scudding foam, had grown part of a teeming, fantastic inner life; and when Michael Robartes pointed to a square ancient-looking house, with a much smaller and newer building under its lee, set out on the very end of a dilapidated and almost deserted pier, and said it was the Temple of the Alchemical Rose, I was possessed with the phantasy that the sea, which kept covering it with showers of white foam, was claiming it as part of some indefinite and passionate life, which had begun to war upon our orderly and careful days, and was about to plunge the world into a night as obscure as that which followed the downfall of the classical world. One part of my mind mocked this phantastic terror, but the other, the part that still lay half plunged in vision, listened to the clash of unknown armies, and shuddered at unimaginable fanaticisms, that hung in those grey leaping waves.

We had gone but a few paces along the pier when we came upon an old man, who was evidently a watchman, for he sat in an overset barrel, close to a place where masons had been lately working upon a break in the pier, and had in front of him a fire such as one sees slung under tinkers' carts. I saw that he was also a voteen, as the peasants say, for there was a rosary hanging from a nail on the rim of the barrel, and as I saw I shuddered, and I did not know why I shuddered. We had passed him a few yards when I heard him cry in Gaelic, 'Idolaters, idolaters, go down to Hell with your witches and your devils; go down to Hell that the herrings may come again into the bay'; and for some moments I could hear him half screaming and half muttering behind us. 'Are you not afraid,' I said, 'that these wild fishing people may do some desperate thing against you?'

'I and mine,' he answered, 'are long past human hurt or help, being incorporate with immortal spirits, and when we die it shall be the consummation of the supreme work. A time will come for these people also, and they will sacrifice a mullet to Artemis, or some other fish to some new divinity, unless indeed their own divinities, the Dagda, with his overflowing cauldron, Lug, with his spear dipped in poppy-juice lest it rush forth hot for battle, Aengus, with the three birds on his shoulder, Bodb and his red swineherd, and all the heroic children of Dana, set up once more their temples of grey stone. Their reign has never ceased, but only waned in power a little, for the Sidhe still pass in every wind, and dance and play at hurley, and fight their sudden battles in every hollow and on every hill; but they cannot build their temples again till there have been martyrdoms and victories, and perhaps even that long-foretold battle in the Valley of the Black Pig.'

Keeping close to the wall that went about the pier on the seaward side, to escape the driving foam and the wind, which threatened every moment to lift us off our feet, we made our way in silence to the door of the square building. Michael Robartes opened it with a key, on which I saw the rust of many salt winds, and led me along a bare passage and up an uncarpeted stair to a little room surrounded with bookshelves. A meal would be brought, but only of fruit, for I must submit to a tempered fast before the ceremony, he explained, and with it a book on the doctrine and method of the Order, over which I was to spend what remained of the winter daylight. He then left me, promising to return an hour before the ceremony. I began searching among the bookshelves, and found one of the most exhaustive alchemical libraries I have ever seen. There were the works of Morienus, who hid his immortal body under a shirt of hair-cloth; of Avicenna, who was a drunkard and yet controlled numberless legions of spirits; of Alfarabi, who put so many spirits into his lute that he could make men laugh, or weep, or fall in deadly trance as he would; of Lully, who transformed himself into the likeness of a red cock; of Flamel, who with his wife Parnella achieved the elixir many hundreds of years ago, and is fabled to live still in Arabia among the Dervishes; and of many of less fame. There were very few mystics but alchemical mystics, and because, I had little doubt, of the devotion to one god of the greater number and of the limited sense of beauty, which Robartes would hold an inevitable consequence; but I did notice a complete set of facsimiles of the prophetical writings of William Blake, and probably because of the multitudes that thronged his illumination and were 'like the gay fishes on the wave when the moon sucks up the dew.' I noted also many poets and prose writers of every age, but only those who were a little weary of life, as indeed the greatest have been everywhere, and who cast their imagination to us, as a something they needed no longer now that they were going up in their fiery chariots.

Presently I heard a tap at the door, and a woman came in and laid a little fruit upon the table. I judged that she had once been handsome, but her cheeks were hollowed by what I would have held, had I seen her anywhere else, an excitement of the flesh and a thirst for pleasure, instead of which it doubtless was an excitement of the imagination and a thirst for beauty. I asked her some question concerning the ceremony, but getting no answer except a shake of the head, saw that I must await initiation in silence. When I had eaten, she came again, and having laid a curiously wrought bronze box on the table, lighted the candles, and took away the plates and the remnants. So soon as I was alone, I turned to the box, and found that the peacocks of Hera spread out their tails over the sides and lid, against a background, on which were wrought great stars, as though to affirm that the heavens were a part of their glory. In the box was a book bound in vellum, and having upon the vellum and in very delicate colours, and in gold, the alchemical rose with many spears thrusting against it, but in vain, as was shown by the shattered points of those nearest to the petals. The book was written upon vellum, and in beautiful clear letters, interspersed with symbolical pictures and illuminations, after the manner of the *Splendor Solis.*

The first chapter described how six students, of Celtic descent, gave themselves separately to the study of alchemy, and solved, one the mystery of the Pelican, another the mystery of the green Dragon, another the mystery of the Eagle, another that of Salt and Mercury. What seemed a succession of accidents, but was, the book declared, the contrivance of preternatural powers, brought them together in the garden of an inn in the South of France, and while they talked together the thought came to them that alchemy was the gradual distillation of the contents of the soul, until they were ready to put off the mortal and put on the immortal. An owl passed, rustling among the vine-leaves overhead, and then an old woman came, leaning upon a stick, and, sitting close to them, took up the thought where they had dropped it. Having expounded the whole principle of spiritual alchemy, and bid them found the Order of the Alchemical Rose, she passed from among them, and when they would have followed was nowhere to be seen. They formed themselves into an Order, holding their goods and making their researches in common, and, as they became perfect in the alchemical doctrine, apparitions came and went among them, and taught them more and more marvellous mysteries. The book then went on to expound so much of these as the neophyte was permitted to know, dealing at the outset and at considerable length with the independent reality of our thoughts, which was, it declared, the doctrine from which all true doctrines rose. If you imagine, it said, the semblance of a living being, it is at once possessed by a wandering soul, and goes hither and thither working good or evil, until the moment of its death has come; and gave many examples, received, it said, from many gods. Eros had taught them how to fashion forms in which a divine soul could dwell, and whisper what they would into sleeping minds; and Ate, forms from which demonic beings could pour madness, or unquiet dreams, into sleeping blood; and Hermes, that if you powerfully imagined a hound at your bedside it would keep watch there until you woke, and drive away all but the mightiest demons, but that if your imagination was weakly, the hound would be weakly also, and the demons prevail, and the hound soon die; and Aphrodite, that if you made, by a strong imagining, a dove crowned with silver and had it flutter over your head, its soft cooing would make sweet dreams of immortal love gather and brood over mortal sleep; and all divinities alike had revealed with many warnings and lamentations that all minds are continually giving birth to such beings, and sending them forth to work health or disease, joy or madness. If you would give forms to the evil powers, it went on, you were to make them ugly, thrusting out a lip, with the thirsts of life, or breaking the proportions of a body with the burdens of life; but the divine powers would only appear in beautiful shapes, which are but, as it were, shapes trembling out of existence, folding up into a timeless ecstasy, drifting with half-shut eyes, into a sleepy stillness. The bodiless souls who descended into these forms were what men call the moods; and worked all great changes in the world; for just as the magician or the artist could call them when he would, so they could call out of the mind of the magician or the artist, or if they were demons, out of the mind of the mad or the ignoble, what shape they would, and through its voice and its gestures pour themselves out upon the world. In this way all great events were accomplished; a mood, a divinity, or a demon, first descending like a faint sigh into men's minds and then changing their thoughts and their actions until hair that was yellow had grown black, or hair that was black had grown yellow, and empires moved their border, as though they were but drifts of leaves. The rest of the book contained symbols of form, and sound, and colour, and their attribution to divinities and demons, so that the initiate might fashion a shape for any divinity or any demon, and be as powerful as Avicenna among those who live under the roots of tears and of laughter.

IV

A couple of hours after sunset Michael Robartes returned and told me that I would have to learn the steps of an exceedingly antique dance because before my initiation could be perfected I had to join three times in a magical dance, for rhythm was the wheel of Eternity, on which alone the transient and accidental could be broken, and the spirit set free. I found that the steps, which were simple enough, resembled certain antique Greek dances, and having been a good dancer in my youth and the master of many curious Gaelic steps, I soon had them in my memory. He then robed me and himself in a costume which suggested by its shape both Greece and Egypt, but by its crimson colour a more passionate life than theirs; and having put into my hands a little chainless censer of bronze, wrought into the likeness of a rose, by some modern crafts-man, he told me to open a small door opposite to the door by which I had entered. I put my hand to the handle, but the moment I did so the fumes of the incense, helped perhaps by his mysterious glamour, made me fall again into a dream, in which I seemed to be a mask, lying on the counter of a little Eastern shop. Many persons, with eyes so bright and still that I knew them for more than human, came in and tried me on their faces, but at last flung me into a corner with a little laughter; but all this passed in a moment, for when I awoke my hand was still upon the handle. I opened the door, and found myself in a marvellous passage, along whose sides were many divinities wrought in a mosaic, not less beautiful than the mosaic in the Baptistery at Ravenna, but of a less severe beauty; the predominant colour of each divinity, which was surely a symbolic colour, being repeated in the lamps that hung from the ceiling, a curiously-scented lamp before every divinity. I passed on, marvelling exceedingly how these enthusiasts could have created all this beauty in so remote a place, and half persuaded to believe in a material alchemy, by the sight of so much hidden wealth; the censer filling the air, as I passed, with smoke of ever-changing colour.

I stopped before a door, on whose bronze panels were wrought great waves in whose shadows were faint suggestions of terrible faces. Those beyond it seemed to have heard our steps, for a voice cried: 'Is the work of the Incorruptible Fire at an end?' and immediately Michael Robartes answered: 'The perfect gold has come from the *athanor*.' The door swung open, and we were in a great circular room, and among men and women who were dancing slowly in crimson robes. Upon the ceiling was an immense rose wrought in mosaic; and about the walls, also in mosaic, was a battle of gods and angels, the gods glimmering like rubies and sapphires, and the angels of the one greyness, because, as Michael Robartes whispered, they had renounced their divinity, and turned from the unfolding of their separate hearts, out of love for a God of humility and sorrow. Pillars supported the roof and made a kind of circular cloister, each pillar being a column of confused shapes, divinities, it seemed, of the wind, who rose as in a whirling dance of more than human vehemence, and playing upon pipes and cymbals; and from among these shapes were thrust out hands, and in these hands were censers. I was bid place my censer also in a hand and take my place and dance, and as I turned from the pillars towards the dancers, I saw that the floor was of a green stone, and that a pale Christ on a pale cross was wrought in the midst. I asked Robartes the meaning of this, and was told that they desired 'To trouble His unity with their mul-titudinous feet.' The dance wound in and out, tracing upon the floor the shapes of petals that copied the petals in the rose overhead, and to the sound of hidden instruments which were perhaps of an antique pattern, for I have never heard the like; and every moment the dance was more passionate, until all the winds of the world seemed to have awakened under our feet. After a little I had grown weary, and stood under a pillar watching the coming and going of those flame-like figures; until gradually I sank into a half-dream, from which I was awakened by seeing the petals of the great rose, which had no longer the look of mosaic, falling slowly through the incense-heavy air, and, as they fell, shaping into the likeness of living beings of an extraordinary beauty. Still faint and cloud-like, they began to dance, and as they danced took a more and more definite shape, so that I was able to distinguish beautiful Grecian faces and august Egyptian faces, and now and again to name a divinity by the staff in his hand or by a bird fluttering over his head; and soon every mortal foot danced by the white foot of an immortal; and in the troubled eyes that looked into untroubled shadowy eyes, I saw the brightness of uttermost desire as though they had found at length, after unreckonable wandering, the lost love of their youth. Sometimes, but only for a moment, I saw a faint solitary figure with a veiled face, and carrying a faint torch, flit among the dancers, but like a dream within a dream, like a shadow of a shadow, and I knew by an understanding born from a deeper fountain than thought, that it was Eros himself, and that his face was veiled because no man or woman from the beginning of the world has ever known what love is, or looked into his eyes, for Eros alone of divinities is altogether a spirit, and hides in passions not of his essence if he would commune with a mortal heart. So that if a man love nobly he knows love through infinite pity, unspeakable trust, unending sympathy; and if ignobly through vehement jealousy, sudden hatred, and unappeasable desire; but unveiled love he never knows. While I thought these things, a voice cried to me from the crimson figures : 'Into the dance! there is none that can be spared out of the dance; into the dance! into the dance! that the gods may make them bodies out of the substance of our hearts'; and before I could answer, a mysterious wave of passion, that seemed like the soul of the dance moving within our souls, took hold of me, and I was swept, neither consenting nor refusing, into the midst. I was dancing with an immortal august woman, who had black lilies in her hair, and her dreamy gesture seemed laden with a wisdom more profound than the darkness that is between star and star, and with a love like the love that breathed upon the waters; and as we danced on and on, the incense drifted over us and round us, covering us away as in the heart of the world, and ages seemed to pass, and tempests to awake and perish in the folds of our robes and in her heavy hair.

Suddenly I remembered that her eyelids had never quivered, and that her lilies had not dropped a black petal, or shaken from their places, and understood with a great horror that I danced with one who was more or less than human, and who was drinking up my soul as an ox drinks up a wayside pool; and I fell, and darkness passed over me.

V

I awoke suddenly as though something had awakened me, and saw that I was lying on a roughly painted floor, and that on the ceiling, which was at no great distance, was a roughly painted rose, and about me on the walls half-finished paintings. The pillars and the censers had gone; and near me a score of sleepers lay wrapped in disordered robes, their upturned faces looking to my imagination like hollow masks; and a chill dawn was shining down upon them from a long window I had not noticed before; and outside the sea roared. I saw Michael Robartes lying at a little distance and beside him an overset bowl of wrought bronze which looked as though it had once held incense. As I sat thus, I heard a sudden tumult of angry men's and women's voices mix with the roaring of the sea; and leaping to my feet, I went quickly to Michael Robartes, and tried to shake him out of his sleep. I then seized him by the shoulder and tried to lift him, but he fell backwards, and sighed faintly; and the voices became louder and angrier; and there was a sound of heavy blows upon the door, which opened on to the pier. Suddenly I heard a sound of rending wood, and I knew it had begun to give, and I ran to the door of the room. I pushed it open and came out upon a passage whose bare boards clattered under my feet, and found in the passage another door which led into an empty kitchen; and as I passed through the door I heard two crashes in quick succession, and knew by the sudden noise of feet and the shouts that the door which opened on to the pier had fallen inwards. I ran from the kitchen and out into a small yard, and from this down some steps which descended the seaward and sloping side of the pier, and from the steps clambered along the water's edge, with the angry voices ringing in my ears. This part of the pier had been but lately refaced with blocks of granite, so that it was almost clear of seaweed; but when I came to the old part, I found it so slippery with green weed that I had to climb up on to the roadway. I looked towards the Temple of the Alchemical Rose, where the fishermen and the women were still shouting, but somewhat more faintly, and saw that there was no one about the door or upon the pier; but as I looked, a little crowd hurried out of the door and began gathering large stones from where they were heaped up in readiness for the next time a storm shattered the pier, when they would be laid under blocks of granite. While I stood watching the crowd, an old man, who was, I think, the voteen, pointed to me, and screamed out something, and the crowd whitened, for all the faces had turned towards me. I ran, and it was well for me that pullers of the oar are poorer men with their feet than with their arms and their bodies; and yet while I ran I scarcely heard the following feet or the angry voices, for many voices of exultation and lamentation, which were forgotten as a dream is forgotten the moment they were heard, seemed to be ringing in the air over my head.

There are moments even now when I seem to hear those voices of exultation and lamentation, and when the indefinite world, which has but half lost its mastery over my heart and my intellect, seems about to claim a perfect mastery; but I carry the rosary about my neck, and when I hear, or seem to hear them, I press it to my heart and say: 'He whose name is Legion is at our doors deceiving our intellects with subtlety and flattering our hearts with beauty, and we have no trust but in Thee'; and then the war that rages within me at other times is still, and I am at peace.

6

Probably no other student of magic wrote so clearly and profoundly about the occult – albeit in fictional form – yet so carefully concealed his actual involvement with the mystic arts as did Arthur Machen. Shortly after his death in 1947 one of his biographers, Wesley Sweetser, paraphrased Machen's life thus : 'His peculiar knowledge of demonology, witchcraft, folklore and occult societies and religions combined with his unique talent for suggesting the indescribable through the creation of atmosphere, has made him the spokesman without peer for sorcery.' Little in this statement can be, or indeed has been, challenged, yet Machen's own derisory remarks made during his lifetime about 'bungling Spiritualists and poor fool occultists' have led many to feel he observed rather than experimented, read rather than practised the secrets of mysticism. Yet his membership of several occult societies – the Golden Dawn being the least of these – clearly indicates he was an adept of no mean standing, if somewhat reticent about the fact.

Arthur Llewellyn Jones (the name Machen was adopted from his mother) was born in 1863 in Caerleon-on-Usk in the heart of the stark Welsh mountains and he felt himself from birth 'beset with the vision of an enchanted land'. In his childhood he delighted in the legendary tales of King Arthur and his knights who had roamed the same valleys, and also found great pleasure in exploring local Roman remains 'which first gave me a vague, indefinable sense of awe and mystery and terror'. In 1880 he moved to London and embarked on a career in bookselling and journalism which kept him in almost constant penury. A solitary man by nature, he quickly found himself drawn to the works of the occultists ('the dictums of those Dark-Robed Masters' he called them) and made friends with one of the leading contemporary writers on the mystic arts, A. E. Waite. His first ventures into the world of fiction began appearing in the late 1880s and, although not widely popular, works such as *The Great God Pan* quickly established him among the initiated as a truly gifted and knowledgeable writer on the occult. He entered the ranks of the Golden Dawn in 1900 and there met W. B. Yeats and the other distinguished writers of the group. Machen considered himself something of an alchemist, with a purpose to 'transform the world of everyday reality into a world of magic and wonder,' and with his short stories of horror and novels like *The Three Impostors* (1895), *The Hill of Dreams* (1907) and *The Terror* (1917) achieved this in no small measure – revealing to ordinary readers secrets of the forbidden sciences they would not easily have found elsewhere in fiction. He felt, also, that 'an enormous mass of occultism, ancient and modern, may be brushed aside at once without the labour of any curious investigation' and that it was the duty of all serious adepts to attempt to explain 'the naked transcendental forces behind human existence'.

As much of Arthur Machen's work is happily in print today it has been difficult to select an item which is not well known and yet illustrative of his absorption with magic. However, in 'Strange Occurrence in Clerkenwell' I believe we have much that is autobiographical and revealing of the hidden sciences. It also admirably complements a further statement by Wesley Sweetser on Machen : 'The mystic is a man alone, living in a world apart; yet as if impelled by a power beyond his control, he has the insatiable urge to communicate his incommunicable experience. . . .'

* * *

Strange Occurrence in Clerkenwell

ARTHUR MACHEN

Mr Dyson had inhabited for some years a couple of rooms in a moderately quiet street in Bloomsbury, where, as he somewhat pompously expressed it, he held his finger on the pulse of life without being deafened with the thousand rumours of the main arteries of London. It was to him a source of peculiar, if esoteric, gratification that from the adjacent corner of Tottenham Court Road a hundred lines of omnibuses went to the four quarters of the town; he would dilate on the facilities for visiting Dalston, and dwell on the admirable line that knew extremist Ealing and the streets beyond Whitechapel.

His rooms, which had been originally 'furnished apartments', he had gradually purged of their more peccant parts; and though one would not find here the glowing splendour of his old chambers in the street off the Strand, there was something of severe grace about the appointments which did credit to his taste. The rugs were old, and of the true faded beauty; the etchings, nearly all of them proofs printed by the artist, made a good show with broad white margins and black frames, and there was no spurious black oak.

Indeed there was but little furniture of any kind: a plain and honest table, square and sturdy stood in one corner; a seventeenth-century settle fronted the hearth; and two wooden elbow-chairs and a book-shelf of the Empire made up the equipment, with no exception worthy of note. For Dyson cared for none of these things; his place was at his own bureau, a quaint old piece of lacquered-work, at which he would sit for hour after hour, with his back to the room, engaged in the desperate pursuit of literature, or, as he termed his profession, the chase of the phrase.

The neat array of pigeon-holes and drawers teemed and overflowed with manuscripts and notebooks, the experiments and efforts of many years; and the inner well, a vast and cavernous receptacle, was stuffed with accumulated ideas. Dyson was a craftsman who loved all the detail and the technique of his work intensely; and if, as has been hinted, he deluded himself a little with the name of artist, yet his amusements were eminently harmless, and, so far as

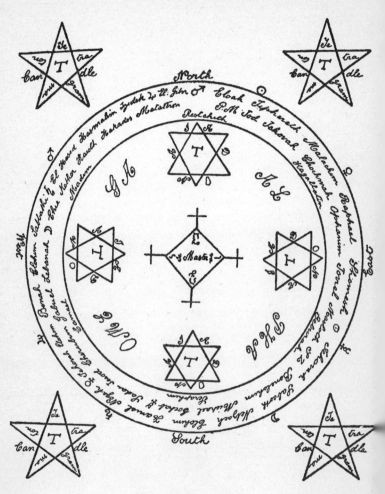

THE MAGICAL CIRCLE

can be ascertained, he (or the publishers) had chosen the good part of not tiring the world with printed matter.

Here, then, Dyson would shut himself up with his fancies, experimenting with words, and striving, as his friend the recluse of Bayswater stove, with the almost invincible problem of style, but always with a fine confidence, extremely different from the chronic depression of the realist. He had been almost continuously at work on some scheme that struck him as well-nigh magical in its possibilities since the night of an adventure with a mysterious tenant from the first floor in Abingdon Grove; and as he laid down the pen with a glow of triumph, he reflected that he had not viewed the streets for five days in succession. With all the enthusiasm of his accomplished labour still working in his brain, he put away his papers and went out, pacing the pavement at first in that rare mood of exultation which finds in every stone upon the way the possibilities of a masterpiece.

It was growing late, and the autumn evening was drawing to a close amidst veils of haze and mist, and in the stilled air the voices, and the roaring traffic, and incessant feet seemed to Dyson like the noise upon the stage when all the house is silent. In the square the leaves rippled down as quick as summer rain, and the street beyond was beginning to flare with the lights in the butchers' shops and the vivid illumination of the greengrocer. It was a Saturday night, and the swarming populations of the slums were turning out in force; the battered women in rusty black had begun to paw the lumps of cagmag, and others gloated over unwholesome cabbages, and there was a brisk demand for four ale.

Dyson passed through these night-fires with some relief; he loved to meditate, but his thoughts were not as De Quincey's after his dose; he cared not two straws whether onions were dear or cheap, and would not have exulted if meat had fallen to two-pence a pound. Absorbed in the wilderness of the tale he had been writing, weighing nicely the points of plot and construction, relishing the recollection of this and that happy phrase, and dreading failure here and there, he left the rush and whistle of the gas-flares behind him, and began to touch upon pavements more deserted.

He had turned, without taking note, to the northward, and was passing through an ancient fallen street, where now notices of floors and offices to let hung out, but still about it lingered the grace and the stiffness of the Age of Wigs – a broad roadway, a broad pavement, and on each side a grave line of houses with long and narrow windows flush with the walls, all of mellowed brickwork. Dyson walked with quick steps, as he resolved that short work must be made of a certain episode; but he was in that happy humour of invention, and another chapter rose in the inner chamber of his brain, and he dwelt on the circumstances he was to write down with curious pleasure.

It was charming to have the quiet streets to walk in, and in his thought he made a whole district the cabinet of his studies, and vowed he would come again. Heedless of his course, he struck off to the east again, and soon found himself involved in a square network of grey two-storied houses, and then in the waste void and elements of brickwork, the passages and unmade roads behind great factory walls, encumbered with the refuse of the neighbourhood, forlorn, ill-lighted, and desperate.

A brief turn, and there rose before him the unexpected, a hill suddenly lifted from the level ground, its steep ascent marked by the lighted lamps, and eager as an explorer, Dyson found his way to the place, wondering where his crooked paths had brought him. Here all was again decorous, but hideous in the extreme. The builder, someone lost in the deep gloom of the early 'twenties, had conceived the idea of twin villas in grey brick, shaped in a manner to recall the outlines of the Parthenon, each with its classic form broadly marked with raised bands of stucco. The name of the street was all strange, and for a further surprise the top of the hill was crowned with an irregular plot of grass and fading trees, called a square, and here again the Parthenon-motive had persisted. Beyond, the streets were curious, wild in their irregularities, here a row of sordid, dingy dwellings, dirty and disreputable in appearance, and there, without warning, stood a house, genteel and prim, with wire blinds and brazen knocker, as clean and trim as if it had been the doctor's house in some benighted little country town. These surprises and discoveries began to exhaust Dyson, and he hailed with delight the blazing windows of a public-house, and went in with the intention of testing the beverage provided for the dwellers in this region, as remote as Libya and Pamphylia and the parts about Mesopotamia.

The babble of voices from within warned him that he was about to assist at the true parliament of the London workman, and he looked about him for that more retired entrance called private. When he had settled himself on an exiguous bench, and had ordered some beer, he began to listen to the jangling talk in the public bar beyond; it was a senseless argument, alternately furious and maudlin, with appeals to Bill and Tom, and mediaeval survivals of speech, words that Chaucer wrote belched out with zeal and relish, and the din of pots jerked down and coppers rapped smartly on the zinc counter made a thorough bass for it all.

Dyson was calmly smoking his pipe between the sips of beer, when an indefinite-looking figure slid rather than walked into the compartment. The man started violently when he saw Dyson placidly sitting in the corner, and glanced keenly about him. He seemed to be on wires, controlled by some electric machine, for he almost bolted out of the door when the barman asked with what he could serve him, and his hand shivered as he took the glass. Dyson inspected him with a little curiosity.

He was muffled up almost to the lips, and a soft felt hat was drawn down over his eyes; he looked as if he shrank from every glance, and a more raucous voice suddenly uplifted in the public bar seemed to find in him a sympathy that made him shake and quiver like a jelly. It was pitiable to see any one so thrilled with nervousness, and Dyson was about to address some trivial remark of casual inquiry to the man, when another person came into the compartment, and, laying his hand on his arm, muttered something in an undertone, and vanished as he came. But Dyson had recognised him as the smooth-tongued and smooth-shaven Burton; and yet he thought little of it, for his whole faculty of observation was absorbed in the lamentable and yet grotesque spectacle before him.

At the first touch of the hand on his arm the unfortunate man had wheeled round as if spun on a pivot, and shrank back with a low, piteous cry, as if some dumb beast were caught in the toils. The blood fled away from the wretch's face, and the skin became grey as if a shadow of death had passed in the air and fallen on it, and Dyson caught a choking whisper –

'Mr Davies! For God's sake, have pity on me, Mr Davies! On my oath, I say –' and his voice sank to silence as he heard the message, and strove in vain to bite his lips, and summon up to his aid some tinge of manhood. He stood there a moment, wavering as the leaves of an aspen, and then he was gone out into the street, as Dyson thought silently, with his doom upon his head. He had not been gone a minute when it suddenly flashed into Dyson's mind that he knew the man; it was undoubtedly the young man with spectacles for whom so many ingenious persons were searching; the spectacles indeed were missing, but the pale face, the dark whiskers, and the timid glances were enough to identify him.

Dyson saw at once that by a succession of hazards he had unawares hit upon the scent of some desperate conspiracy, wavering as the track of a loathsome snake in and out of the highways and byways of the London cosmos; the truth was instantly pictured before him, and he divined that all unconscious and unheeding he had been privileged to see the shadows of hidden forms, chasing and hurrying, and grasping and vanishing across the bright curtain of common life, soundless and silent, or only babbling fables and pretences.

For him in an instant the jargoning of voices, the garish splendour, and all the vulgar tumult of the public-house became part of magic; for here before his eyes a scene in this grim mystery play had been enacted, and he had seen human flesh grow cold with a palsy of fear; the very hell of cowardice and terror had gaped wide within an arm's breadth. In the midst of these reflections the barman came up and stared at him as if to hint that he had exhausted his right to take his ease, and Dyson bought another lease of the seat by an order for more beer. As he pondered the brief glimpse of tragedy, he recollected that with his first start of haunted fear the young man with whiskers had drawn his hand swiftly from his greatcoat pocket, and that he had heard something fall to the ground; and pretending to have dropped his pipe, Dyson began to grope in the corner, searching with his fingers. He touched something and drew it gently to him, and with one brief glance, as he put it quietly in his pocket, he saw it was a little old-fashioned notebook, bound in faded green morocco.

He drank down his beer at a gulp, and left the place, overjoyed at his fortunate discovery, and busy with conjecture as to the possible importance of the find. By turns he dreaded to find perhaps mere blank leaves, or the laboured follies of a betting-book, but the faded morocco cover seemed to promise better things, and to hint at mysteries. He piloted himself with no little difficulty out of the sour and squalid quarter he had entered with a light heart, and emerging at Gray's Inn Road, struck off down Guilford Street and hastened home, only anxious for a lighted candle and solitude.

Dyson sat down at his bureau, and placed the little book before him; it was an effort to open the leaves and dare disappointment. But in desperation at last he laid his fingers between the pages at haphazard, and rejoiced to see a compact range of writing with a margin, and as it chanced, three words caught his glance and stood out apart from the mass. Dyson read –

'the Gold Tiberius'

and his face flushed with fortune and the lust of the hunter.

He turned at once to the first leaf of the pocket-book, and proceeded to read with rapt interest the

HISTORY OF THE YOUNG MAN WITH SPECTACLES

From the filthy and obscure lodgings, situated, I verily believe, in one of the foulest slums of Clerkenwell, I indite this history of a life which, daily threatened, cannot last very much longer. Every day – nay, every hour, I know too well my enemies are drawing their nets closer about me; even now I am condemned to be a close prisoner in my squalid room, and I know that when I go out I shall go to my destruction. This history, if it chance to fall into good hands, may, perhaps, be of service in warning young men of the dangers and pitfalls that most surely must accompany any deviation from the ways of rectitude.

My name is Joseph Walters. When I came of age I found myself in possession of a small but sufficient income, and I determined that I would devote my life to scholarship. I do not mean the scholarship of these days; I had no intention of associating myself with men whose lives are spent in the unspeakably degrading occupation of 'editing' classics, befouling the fair margins of the fairest books with idle and superfluous annotation, and doing their utmost to give a lasting disgust of all that is beautiful. An abbey church turned to the base use of a stable or bakehouse is a sorry sight; but more pitiable still is a masterpiece spluttered over with the commentator's pen, and his hideous mark 'cf.'.

For my part, I chose the glorious career of scholar in its ancient sense; I longed to possess encyclopaedic learning, to grow old amongst books, to distil day by day, and year after year, the inmost sweetness of all worthy writings. I was not rich enough to collect a library, and I was therefore forced to betake myself to the reading-room of the British Museum.

O dim, far-lifted, and mighty dome, Mecca of many minds, mausoleum of many hopes, sad house where all desires fail! For there men enter in with hearts uplifted, and dreaming minds, seeing in those exalted stairs a ladder to fame, in that pompous portico the gate of knowledge, and going in, find but vain vanity, and all but in vain. There, when the long streets are ringing, is silence, there eternal twilight, and the odour of heaviness. But there the blood flows thin and cold, and the brain burns adust; there is the hunt of shadows, and the chase of embattled phantoms, a striving against ghosts and a war that has no victory. O dome, tomb of the quick! surely in thy galleries, where no reverberant voice can call, sighs whisper ever, and mutterings of dead hopes; and there men's souls mount like moths towards the flame, and fall scorched and blackened beneath thee, O dim, far-lifted, and mighty dome!

Bitterly do I now regret the day when I took my place at a desk for the first time, and began my studies. I had not been an habitué of the place for many months, when I became acquainted with a serene and benevolent gentleman, a man somewhat past middle age, who nearly always occupied a desk next to mine. In the reading-room it takes little to make an acquaintance – a casual offer of assistance, a hint as to the search in the catalogue, and the ordinary politeness of men who constantly sit near each other; it was thus I came to know the man calling himself Dr Lipsius. By degrees I grew to look for his presence, and to miss him when he was away, as was sometimes the case, and so a friendship sprang up between us. His immense range of learning was placed freely at my service; he would often astonish me by the way in which he would sketch out in a few minutes the bibliography of a given subject, and before long I had confided to him my ambitions.

'Ah,' he said, 'you should have been a German. I was like that myself when I was a boy. It is a wonderful resolve, an infinite career. I will know all things; yes, it is a device indeed. But it means this – a life of labour without end, and a desire unsatisfied at last. The scholar has to die, and die saying, "I know very little!" '

Gradually, by speeches such as these, Lipsius seduced me : he would praise the career, and at the same time hint that it was as hopeless as the search for the philosopher's stone, and so by artful suggestions, insinuated with infinite address, by degrees he succeeded in undermining all my principles. 'After all,' he used to say, 'the greatest of all sciences, the key to all knowledge, is the science and art of pleasure. Rabelais was perhaps the greatest of all the encyclopaedic scholars; and he, as you know, wrote the most remarkable book that has ever been written. And what does he teach men in this book? Surely the joy of living.

'I need not remind you of the words, suppressed in most of the editions, the key of all the Rabelaisian mythology, of all the enigmas of his grand philosophy, *Vivez joyeux*. There you have all his learning; his work is the institutes of pleasure as the fine art; the finest art there is : the art of all arts. Rabelais had all science, but he had all life too. And we have gone a long way since his time. You are enlightened, I think; you do not consider all the petty rules and by-laws that a corrupt society has made for its own selfish convenience as the immutable decrees of the Eternal.'

Such were the doctrines that he preached; and it was by such insidious arguments, line upon line, here a little and there a little, that he at last succeeded in making me a man at war with the whole social system. I used to long for some opportunity to break the chains and to live a free life, to be my own rule and measure. I viewed existence with the eyes of a pagan, and Lipsius understood to perfection the art of stimulating the natural inclinations of a young man hitherto a hermit. As I gazed up at the great dome I saw it flushed with the flames and colours of a world of enticement unknown to me, my imagination played me a thousand wanton tricks, and the forbidden drew me as surely as a loadstone draws on iron. At last my resolution was taken, and I boldly asked Lipsius to be my guide.

He told me to leave the Museum at my usual hour, half past four, to walk slowly along the northern pavement of Great Russell Street, and to wait at the corner of the street till I was addressed, and then to obey in all things the instructions of the person who came up to me. I carried out these directions, and stood at the corner looking about me anxiously, my heart beating fast, and my breath coming in gasps. I waited there for some time, and had begun to fear I had been made the object of a joke, when I suddenly became conscious of a gentleman who was looking at me with evident amusement from the opposite pavement of Tottenham Court Road. He came over and, raising his hat, politely begged me to follow him, and I did so without a word wondering where we were going, and what was to happen.

I was taken to a house of quiet and respectable aspect in a street lying to the north of Oxford Street, and my guide rang a bell. A servant showed us into a large room quietly furnished, on the ground floor. We sat there in silence for some time, and I noticed that the furniture, though unpretending, was extremely valuable. There were large oak presses, two book-cases of extreme elegance, and in one corner a carved chest which must have been mediaeval.

Presently, Dr Lipsius came in and welcomed me with his usual manner, and after some desultory conversation my guide left the room. Then an elderly man dropped in, and began talking to Lipsius, and from their conversation I understood that my friend was a dealer in antiques; they spoke of the Hittite seal, and of the prospects of further discoveries, and later, when two or three more persons joined us, there was an argument as to the possibility of a systematic exploration of the pre-Celtic monuments in England. I was, in fact, present at an archaeological reception of an informal kind, and at nine o'clock, when the antiquaries were gone, I stared at Lipsius in a manner that showed I was puzzled, and sought an explanation.

'Now,' he said, 'we will go upstairs.'

As we passed up the stairs, Lipsius lighting the way with a hand-lamp, I heard the sound of a jarring lock and bolts and bars shot on at the front door. My guide drew back a baize door and we went down a passage, and I began to hear odd sounds, a noise of curious mirth; then he pushed me through a second door, and my initiation began. I cannot write down what I witnessed that night; I cannot bear to recall what went on in those secret rooms fast shuttered and curtained so that no light should escape into the quiet street; they gave me red wine to drink, and a woman told me as I sipped it that it was wine of the Red Jar that Avallaunius had made. Another asked me how I liked the wine of the Fauns, and I heard a dozen fantastic names, while the stuff boiled in my veins, and stirred, I think, something that had slept within me from the moment I was born.

It seemed as if my self-consciousness deserted me; I was no

longer a thinking agent, but at once subject and object; I mingled
in the horrible sport, and watched the mystery of the Greek groves
and fountains enacted before me, saw the reeling dance and heard
the music calling as I sat beside my mate, and yet I was outside it
all, and viewed my own part an idle spectator. Thus with strange
rites they made me drink the cup, and when I woke up in the
morning I was one of them, and had sworn to be faithful.

At first I was shown the enticing side of things; I was bidden
to enjoy myself and care for nothing but pleasure, and Lipsius himself indicated to me as the acutest enjoyment the spectacle of the
terrors of the unfortunate persons who were from time to time
decoyed into the evil house. But after a time it was pointed out to
me that I must take my share in the work, and so I found myself
compelled to be in my turn a seducer; and thus it is on my conscience that I have helped many to the depths of the pit.

One day Lipsius summoned me to his private room, and told me
that he had a difficult task to give me. He unlocked a drawer and
gave me a sheet of typewritten paper, and bade me read it.

It was without place, or date, or signature, and ran as follows :

Mr James Headley, F.S.A., will receive from his agent in
Armenia, on the 12th inst., a unique coin, the gold Tiberius. It
bears on the reverse a faun with the legend *Victoria*. It is believed
that this coin is of immense value. Mr Headley will come up to
town to show the coin to his friend, Professor Memys, of Chenies
Street, Oxford Street, on some date between the 13th and the
18th.

Dr Lipsius chuckled at my face of blank surprise when I laid down
this singular communication.

'You will have a good chance of showing your discretion,' he
said. 'This is not a common case; it requires great management and
infinite tact. I am sure I wish I had a Panurge in my service, but
we will see what you can do.'

'But is it not a joke?' I asked him. 'How can you know – or
rather, how can this correspondent of yours know – that a coin
has been despatched from Armenia to Mr Headley? And how is it
possible to fix the period in which Mr Headley will take it into his

brain to come up to town? It seems to me a lot of guesswork.'

'My dear Mr Walters,' he replied, 'we do not deal in guesswork here. It would bore you if I went into all these little details, the cogs and wheels, if I may say so, which move the machine. Don't you think it is much more amusing to sit in front of the house and be astonished than to be behind the scenes and see the mechanics? Better tremble at the thunder, believe me, than see the man rolling the cannon-ball. But, after all, you needn't bother about the how and why; you have your share to do. Of course I shall give you full instructions, but a great deal depends on the way the thing is carried out. I have often heard very young men maintain that style is everything in literature, and I can assure you that the same maxim holds good in our far more delicate profession. With us style is absolutely everything, and that is why we have friends like yourself.'

I went away in some perturbation : he had no doubt designedly left everything in mystery, and I did not know what part I should have to play. Though I had assisted at scenes of hideous revelry, I was not yet dead to all echo of human feeling, and I trembled lest I should receive the order to be Mr Headley's executioner.

A week later, it was on the sixteenth of the month, Dr Lipsius made me a sign to come into his room.

'It is for tonight,' he began. 'Please to attend carefully to what I am going to say, Mr Walters, and on peril of your life, for it is a dangerous matter – on peril of your life, I say, follow these instructions to the letter. You understand? Well, tonight at about half past seven, you will stroll quietly up the Hampstead Road till you come to Vincent Street. Turn down here and walk along, taking the third turning to your right, which is Lambert Terrace. Then follow the terrace, cross the road, and go along Hertford Street, and so into Lillington Square. The second turning you will come to in the Square is called Sheen Street; but in reality it is more a passage between blank walls than a street.

'Whatever you do, take care to be at the corner of this street at eight o'clock precisely. You will walk along it, and just at the bend where you lose sight of the square you will find an old gentleman with white beard and whiskers. He will in all probability be abusing a cabman for having brought him to Sheen Street instead of Chenies Street. You will go up to him quietly and offer your services; he will tell you where he wants to go, and you will be so courteous as to offer to show him the way. I may say that Professor Memys moved into Chenies Street a month ago; thus Mr Headley has never been to see him there, and, moreover, he is very short-sighted, and knows little of the topography of London. Indeed, he has quite lived the life of a learned hermit at Audley Hall.

'Well, need I say more to a man of your intelligence? You will bring him to this house, he will ring the bell, and a servant in quiet livery will let him in. Then your work will be done, and I am sure done well. You will leave Mr Headley at the door, and simply continue your walk, and I shall hope to see you the next day. I really don't think there is anything more I can tell you.'

These minute instructions I took care to carry out to the letter. I confess that I walked up the Tottenham Court Road by no means blindly, but with an uneasy sense that I was coming to a decisive point in my life. The noise and rumour of the crowded pavements were to me but dumb show; I revolved again and again in ceaseless iteration the task that had been laid on me, and I questioned myself as to the possible results. As I got near the point of turning, I asked myself whether danger were not about my steps; the cold thought struck me that I was suspected and observed, and every chance foot-passenger who gave me a second glance seemed to me an officer of police. My time was running out, the sky had darkened, and I hesitated, half resolved to go no farther but to abandon Lipsius and his friends forever. I had almost determined to take this course, when the conviction suddenly came to me that the whole thing was a gigantic joke, a fabrication of rank improbability. Who could have procured the information about the Armenian agent? I asked myself. By what means could Lipsius have known the particular day and the very train that Mr Headley was to take? How engage him to enter one special cab amongst the dozens waiting at Paddington?

I vowed it a mere Milesian tale, and went forward merrily, turned down Vincent Street, and threaded out the route that Lipsius had so carefully impressed upon me. The various streets he had named were all places of silence and an oppressive cheap gentility; it was dark, and I felt alone in the musty squares and crescents, where people pattered by at intervals, and the shadows were growing blacker.

I entered Sheen Street, and found it as Lipsius had said, more a passage than a street; it was a byway, on one side a low wall and neglected gardens, and grim backs of a line of houses, and on the other a timber-yard. I turned the corner, and lost sight of the square, and then, to my astonishment, I saw the scene of which I had been told. A hansom cab had come to a stop beside the pavement, and an old man, carrying a handbag, was fiercely abusing the cabman, who sat on his perch the image of bewilderment.

'Yes, but I'm sure you said Sheen Street, and that's where I brought you,' I heard him saying as I came up, and the old gentleman boiled in a fury, and threatened police and suits at law.

The sight gave me a shock, and in an instant I resolved to go through with it. I strolled on, and without noticing the cabman, lifted my hat politely to old Mr Headley.

'Pardon me, sir,' I said, 'but is there any difficulty? I see you are a traveller; perhaps the cabman has made a mistake. Can I direct you?'

The old fellow turned to me, and I noticed that he snarled and showed his teeth like an ill-tempered cur as he spoke.

'This drunken fool has brought me here,' he said. 'I told him to drive to Chenies Street, and he brings me to this infernal place. I won't pay him a farthing, and I meant to have given him a handsome sum. I am going to call for the police and give him in charge.'

At this threat the cabman seemed to take alarm; he glanced around, as if to make sure that no policeman was in sight, and drove off grumbling loudly, and Mr Headley grinned savagely with satisfaction at having saved his fare, and put back one and sixpence into his pocket, the 'handsome sum' the cabman had lost.

'My dear sir,' I said, 'I am afraid this piece of stupidity has annoyed you a great deal. It is a long way to Chenies Street, and you will have some difficulty in finding the place unless you know London pretty well.'

'I know it very little,' he replied. 'I never come up except on important business, and I've never been to Chenies Street in my life.'

'Really? I should be happy to show you the way. I have been for a stroll, and it will not at all inconvenience me to take you to your destination.'

'I want to go to Professor Memys, at No. 15. It's most annoying to me; I'm short-sighted, and I can never make out the numbers on the doors.'

'This way if you please,' I said, and we set out.

I did not find Mr Headley an agreeable man; indeed, he grumbled the whole way. He informed me of his name, and I took care to say, 'The well-known antiquary?' and thenceforth I was compelled to listen to the history of his complicated squabbles with publishers, who treated him, as he said, disgracefully; the man was a chapter in the Irritability of Authors. He told me that he had been on the point of making the fortune of several firms, but had been compelled to abandon the design owing to their rank ingratitude.

Besides these ancient histories of wrong, and the more recent misadventure of the cabman, he had another grievous complaint to make. As he came along in the train, he had been sharpening a pencil, and the sudden jolt of the engine as it drew up at a station had driven the penknife against his face, inflicting a small triangular wound just on the cheekbone, which he showed me. He denounced the railway company, heaped imprecations on the head of the driver, and talked of claiming damages. Thus he grumbled all the way, not noticing in the least where he was going; and so unamiable did his conduct seem to me, that I began to enjoy the trick I was playing on him.

Nevertheless, my heart beat a little faster as we turned into the street where Lipsius was waiting. A thousand accidents, I thought, might happen; some chance might bring one of Headley's friends to meet us; perhaps, though he knew not Chenies Street, he might know the street where I was taking him; in spite of his short sight, he might possibly make out the number, or, in a sudden fit of suspicion, he might make an enquiry of the policeman at the corner. Thus every step upon the pavement, as we drew nearer to the goal, was to me a pang and a terror, and every approaching passenger carried a certain threat of danger. I gulped down my excitement with an effort, and made shift to say pretty quietly –

'No. 15, I think you said? That is the third house from this. If you will allow me, I will leave you now; I have been delayed a little, and my way lies on the other side of Tottenham Court Road.'

He snarled out some kind of thanks, and I turned my back and walked swiftly in the opposite direction. A minute or two later I looked round and saw Mr Headley standing on the doorstep, and then the door opened and he went in. For my part, I gave a sigh of relief; I hastened to get away from the neighbourhood, and endeavoured to enjoy myself in merry company.

The whole of the next day I kept away from Lipsius. I felt anxious, but I did not know what had happened, or what was happening, and a reasonable regard for my own safety told me that I should do well to remain quietly at home. My curiosity, however, to learn the end of the odd drama in which I had played a part stung me to the quick, and late in the evening I made up my mind to see how events had turned out. Lipsius nodded when I came in, and asked if I could give him five minutes' talk. We went to his room, and he began to walk up and down, while I sat waiting for him to speak.

'My dear Mr Walters,' he said at length, 'I congratulate you warmly; your work was done in the most thorough and artistic manner. You will go far. Look.'

He went to his *escritoire* and pressed a secret spring; a drawer flew out, and he laid something on the table. It was a gold coin! I took it up and examined it eagerly, and read the legend about the figure of the faun.

'Victoria,' I said, smiling.

'Yes; it was a great capture, which we owe to you. I had great difficulty in persuading Mr Headley that a little mistake had been made, that was how I put it. He was very disagreeable, and indeed ungentlemanly, about it; didn't he strike you as a very cross old man?'

I held the coin, admiring the choice and rare design, clear cut as if from the mint; and I thought the fine gold glowed and burnt like a lamp.

'And what finally became of Mr Headley?' I said at last.

Lipsius smiled and shrugged.

'What on earth does it matter?' he said. 'He might be here, or there, or anywhere; but what possible consequence could it be? Besides, your question rather surprises me; you are an intelligent man, Mr Walters. Just think it over, and I'm sure you won't repeat the question.'

'My dear sir,' I said, 'I hardly think you are treating me fairly. You have paid me some handsome compliments on my share in the capture, and I naturally wish to know how the matter ended. From what I saw of Mr Headley I should think you must have had some difficulty with him.'

He gave me no answer for the moment, but began again to walk up and down the room, apparently absorbed in thought.

'Well,' he said at last, 'I suppose there is something in what you say. We are certainly indebted to you. I have said that I have a high opinion of your intelligence, Mr Walters. Just look here, will you?'

He opened a door communicating with another room, and pointed.

There was a great box lying on the floor, a queer, coffin-shaped thing. I looked at it, and saw it was a mummy case, like those in the British Museum, vividly painted in the brilliant Egyptian colours, with I knew not what proclamation of dignity or hopes of life immortal. The mummy swathed about in the robes of death was lying within, and the face had been uncovered.

'You are going to send this away?' I said, forgetting the question I had put.

'Yes; I have an order from a local museum. Look a little more closely.'

Puzzled by his manner, I peered into the face, while he held the lamp. The flesh was black with the passing of the centuries; but as I looked I saw upon the right cheek bone a small triangular scar, and the secret of the mummy flashed upon me : I was looking at the dead body of the man whom I had decoyed into that house.

There was no thought or design of action in my mind. I held the accursed coin in my hand, burning me with a foretaste of hell, and I fled as I would have fled from pestilence and death, and dashed into the street in blind horror, not knowing where I went. I felt the gold coin grasped in my clenched fist, and throwing it away, I knew not where, I ran on and on through by-streets and dark ways, till at last I issued out into a crowded thoroughfare and checked myself. Then as consciousness returned I realised my instant peril, and understood what would happen if I fell into the hands of Lipsius. I knew that I had put forth my finger to thwart a relentless mechanism rather than a man.

My recent adventure with the unfortunate Mr Headley had taught me that Lipsius had agents in all quarters; and I foresaw that if I fell into his hands, he would remain true to his doctrine of style, and cause me to die a death of some horrible and ingenious torture. I bent my whole mind to the task of outwitting him and his emissaries, three of whom I knew to have proved their ability for tracking down persons who for various reasons preferred to remain obscure. These servants of Lipsius were two men and a woman, and the woman was incomparably the most subtle and the most deadly. Yet I considered that I too had some portion of craft, and I took my resolve. Since then I have matched myself day by day against the ingenuity of Lipsius and his myrmidons.

For a time I was successful; though they beat furiously after me in the covert of London, I remained *perdu,* and watched with some amusement their frantic efforts to recover the scent lost in two or three minutes. Every lure and wile was put forth to entice me from my hiding-place; I was informed by the medium of the public prints that what I had taken had been recovered, and meetings were proposed in which I might hope to gain a great deal without the slightest risk. I laughed at their endeavours, and began a little to despise the organisation I had so dreaded, and ventured more abroad. Not once or twice, but several times, I recognised the two men who were charged with my capture, and I succeeded in eluding them at close quarters; and a little too hastily I decided that I had nothing to dread, and that my craft was greater than theirs.

But in the meanwhile, while I congratulated myself on my cunning, the third of Lipsius's emissaries was weaving her nets; and in an evil hour I paid a visit to an old friend, a literary man named Russell, who lived in a quiet street in Bayswater. The woman, as I found out too late, a day or two ago occupied rooms in the same house, and I was followed and tracked down. Too late, as I have said, I recognised that I had made a fatal mistake, and that I was besieged.

Sooner or later I shall find myself in the power of an enemy without pity; and so surely as I leave this house I shall go to receive doom. I hardly dare to guess how it will at last fall upon me; my imagination, always a vivid one, paints to me appalling pictures of the unspeakable torture which I shall probably endure; and I know that I shall die with Lipsius standing near and gloating over the refinements of my suffering and my shame.

Hours, nay minutes, have become precious to me. I sometimes pause in the midst of anticipating my tortures, to wonder whether even now I cannot hit upon some supreme stroke, some design of infinite subtlety, to free myself from the toils. But I find that the faculty of combination has left me; I am as the scholar of the old

myth, deserted by the power which has helped me hitherto. I do
not know when the supreme moment will come, but sooner or later,
it is inevitable; before long I shall receive sentence, and from the
sentence to execution will not be long. . . .

*

I cannot remain here a prisoner any longer. I shall go out tonight
when the streets are full of crowds and clamours, and make a last
effort to escape. . . .

*

It was with profound astonishment that Dyson closed the little
book, and thought of the strange series of incidents which had
brought him into touch with the plots and counterplots connected
with the Gold Tiberius. He had bestowed the coin carefully away,
and he shuddered at the bare possibility of its place of deposit
becoming known to the evil band who seemed to possess such
extraordinary sources of information.

It had grown late while he read, and he put the pocket-book
away, hoping with all his heart that the unhappy Walters might
even at the eleventh hour escape the doom he dreaded.

'A wonderful story, as you say, an extraordinary sequence and play
of coincidence. I confess that your expressions when you first
showed me the Gold Tiberius were not exaggerated. But do you
think that Walters has really some fearful fate to dread?'

'I cannot say. Who can presume to predict events when life itself
puts on the robe of coincidence and plays at drama? Perhaps we have
not yet reached the last chapter in the queer story. But, look, we
are drawing near to the verge of London; there are gaps, you see,
in the serried ranks of brick, and a vision of green fields beyond.'

Dyson had persuaded the ingenious Mr Phillipps to accompany
him on one of those aimless walks to which he was himself so
addicted. Starting from the very heart of London, they had made
their way westward through the stony avenues, and were now just
emerging from the red lines of an extreme suburb, and presently
the half-finished road ended, a quiet land began, and they were

beneath the shade of elm trees. The yellow autumn sunlight that had lit up the bare distance of the suburban street now filtered down through the boughs of the trees and shone on the glowing carpet of fallen leaves, and the pools of rain glittered and shot back the gleam of light. Over all the broad pastures there was peace and the happy rest of autumn before the great winds begin, and afar off London lay all vague and immense amidst the veiling mist; here and there a distant window catching the sun and kindling with fire, and a spire gleaming high, and below the streets in shadow, and the turmoil of life. Dyson and Phillipps walked on in silence beneath the high hedges, till at a turn of the lane they saw a mouldering and ancient gate. standing open, and the prospect of a house at the end of a moss-grown carriage drive.

'There is a survival for you,' said Dyson; 'it has come to its last days, I imagine. Look how the laurels have grown gaunt and weedy, and black and bare beneath; look at the house, covered with yellow wash, and patched with green damp. Why, the very notice-board, which informs all and singular that the place is to be let, has cracked and half fallen.'

'Suppose we go in and see it,' said Phillipps; 'I don't think there is anybody about.'

They turned up the drive, and walked slowly towards this remnant of old days. It was a large, straggling house, with curved wings at either end, and behind a series of irregular roofs and projections, showing that the place had been added to at divers dates; the two wings were roofed in cupola fashion, and at one side, as they came nearer, they could see a stableyard, and a clock turret with a bell, and the dark masses of gloomy cedars. Amidst all the lineaments of dissolution there was but one note of contrast : the sun was setting beyond the elm trees, and all the west and south were in flames; on the upper windows of the house the glow shone reflected, and it seemed as if blood and fire were mingled. Before the yellow front of the mansion, stained, as Dyson had remarked, with gangrenous patches, green and blackening, stretched what had once been, no doubt, a well-kept lawn, but it was now rough and ragged, and nettles and great docks, and all manner of coarse weeds, struggled in the places of the flower-beds.

The urns had fallen from their pillars beside the walk, and lay broken in shards upon the ground, and everywhere from grass-plot and path a fungoid growth had sprung up and multiplied, and lay dank and slimy like a festering sore upon the earth. In the middle of the rank grass of the lawn was a desolate fountain; the rim of the basin was crumbling and pulverised with decay, and within the water stood stagnant, with green scum for the lilies that had once bloomed there; rust had eaten into the bronze flesh of the Triton that stood in the middle, and the conch-shell he held was broken.

'Here,' said Dyson, 'one might moralise over decay and death. Here all the stage is decked out with the symbols of dissolution; the cedarn gloom and twilight hang heavy around us, and everywhere within the pale darkness has found a harbour, and the very air is changed and brought to accord with the scene. To me, I confess, this deserted house is as moral as a graveyard, and I find something sublime in that lonely Triton, deserted in the midst of his water-pool. He is the last of the gods; they have left him, and he remembers the sound of water falling on water, and the days that were sweet.'

'I like your reflections extremely,' said Phillipps; 'but I may mention that the door of the house is open.'

'Let us go in, then.'

The door was just ajar, and they passed into the mouldy hall and looked in at a room on one side. It was a large room, going far back, and the rich, old, red flock paper was peeling from the walls in long strips, and blackened with vague patches of rising damp; the ancient clay, the dank reeking earth rising up again, and subduing all the work of men's hands after the conquest of many years. The floor was thick with the dust of decay, and the painted ceiling fading from all gay colours and light fancies of cupids in a career, and disfigured with sores of dampness, seemed transmuted into other work.

No longer the amorini chased one another pleasantly, with limbs that sought not to advance and hands that merely simulated the act of grasping at the wreathed flowers; but it appeared some savage burlesque of the old careless world and of its cherished conventions, and the dance of the Lovers had become a Dance of Death; black pustules and festering sores swelled and clustered on fair limbs and smiling faces showed corruption, and the fairy blood had boiled with the germs of foul disease; it was a parable of the leaven working, and worms devouring for a banquet the heart of a rose.

Strangely, under the painted ceiling, against the decaying walls, two old chairs still stood alone, the sole furniture of the empty place. High-backed, with curving arms and twisted legs, covered with faded gold leaf, and upholstered in tattered damask, they too were a part of the symbolism, and struck Dyson with surprise. 'What have we here?' he said. 'Who has sat in these chairs? Who, clad in peach-blossom satin, with lace ruffles and diamond buckles, all golden, *a conté fleurettes* to his companion? Phillipps, we are in another age. I wish I had some snuff to offer you, but failing that I beg to offer you a seat, and we will sit and smoke.'

They sat down on the queer old chairs, and looked out of the dim and grimy panes to the ruined lawn, and the fallen urns, and the deserted Triton.

'It's a foolish fancy,' Dyson said then; 'but I keep thinking I hear a noise like some one groaning. Listen; no, I can't hear it now. There it is again! Did you notice it, Phillipps?'

'No, I can't say I heard anything. But I believe that old places like this are like shells from the shore, ever echoing with noises. The old beams, mouldering piecemeal, yield a little and groan; and such a house as this I can fancy all resonant at night with voices, the voices of matter so slowly and so surely transformed into other shapes, the voice of the worm that gnaws at last the very heart of the oak, the voice of stone grinding on stone, and the voice of the conquest of Time.'

They sat still in the old arm-chairs, and grew graver in the musty ancient air.

'I don't like the place,' said Phillipps, after a long pause. 'To me it seems as if there were a sickly, unwholesome smell about it, a smell of something burning.'

'You are right; there is an evil odour here. Hark! Did you hear that?'

A hollow sound, a noise of infinite sadness and infinite pain, broke in upon the silence, and the two men looked fearfully at one another, horror, and the sense of unknown things, glimmering in their eyes.

'Come,' said Dyson, 'we must see into this,' and they went into the hall.

'Do you know,' said Phillipps, 'it seems absurd, but I could almost fancy that the smell is that of burning flesh.'

They went up the hollow-sounding stairs, and the odour became thick and noisome, stifling the breath, and a vapour, sickening as the smell of the chamber of death, choked them. A door was open, and they entered the large upper room, and clung hard to one another, shuddering at the sight they saw.

A naked man was lying on the floor, his arms and legs stretched wide apart, and bound to pegs that had been hammered into the boards. The body was torn and mutilated in the most hideous fashion, scarred with the marks of red-hot irons, a shameful ruin of the human shape. But upon the middle of the body a fire of coals was smouldering; the flesh had been burnt through. The man was dead, but the smoke of his torment mounted still, a black vapour.

'The young man with spectacles,' said Mr Dyson.

7

Perhaps not surprisingly there have been few women to attain
the status of Magus in the ranks of occult practitioners. A
great many ladies have absorbed themselves (and indeed still
do) in astrology, palmistry, clairvoyancy, fortune-telling and
a hundred and one fringe magical practices, but with the
exception of Madame Blavatsky, whom we have already
studied, and 'Dion Fortune', whom we come to next, the
history of modern occultism is devoid of their presence. This
may well be due to the fact that the women's role has always
been subservient to man's in ritual magic (except in the case
of witchcraft where the woman, representing the Great Mother
or Fertility Goddess, does dominate the ceremony), and man
has deliberately kept her in ignorance of the prime secrets. To
succeed to the highest plain, then, she has virtually had to
venture alone. Such a determined personality was Violet
Firth (1890-1946) who wrote and practised the occult arts
under the pseudonym of Dion Fortune.

Like Madame Blavatsky, Dion Fortune was a forceful,
intelligent and dedicated young woman who refused to be
overawed or excluded from the world of magic which so
clearly fascinated her. From a quite early age we know that
she displayed marked mediumistic powers and came to be
regarded as something of a celebrity in her home town. Her
interest in the Occult began just after the First World War
when she joined the sadly waning Order of the Golden Dawn.
The mainstay of this group, MacGregor Mathers, had died
during the war (Crowley and Yeats, of course, had long since
left it) and his widow Moina was now the titular head. Miss
Fortune's quick mind and determination soon gained her
initiation in 1919 (she received the name *Deo Non Fortuna*,
later simplified for her pen-name), but equally quickly led to
her disillusionment with the Order. She complained of the
lack of real teaching by the leaders: 'One was put through
the ceremonies,' she later wrote, 'given the bare bones of the

system, a few commentaries for the most part of very inferior quality, and left to one's own devices.' But her 'own devices' proved to be considerable and when the first flaws in the relationship between Mrs Mathers and herself became evident, she had probably surpassed all other members – male and female – in terms of proficiency and learning. She had also reached the conclusion that it was time the Golden Dawn – indeed all forms of ritual magic and occultism – were explained to the public, so that they could win some general support and understanding, hitherto lacking. She proposed, and went ahead to found, a new mystic society, The Fraternity of the Inner Light; Mrs Mathers was incensed and immediately expelled her one-time favourite from the Order. (Dion Fortune maintained later that Mrs Mathers had also used black magic against her as a punishment, one night sending a huge phantom cat which left claw-marks on her back and legs while she slept.)

As the Golden Dawn fell further into internal strife, the new Fraternity developed apace and Dion Fortune's rush of books and magazine articles brought her plenty of new followers. Apart from her many works of fiction, she also wrote *The Mystical Qabalah* which, like Crowley's *Magick in Theory and Practice*, was a book of major importance to all students of the Occult. A marriage late in life to a doctor somewhat curtailed her magical and mediumistic practices, but the Society she had formed and the determination she gave it to encourage openly all those interested in studying the Occult, are still influential today.

Dion Fortune is currently finding a new readership for her novels, as these are being reprinted steadily by an enterprising London publisher. In them she incorporated much of what she learned in her study – as indeed she did in the following story which doubtless draws some of its inspiration from the unsettled days in the life of the Order of the Golden Dawn. The tale features Dion Fortune's *alter ego* Dr Taverner, an enquirer into all things occult; it also brings us into contact for the first time with those mysterious manuscripts of occult ritual, the inherent power in them and the dangers they present when in the wrong hands. . . .

* * *

The Return of the Ritual

DION FORTUNE

It was Dr Taverner's custom, at certain times and seasons, to do what I should call hypnotise himself; he, however, called it 'going subconscious', and declared that, by means of concentration, he shifted the focus of his attention from the external world to the world of thought. Of the different states of consciousness to which he thus obtained access, and of the work that could be performed in each one, he would talk by the hour, and I soon learnt to recognise the phases he passed through during this extraordinary process.

Night after night I have watched beside the unconscious body of my colleague as it lay twitching on the sofa while thoughts that were not derived from his mind influenced the passive nerves. Many people can communicate with each other by means of thought, but I had never realised the extent to which this power was employed until I heard Taverner use his body as the receiving instrument of such messages.

One night while he was drinking some hot coffee I had given him (for he was always chilled to the bone after these performances) he said to me : 'Rhodes, there is a very curious affair afoot.'

I enquired what he meant.

'I am not quite sure,' he replied. 'There is something going on which I do not understand, and I want you to help me to investigate it.'

I promised my assistance, and asked the nature of the problem.

'I told you when you joined me,' he said, 'that I was a member of an occult brotherhood, but I did not tell you anything about it, because I am pledged not to do so, but for the purpose of our work together I am going to use my discretion and explain certain things to you.

'You know, I daresay, that we make use of ritual in our work. This is not the nonsense you may think it to be, for ritual has a profound effect on the mind. Anyone who is sufficiently sensitive can feel vibrations radiating whenever an occult ceremonial is being performed. For instance, I have only got to listen mentally for a moment to tell whether one of the Lhassa Lodges is working its terrific ritual.

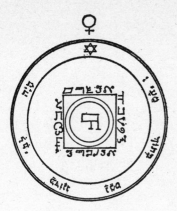

A RITUAL PENTACLE

'When I was subconscious just now I heard one of the rituals of my own Order being worked, but worked as no Lodge I have ever sat in would perform it. It was like a rendering of Tchaikovsky picked out on the piano with one finger by a child, and unless I am very much mistaken, some unauthorised person has got hold of that ritual and is experimenting with it.'

'Someone has broken his oath and given away your secrets,' I said.

'Evidently,' said Taverner. 'It has not often been done, but instances have occured, and if any of the Black Lodges, who would know how to make use of it, should get hold of the ritual the results might be serious, for there is great power in these old ceremonies, and while that power is safe in the hands of the carefully picked students whom we initiate, it would be a very different matter in those of unscrupulous men.'

'Shall you try to trace it?' I enquired.

'Yes,' said Taverner, 'but it is easier said than done. I have absolutely nothing to guide me. All I can do is to send round word among the Lodges to see whether a copy is missing from their archives; that will narrow our zone of search somewhat.'

Whether Taverner made use of the post or of his own peculiar methods of communication I do not know, but in a few days' time he had the information he required. None of the carefully guarded rituals was missing from any of the Lodges, but when search was made among the records at headquarters it was discovered that a ritual had been stolen from the Florentine Lodge during the middle ages by the custodian of the archives and sold (it was believed) to the Medici; at any rate, it was known to have been worked in Florence during the latter half of the fifteenth century. What became of it after the Medician manuscripts were dispersed at the plundering of Florence by the French was never known; it was lost sight of and was always believed to have been destroyed. Now, however, after the lapse of so many centuries someone was waking its amazing power.

As we were passing down Harley Street a few days later, Taverner asked me if I would mind turning aside with him into the Marylebone Lane, where he wished to call at a secondhand bookshop. I was surprised that a man of the type of my colleague should patronise such a place, for it appeared to be stocked chiefly with tattered paper-covered Ouidas and out-of-date piousness, and the alacrity with which the shopboy went to fetch the owner showed that my companion was a regular and esteemed customer.

The owner when he appeared was an even greater surprise than his shop; unbelievably dusty, his frockcoat, beard and face all appeared to be of a uniform grey-green, yet when he spoke his voice was that of a cultured man, and, though my companion addressed him as an equal, he answered as to a superior.

'Have you received any reply to the advertisement I asked you to insert for me?' asked Taverner of the snuff-coloured individual who confronted us.

'I have not; but I have got some information for you – you are not the only purchaser in the market for the manuscript.'

'My competitor being – ?'

'A man named Williams.'

'That does not tell us very much.'

'The postmark was Chelsea,' said the old bookseller with a significant look.

'Ah!' said my employer. 'If that manuscript should come into the market I will not limit you as to price.'

'I think we are likely to have a little excitement,' observed Taverner as we left the shop, its dust-covered occupant bowing behind us. 'The Chelsea Black Lodges have evidently heard what I heard and are also making a bid for the ritual.'

'You do not suppose that it is one of the Chelsea Lodges that has got it at the present moment?' I enquired.

'I do not,' said Taverner, 'for they would have made a better job of it. Whatever may be said against their morals, they are not fools, and know what they are about. No, some person or group of persons who dabbles in the occult without any real knowledge has got hold of that manuscript. They know enough to recognise a ritual when they see it, and are playing about with it to see what will happen. Probably no one would be more astonished than they if anything *did* happen.

'Were the ritual confined to such hands as those I should not be worried about it; but it may get into the possession of people who will know how to use it and abuse its powers, and then the consequences will be much more serious than you can realise. I will even go so far as to say that the course of civilisation would be affected if such a thing occurred.'

I saw that Taverner was profoundly moved. Regardless of traffic he plunged into the roadway, making a bee-line for his rooms.

'I would give any price for that manuscript if I could lay my hands on it, and if it were not for sale I would not hesitate to steal it; but how in the name of Heaven am I to trace the thing?'

We had regained the consulting-room, and Taverner was pacing up and down the floor with long strides. Presently he took up the telephone and rang up his Hindhead nursing home and told the matron that we should be spending the night in town. As there was no sleeping accommodation at the house in Harley Street, where he had his London headquarters, I guessed that a night of vigil was in contemplation.

I was fairly used to these watch-nights now; I knew that my duty would be to guard Taverner's vacated body while his soul ranged through outer darkness on some strange quest of its own and talked to its peers – men who were also able to leave their bodies at will and walk the starry ways with him, or others who had died centuries ago, but were still concerned with the welfare of their fellow men whom they had lived to serve.

We dined at a little restaurant in a back street off Soho, where the head waiter argued metaphysics in Italian with Taverner between courses, and returned to our Harley Street quarters to wait until the great city about us should have gone to sleep and left the night quiet for the work we were about to embark upon. It was not till well after midnight that Taverner judged the time was suitable, and then he settled himself upon the broad consulting-room couch, with myself at his feet.

In a few minutes he was asleep, but as I watched him I saw his breathing alter, and sleep gave way to trance. A few muttered words, stray memories of his previous earthly lives, came from his lips; then a deep and sibilant breath marked a second change of level, and I saw that he was in the state of consciousness that occultists use when they communicate with each other by means of telepathy. It was exactly like 'listening in' with a wireless telephone; Lodge called to Lodge across the deeps of the night, and the passive brain picked up the vibrations and passed them on to the voice, and Taverner spoke.

The jangle of messages, however, was cut off in the middle of a sentence. This was not the level on which Taverner meant to work tonight. Another sibilant hiss announced that he had gone yet deeper into the hypnotic condition. There was a dead stillness in the room, and then a voice that was not Taverner's broke the silence.

'The level of the records,' it said, and I guessed what Taverner meant to do; no brain but his could have hit upon the extraordinary scheme of tracing the manuscript by examining the subconscious mind of the human race. Taverner, in common with his fellow psychologists, held that every thought and every act have their images stored in the person's subconscious mind, but he also held that records of them are stored in the mind of Nature; and it was these records that he was seeking to read.

Broken fragments of sentences, figures, and names, fell from the lips of the unconscious man, and then he got his focus and steadied to his work.

'*Il cinquecento, Firenze, Italia, Pierro della Costa,*'* came a deep-level voice; then followed a long-drawn-out vibrating sound half-way between a telephone bell and the note of a 'cello, and the voice changed.

'Two forty-five, November the fourteenth, 1898, London, England.'

For a time there was silence, but almost immediately Taverner's voice cut across it.

---

* The fifteenth century, Florence, Italy, Peter della Costa.

'I want Pierro della Costa, who was reborn November the fourteenth, 1898, at two forty-five a.m.'

Silence. And then Taverner's voice again calling as if over a telephone: 'Hullo! Hullo! Hullo!' Apparently he received an answer, for his tone changed. 'Yes; it is the Senior of Seven who is speaking.'

Then his voice took on an extraordinary majesty and command. 'Brother, where is the ritual that was entrusted to thy care?'

What answer was given I could not divine; but after a pause Taverner's voice came again. 'Brother, redeem thy crime and return the ritual whence it was taken.' Then he rolled over on to his side, and the trance condition passed into natural sleep, and so to an awakening.

Dazed and shivering, he recovered consciousness, and I gave him hot coffee from a thermos flask, such as we always kept handy for these midnight meals. I recounted to him what had passed, and he nodded his satisfaction between sips of the steaming liquid.

'I wonder how Pierro della Costa will effect his task,' he said. 'The present-day personality will probably not have the faintest idea as to what is required of it, and will be blindly urged forward by the subconscious.'

'How will it locate the manuscript?' I enquired. 'Why should he succeed where you failed?'

'I failed because I could not at any point establish contact with the manuscript. I was not on earth at the time it was stolen, and I could not trace it in the racial memories for the same reason. One must have a jumping-off place, you know. Occult work is not performed by merely waving a wand.'

'How will the present-day Pierro go to work?' I enquired.

'The present-day Pierro won't do anything,' said Taverner, 'because he does not know how, but his subconscious mind is that of the trained occultist, and under the stimulus I have given it, will perform its work; it will probably go back to the time when the manuscript was handed over to the Medici, and then trace its subsequent history by means of the racial memories – the subconscious memory of Nature.'

'And how will he go to work to recover it?'

'As soon as the subconscious has located its quarry, it will send an impulse through into the conscious mind, bidding it take the body upon the quest, and a very puzzled modern young man may find himself in a difficult situation.'

'How will he know what to do with the manuscript when he has found it?'

'Once an Initiate, always an Initiate. In all moments of difficulty and danger the Initiate turns to his Master. Something in that boy's soul will reach out to make contact, and he will be brought back to his own Fraternity. Sooner or later he will come across one of the Brethren, who will know what to do with him.'

I was thankful enough to lie down on the sofa and get a couple of hours' sleep, until such time as the charwoman should disturb me; but Taverner, upon whom 'going subconscious' always seemed to have the effect of a tonic, announced his intention of seeing the sun rise from London Bridge, and left me to my own devices.

He returned in time to take me out to breakfast, and I discovered that he had given instructions for every morning paper and each successive edition of the evening ones to be sent in to us. All day long the stream of printed matter poured in, and had to be gone over, for Taverner was on the lookout for Pierro della Costa's effort to recover the ritual.

'His first attempt upon it is certain to be some blind lunatic outburst,' said Taverner, 'and it will probably land him in the hands of the police, whence it will be our duty as good Brethren, to rescue him; but it will have served its purpose, for he will, as it were, have "pointed" the manuscript after the fashion of a sporting dog.'

Next morning our vigilance was rewarded. An unusual case of attempted burglary was reported from St John's Wood. A young bank clerk of hitherto exemplary character had effected an entry into the house of a Mr Joseph Coates by the simple expedient of climbing on to the dining-room window-sill from the area steps, and, in full view of the entire street, kicking the glass out of the window. Mr Coates, aroused by the din, came down armed with a stick, which, however, was not required, the would-be burglar (who could give no explanation of his conduct) meekly waiting to be taken to the police station by the policeman whom the commotion he made had also attracted to the spot.

Taverner immediately telephoned to find out what time the case would be coming on at the police court, and we forthwith set out upon our quest. We sat in the enclosure reserved for the general public while various cases of wife-beaters and disorderly drunkards were disposed of, and I watched my neighbours.

Not far from us a girl of a different type from the rest of the sordid audience was seated; her pale oval face seemed to belong to another race from the irregular Cockney features about her. She looked like some mediaeval saint from an Italian fresco, and it only needed the stiff brocaded robes to complete the resemblance.

' "Look for the woman," ' said Taverner's voice in my ear. 'Now we know why Pierro della Costa fell to a bribe.'

The usual riff-raff having been dealt with, a prisoner of a different type was placed in the dock. A young fellow, refined, highly strung, looked round him in bewilderment at his unaccustomed surroundings, and then, catching sight of the olive-cheeked madonna in the gallery, took heart of grace.

He answered the magistrate's questions collectedly enough, giving his name as Peter Robson, and his profession as clerk. He listened attentively to the evidence of the policeman who had arrested him, and to Mr Joseph Coates, and when asked for his explanation, said he had none to give. In answer to questions, he declared that he had never been in that part of London before; he had no motive for going there, and he did not know why he had attempted to enter the window.

The magistrate, who at first had seemed disposed to deal leniently with the case, appeared to think that this persistent refusal of all explanation must conceal some motive, and proceeded to press the prisoner somewhat sharply. It looked as if matters were going hard with him, when Taverner, who had been scribbling on the back of a visiting card, beckoned an usher and sent the message up to the magistrate. I saw him read it, and turn the card over. Taverner's degrees and the Harley Street address were enough for him.

'I understand,' said he to the prisoner, 'that you have a friend here who can offer an explanation of the affair, and is prepared to go surety for you.'

The prisoner's face was a study; he looked round, seeking some familiar face, and when Taverner, well-dressed and of imposing appearance, entered the witness box, his perplexity was comical; and then, through all his bewilderment, a flash of light suddenly shot into the boy's eyes. Some gleam from the subconscious reached him, and he shut his mouth and awaited events.

My colleague, giving his name as John Richard Taverner, doctor of medicine, philosophy and science, master of arts and bachelor at law, said that he was a distant relation of the prisoner who was subject to that peculiar malady known as double personality. He was satisfied that this condition was quite sufficient to account for the attempt at burglary, some freak of the boy's other self having led to the crime.

Yes, Taverner was quite prepared to go surety for the boy, and the magistrate, evidently relieved at the turn affairs had taken, forthwith bound the prisoner over to come up for judgment if called upon, and within ten minutes of Taverner's entry upon the scene we were standing on the steps of the court, where the Florentine madonna joined us.

'I don't know who you are, sir,' the boy was saying, 'nor why you should help me, but I am very grateful to you. May I introduce my fiancée, Miss Fenner? She would like to thank you, too.'

Taverner shook hands with the girl.

'I don't suppose you two have eaten much breakfast with this affair hanging over your heads,' he said. They admitted that they had not.

'Then,' said he, 'you must be my guests for an early lunch.'

We all packed into a taxi, and drove to the restaurant where the metaphysical head waiter held sway. Here Peter Robson immediately tackled Taverner.

'Look here, sir,' he said, 'I am exceedingly grateful to you for what you have done for me, but I should very much like to know why you did it.'

'Do you ever weave daydreams?' enquired Taverner irrelevantly. Robson stared at him in perplexity, but the girl at his side suddenly exclaimed :

'I know what you mean. Do you remember, Peter, the stories we used to make up when we were children? How we belonged to a secret society that had its headquarters in the woodshed, and had only to make a certain sign and people would know we were members and be afraid of us? I remember once, when we had been locked in the scullery because we were naughty, you said that if you made this sign, the policeman would come in and tell your father he had got to let us out, because we belonged to a powerful Brotherhood that did not allow its members to be locked in sculleries. That is exactly what has happened; it is your daydream come true. But what is the meaning of it all?'

'Ah, what, indeed?' said Taverner. Then turning to the boy : 'Do you dream much?' he asked.

'Not as a rule,' he replied, 'but I had a most curious dream the night before last, which I can only regard as prophetic in the light of subsequent events. I dreamt that someone was accusing me of a crime, and I woke up in a dreadful way about it.'

'Dreams are curious things,' said Taverner, 'both day dreams and night dreams. I don't know which are the stranger. Do you believe in the immortality of the soul, Mr. Robson?'

'Of course I do.'

'Then has it ever struck you the eternal life must stretch both ways?'

'You mean,' said Robson under his breath, 'that it wasn't all imagination. It might be – memory?'

'Other people have had the same dream,' said Taverner, 'myself among them.' Then he leant across the narrow table and stared into the lad's eyes.

'Supposing I told you that just such an organisation as you imagined exists; that if, as a boy even, you had gone out into the main street and made that sign, someone would have been almost certain to answer it?'

'Supposing I told you that the impulse which made you break that window was not a blind instinct, but an attempt to carry out an order from your Fraternity, would you believe me?'

'I think I should,' said the lad opposite him. 'At any rate, if it isn't true, I wish it were, for it appeals to me more than anything I have ever heard.'

'If you care to go deeper into the matter,' said Taverner, 'will you come this evening to my place in Harley Street, and then we can talk the matter over?'

Robson accepted with eagerness. What man would refuse to follow his daydreams when they began to materialise.

After we had parted from our new acquaintance, we took a taxi to St John's Wood and stopped at a house whose front ground-floor window was in process of being reglazed. Taverner sent in his card, and we were ushered into a room decorated with large bronze Buddhas, statuettes from Egyptian tombs, and pictures by Watts. In a few minutes Mr Coates appeared.

'Ah, Dr Taverner,' he said, 'I presume you have come about the extraordinary matter of your young relative who broke into my house last evening?'

'That is so, Mr Coates,' replied my companion. 'I have come to offer you my sincere apologies on behalf of the family.'

'Don't mention it,' said our host, 'the poor lad was suffering from mental trouble, I take it?'

'A passing mania,' said Taverner, brushing it away with a wave of his hand. He glanced round the room. 'I see by your books that you are interested in a hobby of my own, the ancient mystery religions. I think I may claim to be something of an Egyptologist.'

Coates rose to the bait at once.

'I came across a most extraordinary document the other day,' said our new acquaintance. 'I should like to show it to you. I think you would be interested.'

He drew from his pocket a bunch of keys, and inserted one in the lock of a drawer in a bureau. To his astonishment the key pushed loosely through the hole, and he pulled the drawer open only to find that the lock had been forced off. He ran his hand to the back of the drawer, and withdrew it empty! Coates looked from Taverner to myself and back again in astonishment.

'That manuscript was there when I went to the police court this morning,' he said. 'What is the meaning of this extraordinary business? First of all a man breaks into my house and makes no attempt to steal anything, and then someone else breaks in and, neglecting many objects of value, takes a thing that can be of no interest to anyone but myself.'

'Then the manuscript which has been stolen is of no particular value?' said Taverner.

'I gave half-a-crown for it,' replied Coates.

'Then you should be thankful to have got off so lightly,' said Taverner.

'This is the devil, Rhodes,' he went on, as we re-entered the waiting taxi. 'Someone from a Chelsea Black Lodge, knowing Coates would be at the police court this morning, has taken that manuscript.'

'What is to be the next move?' I enquired.

'Get hold of Robson; we can only work through him.'

I asked him how he intended to deal with the situation that had arisen.

'Are you going to send Robson after the manuscript again?' I enquired.

'I shall have to,' said Taverner.

'I do not think there is the makings of a successful buccaneer in Robson.'

'Neither do I,' agreed Taverner; 'we shall have to fall back on Pierro della Costa.'

Robson met us at Harley Street, and Taverner took him out to dinner.

After dinner we returned to the consulting room, where Taverner handed round cigars, and set himself to be an agreeable host, a task in which he succeeded to perfection, for he was one of the most interesting talkers I have ever met.

Presently the talk led round to Italy during the Renaissance, and the great days of Florence and the Medici; and then he began to tell the story of one, Pierro della Costa, who had been a student of the occult arts in those days, and had brewed love philtres for the ladies of the Florentine court. He told the story with considerable vividness, and in great detail, and I was surprised to see that the attention of the lad was wandering, and that he was apparently pursuing a train of thought of his own, oblivious of his surroundings. Then I realised that he was sliding off into that trance condition with which my experience of my colleague had made me familiar.

Still Taverner talked on, telling the history of the old Florentine to the unconscious boy – how he rose to be custodian of the archives, was offered a bribe, and betrayed his trust in order that he might buy the favour of the woman he loved. Then, as he came to the end of the story, his voice changed, and he addressed the unconscious lad by name.

'Pierro della Costa,' he said, 'why did you do it?'

'Because I was tempted,' came the answer, but not in the voice in which the boy had talked to us; it was a man's voice, calm, deep, and dignified, vibrating with emotion.

'Do you regret it?' asked Taverner.

'I do,' returned the voice that was not the boy's voice. 'I have asked of the Great Ones that I may be permitted to restore that which I stole.'

'Thy request is granted,' said Taverner. 'Do that which thou has to do, and the blessing of the Great Ones be upon thee.'

Slowly the boy rolled over and sat up, but I saw at a glance that it was not the same individual who confronted us : a man, mature, of strong character and determined purpose, looked out of the boy's blue eyes.

'I go,' he said, 'to restore that which I took. Give me the means.' We went round, he and Taverner and I, to the garage, and got out the car. 'Which way do you want to go?' asked my colleague. The lad pointed to the south-west, and Taverner turned the car in the direction of the Marble Arch. Piloted by the man who was not Robson, we went south down Park Lane, and finally came out in the tangle of mean streets behind Victoria Station; thence we turned east. We pulled up behind the Tate Gallery, and the boy got out.

'From here,' he said, 'I go on alone,' and he disappeared down a side street.

Although we waited for a matter of half an hour, Taverner did not stop the engine. 'We may want to get out of here quick,' he said. Then, just as I was beginning to wonder if we were going to spend the night in the open, we heard running footsteps coming down the street, and Robson leapt into the car. That Taverner's precaution in not stopping the engine was justified was proved by the fact that close upon Robson's heels other footsteps sounded.

'Quick, Rhodes,' cried Taverner. 'Hang the rug over the back.' I did as I was bid, and succeeded in obscuring the number plate, and as the first of our pursuers rounded the corner, the big car leapt into its stride, and we drew clear.

No one spoke on the journey down to Hindhead.

We entered the sleeping house as quietly as might be, and as Taverner turned on the office lights, I saw that Robson carried a curious-looking volume bound in vellum. We did not tarry in the office, however, for Taverner led us through the sleeping house to a door which I knew led down to the cellar stairs.

'Come too, Rhodes,' said Taverner. 'You have seen the beginning of this matter, and you shall see the end, for you have shared in the risk, and although you are not one of Us, I know that I can rely on your discretion.'

We passed down the spiral stone stairs and along a flagged passage. Taverner unlocked a door, and admitted us to a wine cellar. He crossed this, and unlocked a further door. A dim point of flame illumined the darkness ahead of us, swaying uneasily in the draught. Taverner turned on a light, and to my intense surprise

I found myself in a chapel. High carved stalls were built into the walls on three sides, and on the fourth was an altar. The flickering light I had seen in the darkness came from the floating wick of a lamp hung above our heads as the centre point of a great Symbol.

Taverner lit the incense in a bronze thurible, and set it swinging. He handed Robson the black robe of an Inquisitor, and he himself assumed another one; then these two cowled figures faced one another across the floor of the empty chapel. Taverner began what was evidently a prayer. I could not gather its substance, for I am unable to follow spoken Latin. Then came a Litany of question and response, Robson, the London clerk, answering in the deep resonant voice of a man accustomed to intone across great buildings. Then he rose to his feet, and with the stately steps of a processional advanced to the altar, and laid thereon the ragged and mildewed manuscript he held in his hands. He knelt, and what absolution the sombre figure that stood over him pronounced, I cannot tell, but he rose to his feet like a man from whose shoulders a great burden has been rolled.

Then, for the first time, Taverner spoke in his native tongue. 'In all moments of difficulty and danger' – the booming of his deep voice filled the room with echoes – 'make this sign.' And I knew that the man who had betrayed his trust had made good and been received back into his old Fraternity.

We returned to the upper world, and the man who was not Robson bade us farewell. 'It is necessary that I should go,' he said.

'It is indeed,' said Taverner. 'You had better be out of England till this matter has blown over. Rhodes, will you undertake to drive him down to Southampton? I have other work to do.'

As we dropped down the long slope that leads to Liphook, I studied the man at my side. By some strange alchemy Taverner had woken the long dead soul of Pierro della Costa and imposed it upon the present-day personality of Peter Robson. Power radiated from him as light from a lamp; even the features seemed changed. Deep lines about the corners of the mouth lent a firmness to the hitherto indefinite chin, and the light blue eyes, now sunken in the head, had taken on the glitter of steel and were as steady as those of a swordsman.

It was just after six in the morning when we crossed the floating bridge into Southampton. The place was already astir, for a dock town never sleeps, and we enquired our way to the little-known inn where Taverner had directed us to go for breakfast. We discovered it to be an unpretentious public-house near the dock gates, and the potman was just drawing the bright curtains of turkey twill as we entered.

It was evident that strangers were not very welcome in the little tavern, and no one offered to take our order. As we stood there irresolute, heavy footsteps thundered down creaking wooden stairs, and a strongly built man wearing the four lines of gold braid denoting the rank of Captain entered the bar parlour. He glanced at us as he came in, and indeed we were sufficiently incongruous to be notable in such a place.

His eyes attracted my attention; he had the keen, outlooking gaze so characteristic of a seaman, but in addition to this he had a curious trick of looking at one without appearing to see one; the focus of the eyes met about a yard behind one's back. It was a thing I had often seen Taverner do when he wished to see the colours of an aura, that curious emanation which, for those who can see it, radiates from every living thing and is so clear an indication of the condition within.

Grey eyes looked into blue as the newcomer took in my companion, and then an almost imperceptible sign passed between them, and the sailor joined us.

'I believe you know my mother,' he remarked by way of introduction. Robson admitted the acquaintanceship, though I am prepared to swear he had never seen the man before, and we all three adjourned to an inner room for breakfast, which appeared in response to the bellowed orders of our new acquaintance.

Without any preamble he enquired our business, and Robson was equally ready to communicate it.

'I want to get out of the country as quietly as possible,' he said. Our new friend seemed to think that it was quite in the ordinary course of events that a man without luggage should be departing in this manner.

'I am sailing at nine this morning, going down the Gold Coast as far as Loango. We aren't exactly the Cunard, but if you care to come you will be welcome. You can't wear that rig, however; you would only draw a crowd, which I take it is what you don't want to do.'

He put his head through a half-door which separated the parlour from the back premises, and in response to his vociferations a little fat man with white chin whiskers appeared. A consultation took place between the two, the newcomer being equally ready to lend his assistance. Very shortly a suit of cheap serge reach-me-downs and a peaked cap were forthcoming, these being, the sailor assured us, the correct costume for a steward, in which capacity it was designed that Peter Robson should go to sea.

Leaving the inn that the mysterious Fellowship had made so hospitable to us, we took our way to the docks, and passing through the wilderness of railway lines, cranes, and yawning gulfs that constitute their scenery, we arrived at our companion's ship, a rusty-sided tramp, her upper works painted a dirty white.

We accompanied her captain to his cabin, a striking contrast to the raffle outside: a solid desk bearing a student's shaded lamp, a copy of Albrecht Dürer's study of the *Praying Hands*, a considerable shelf of books, and, perceptible beneath the all-pervading odour of strong tobacco, the faint spicy smell that clings to a place where incense is regularly burnt. I studied the titles of the books, for they tell one more of a man than anything else; *Isis Unveiled* stood cheek by jowl with *Creative Evolution* and two fat tomes of Eliphas Levi's *History of Magic*.

On the drive back to Hindhead I thought much of the strange side of life with which I had come in contact.

Yet another example was afforded me of the widespread ramifications of the Society. At Taverner's request I looked up the sea captain on his return from the voyage and asked him for news of Robson. This he was unable to give me, however; he had put the lad ashore at some mudhole on the West Coast. Standing on the quay stewing in the sunshine he had made the Sign. A half-caste Portuguese had touched him on the shoulder, and the two had vanished in the crowd. I expressed some anxiety as to the fate of an inexperienced lad in a strange land.

'You needn't worry,' said the sailor. 'That sign would take him right across Africa and back again.'

When I was talking the matter over with Taverner, I said to him: 'What made you and the captain claim relationship with Robson? It seemed to me a perfectly gratuitous lie.'

'It was no lie, but the truth,' said Taverner. 'Who is my Mother, and who are my Brethren but the Lodge and the Initiates thereof?'

8

In that complex and perhaps most controversial area of the Occult, spiritualism, one name towers over all others during the past one hundred years : Sir Arthur Conan Doyle. Others might well have practised it with more renown and deeper involvement, but without his contribution the subject would never have gained such widespread acceptance – if not understanding – among people of all classes throughout Europe and America. Conan Doyle's interest in the Occult dated from the years immediately after the First World War and, since he enjoyed the reputation of a skilled and far-famed writer, he helped bring credibility to a practice widely held to be the dominion of deceivers and frauds.

Ever since the heyday of Queen Victoria, spiritualism, the holding of seances and attempted communication with the spirits of the dead, had been the consuming passion of many men and women. Needless to say, phoney mediums proliferated and all manner of 'rigged' equipment and concealed assistants were used to fool the innocent. Conan Doyle saw clearly the truth from the fiction and campaigned relentlessly on behalf of the 'true Art' for the rest of his life.

Arthur Conan Doyle (1859-1930) began his career as a doctor, for a time running a general practice in Southsea. Financial difficulties, however, made him seek a secondary source of income and he turned to writing, evolving shortly thereafter the character who was to make him immortal among story-tellers, Sherlock Holmes. The success of the master detective freed him from worry and allowed him to continue writing and indulge his great passion for travel. Profoundly shocked by the horrors of the 1914-18 war, and still seeking his own personal fulfilment, Conan Doyle was introduced to spiritualism in 1920. He attended seances, met the leading practitioners and had soon embraced the art enthusiastically. His desire to communicate his convictions to a wider public resulted in his book *The Wanderings of a*

Spiritualist, which was published in 1921. For the next five years he worked on a two-volume *History of Spiritualism*, which was greeted on publication as being the standard work. The *Morning Post*, not normally given to praise anything connected with the Occult, enthused : 'It is needed because the time has come when most sensible people want to know something definite and accurate about a movement which is *of the utmost importance to the human race*.' (The italics are mine.) In later years Sir Arthur continued to write further on the subject and was a frequent guest at seances throughout Britain and America. At one of these he posed for a photograph with a medium and, on the resulting print, a 'spirit face' was seen floating above his head. (The picture is reproduced opposite p. 96.) The authenticity of this has since been much debated. He never lost his ability to be sceptical, however, and in perhaps his best story about the Occult, 'Playing with Fire', draws on his own experiences and a natural caution to recount an extraordinary tale of materialisation.

While to many Sir Arthur Conan Doyle is best remembered as the creator of Sherlock Holmes, to others he stands firmly as one of the master occultists of the twentieth century.

* * *

Playing with Fire

Sir Arthur Conan Doyle

I cannot pretend to say what occurred on 14th April last at No. 17 Badderly Gardens. Put down in black and white, my surmise might seem too crude, too grotesque, for serious consideration. And yet that something did occur, and that it was of a nature which will leave its mark upon every one of us for the rest of our lives, is as certain as the unanimous testimony of five witnesses can make it. I will not enter into any argument or speculation. I will only give a plain statement, which will be submitted to John Moir, Harvey Deacon, and Mrs Delamere, and withheld from publication unless they are prepared to corroborate every detail. I cannot obtain the sanction of Paul Le Duc, for he appears to have left the country.

It was John Moir (the well-known senior partner of Moir, Moir and Sanderson) who had originally turned our attention to occult subjects. He had, like many very hard and practical men of business, a mystic side to his nature, which had led him to the examination, and eventually to the acceptance, of those elusive phenomena which are grouped together with much that is foolish, and much that is fraudulent, under the common heading of spiritualism. His researches, which had begun with an open mind, ended unhappily in dogma, and he became as positive and fanatical as any other bigot. He represented in our little group the body of men who have turned these sinister phenomena into a new religion.

Mrs Delamere, our medium, was his sister, the wife of Delamere, the rising sculptor. Our experience had shown us that to work on these subjects without a medium was as futile as for an astronomer to make observations without a telescope. On the other hand, the introduction of a paid medium was hateful to all of us. Was it not obvious that he or she would feel bound to return some result for money received, and that the temptation to fraud would be an overpowering one? No phenomena could be relied upon which were produced at a guinea an hour. But, fortunately, Moir had discovered that his sister was mediumistic – in other words, that she was a battery of that animal magnetic force which is the only form of energy that is subtle enough to be acted upon from the

THE SIGN USED BY A MAGICIAN TO
'RID' HIMSELF OF A SPELL

spiritual plane as well as from our own material one. Of course, when I say this, I do not mean to beg the question; but I am simply indicating the theories upon which we were ourselves, rightly or wrongly, explaining what we saw. The lady came, not altogether with the approval of her husband, and though she never gave indications of any very great psychic force, we were able, at least, to obtain those usual phenomena of message-tilting which are at the same time so puerile and so inexplicable. Every Sunday evening we met in Harvey Deacon's studio at Badderly Gardens, the next house to the corner of Merton Park Road.

Harvey Deacon's imaginative work in art would prepare anyone to find that he was an ardent lover of everything which was *outré* and sensational. A certain picturesqueness in the study of the occult had been the quality which had originally attracted him to it, but his attention was speedily arrested by some of those phenomena to which I have referred, and he was coming rapidly to the conclusion that what he had looked upon as an amusing romance and an after-dinner entertainment was really a very formidable reality. He is a man with a remarkably clear and logical brain – a true descendant of his ancestor, the well-known Scotch professor – and he represented in our small circle the critical element, the man who has no prejudices, is prepared to follow facts as far as he can see them, and refuses to theorise in advance of his data. His caution annoyed

Moir as much as the latter's robust faith amused Deacon, but each in his own way was equally keen upon the matter.

And I? What am I to say that I represented? I was not the devotee. I was not the scientific critic. Perhaps the best that I can claim for myself is that I was the dilettante man about town, anxious to be in the swim of every fresh movement, thankful for any new sensation which would take me out of myself and open up fresh possibilities of existence. I am not an enthusiast myself, but I like the company of those who are. Moir's talk, which made me feel as if we had a private pass-key through the door of death, filled me with a vague contentment. The soothing atmosphere of the seance with the darkened lights was delightful to me. In a word, the thing amused me, and so I was there.

It was, as I have said, upon 14th April last that the very singular event which I am about to put upon record took place. I was the first of the men to arrive at the studio, but Mrs Delamere was already there, having had afternoon tea with Mrs Harvey Deacon. The two ladies and Deacon himself were standing in front of an unfinished picture of his upon the easel. I am not an expert in art, and I have never professed to understand what Harvey Deacon meant by his pictures; but I could see in this instance that it was all very clever and imaginative, fairies and animals and allegorical figures of all sorts. The ladies were loud in their praises, and indeed the colour effect was a remarkable one.

'What do you think of it, Markham?' he asked.

'Well, it's above me,' said I. 'These beasts – what are they?'

'Mythical monsters, imaginary creatures, heraldic emblems – a sort of weird, bizarre procession of them.'

'With a white horse in front!'

'It's not a horse,' said he, rather testily – which was surprising, for he was a very good-humoured fellow as a rule, and hardly ever took himself seriously.

'What is it, then?'

'Can't you see the horn in front? It's a unicorn. I told you they were heraldic beasts. Can't you recognise one?'

'Very sorry, Deacon,' said I, for he really seemed to be annoyed.

He laughed at his own irritation.

'Excuse me, Markham!' said he; 'the fact is that I have had an awful job over the beast. All day I have been painting him in and painting him out, and trying to imagine what a real live, ramping unicorn would look like. At last I got him, as I hoped; so when you failed to recognise it, it took me on the raw.'

'Why, of course it's a unicorn,' said I, for he was evidently depressed at my obtuseness. 'I can see the horn quite plainly, but I never saw a unicorn except beside the Royal Arms, and so I never thought of the creature. And these others are griffins and cockatrices, and dragons of sorts?'

'Yes, I had no difficulty with them. It was the unicorn which bothered me. However, there's an end of it until tomorrow.' He turned the picture round upon the easel, and we all chatted about other subjects.

Moir was late that evening, and when he did arrive he brought with him, rather to our surprise, a small, stout Frenchman, whom he introduced as Monsieur Paul Le Duc. I say to our surprise, for we held a theory that any intrusion into our spiritual circle deranged the conditions, and introduced an element of suspicion. We knew that we could trust each other, but all our results were vitiated by the presence of an outsider. However, Moir soon reconciled us to the innovation. Monsieur Paul Le Duc was a famous student of occultism, a seer, a medium, and a mystic. He was travelling in England with a letter of introduction to Moir from the President of the Parisian brothers of the Rosy Cross. What more natural than that he should bring him to our little seance, or that we should feel honoured by his presence?

He was, as I have said, a small, stout man, undistinguished in appearance, with a broad, smooth, clean-shaven face, remarkable only for a pair of large, brown, velvety eyes, staring vaguely out in front of him. He was well dressed, with the manners of a gentleman and his curious little turns of English speech set the ladies smiling. Mrs Deacon had a prejudice against our researches and left the room, upon which we lowered the lights, as was our custom, and drew up our chairs to the square mahogany table which stood in the centre of the studio. The light was subdued, but sufficient to allow us to see each other quite plainly. I remember that I could even observe the curious, podgy little square-topped hands which the Frenchman laid upon the table.

'What a fun!' said he. 'It is many years since I have sat in this fashion, and it is to me amusing. Madame is medium. Does madame make the trance?'

'Well hardly that,' said Mrs Delamere. 'But I am always conscious of extreme sleepiness.'

'It is the first stage. Then you encourage it, and there comes the trance. When the trance comes, then out jumps your little spirit and in jumps another little spirit, and so you have direct talking or writing. You leave your machine to be worked by another. *Hein?* But what have unicorns to do with it?'

Harvey Deacon started in his chair. The Frenchman was moving his head slowly round and staring into the shadows which draped the walls.

'What a fun!' said he. 'Always unicorns. Who has been thinking so hard upon a subject so bizarre?'

'This is wonderful!' cried Deacon. 'I have been trying to paint one all day. But how could you know it?'

'You have been thinking of them in this room.'

'Certainly.'

'But thoughts are things, my friend. When you imagine a thing you make a thing. You did not know, *hein?* But I can see your unicorns because it is not only with my eye that I can see.'

'Do you mean to say that I create a thing which has never existed by merely thinking of it?'

'But certainly. It is the fact which lies under all other facts. That is why an evil thought is also a danger.'

'They are, I suppose, upon the astral plane?' said Moir.

'Ah, well, these are but words, my friends. They are there – somewhere – everywhere – I cannot tell myself. I see them. I could touch them.'

'You could not make *us* see them.'

'It is to materialise them. Hold! It is an experiment. But the power is wanting. Let us see what power we have, and then arrange what we shall do. May I place you as I wish?'

'You evidently know a great deal more about it than we do,' said Harvey Deacon; 'I wish that you would take complete control.'

'It may be that the conditions are not good. But we will try what we can do. Madame will sit where she is, I next, and this gentleman beside me. Meester Moir will sit next to madame, because it is well to have blacks and blondes in turn. So! And now with your permission I will turn the lights all out.'

'What is the advantage of the dark?' I asked.

'Because the force with which we deal is a vibration of ether and so also is light. We have the wires all for ourselves now – *hein*? You will not be frightened in the darkness, madame? What a fun is such a seance!'

At first the darkness appeared to be absolutely pitchy, but in a few minutes our eyes became so far accustomed to it that we could just make out each other's presence – very dimly and vaguely, it is true. I could see nothing else in the room – only the black loom of the motionless figures. We were all taking the matter much more seriously than we had ever done before.

'You will place your hands in front. It is hopeless that we touch, since we are so few round so large a table. You will compose yourself, madame, and if sleep should come to you you will not fight against it. And now we sit in silence and we expect – *hein*?

So we sat in silence and expected, staring out into the blackness in front of us. A clock ticked in the passage. A dog barked intermittently far away. Once or twice a cab rattled past in the street, and the gleam of its lamps through the chink in the curtains was a cheerful break in that gloomy vigil. I felt those physical symptoms with which previous seances had made me familiar – the coldness of the feet, the tingling in the hands, the glow of the palms, the feeling of a cold wind upon the back. Strange little shooting pains came in my forearms, especially as it seemed to me in my left one, which was nearest to our visitor – due no doubt to disturbance of the vascular system, but worthy of some attention all the same. At the same time I was conscious of a strained feeling of expectancy which was almost painful. From the rigid, absolute silence of my companions I gathered that their nerves were as tense as my own.

And then suddenly a sound came out of the darkness – a low, sibilant sound, the quick, thin breathing of a woman. Quicker and thinner yet it came, as between clenched teeth, to end in a loud gasp with a dull rustle of cloth.

'What's that? Is all right?' someone asked in the darkness.

'Yes, all is right,' said the Frenchman. 'It is madame. She is in her trance. Now, gentlemen, if you will wait quiet you will see something, I think, which will interest you much.'

Still the ticking in the hall. Still the breathing, deeper and fuller now, from the medium. Still the occasional flash, more welcome than ever, of the passing lights of the hansom. What a gap we were bridging, the half-raised veil of the eternal on the one side and the cabs of London on the other. The table was throbbing with a mighty pulse. It swayed steadily, rhythmically, with an easy swooping, scooping motion under our fingers. Sharp little raps and cracks came from its substance, file-firing, volley-firing, the sounds of a faggot burning briskly on a frosty night.

'There is much power,' said the Frenchman. 'See it on the table!'

I had thought it was some delusion of my own, but all could see it now. There was a greenish-yellow phosphorescent light – or I should say a luminous vapour rather than a light – which lay over the surface of the table. It rolled and wreathed and undulated in dim glimmering folds, turning and swirling like clouds of smoke. I could see the white, square-ended hands of the French medium in this baleful light.

'What a fun!' he cried. 'It is splendid!'

'Shall we call the alphabet?' asked Moir.

'But no – for we can do much better,' said our visitor. 'It is but a clumsy thing to tilt the table for every letter of the alphabet, and with such a medium as madame we should do better than that.'

'Yes, you will do better,' said a voice.

'Who was that? Who spoke? Was that you, Markham?'

'No, I did not speak.'

'It was madame who spoke.'

'But it was not her voice.'

'Is that you, Mrs Delamere?'

'It is not the medium, but it is the power which uses the organs of the medium,' said the strange, deep voice.

'Where is Mrs Delamere? It will not hurt her, I trust.'

'The medium is happy in another plane of existence. She has taken my place, as I have taken hers.'

'Who are you?'

'It cannot matter to you who I am. I am one who has lived as you are living, and who has died as you will die.'

We heard the creak and grate of a cab pulling up next door. There was an argument about the fare, and the cabman grumbled hoarsely down the street. The green-yellow cloud still swirled faintly over the table, dull elsewhere, but glowing into a dim luminosity in the direction of the medium. It seemed to be piling itself up in front of her. A sense of fear and cold struck into my heart. It seemed to me that lightly and flippantly we had approached the most real and august of sacraments, that communion with the dead of which the Fathers of the Church had spoken.

'Don't you think we are going too far? Should we not break up this seance?' I cried.

'But the others were all earnest to see the end of it. They laughed at my scruples.

'All the powers are made for use,' said Harvey Deacon. 'If we *can* do this, we *should* do this. Every new departure of knowledge has been called unlawful in its inception. It is right and proper that we should enquire into the nature of death.'

'It is right and proper,' said the voice.

'There, what more could you ask?' cried Moir, who was much excited. 'Let us have a test. Will you give us a test that you are really there?'

'What test do you demand?'

'Well now – I have some coins in my pocket. Will you tell me how many?'

'We come back in the hope of teaching and of elevating, and not to guess childish riddles.'

'Ha, ha, Meester Moir, you catch it that time,' cried the Frenchman. 'But surely this is very good sense what the Control is saying.'

'It is a religion, not a game,' said the cold, hard voice.

'Exactly – the very view I take of it,' cried Moir. 'I am sure I am very sorry if I have asked a foolish question. You will not tell me who you are?'

'What does it matter?'

'Have you been a spirit long?'

'Yes.'

'How long?'

'We cannot reckon time as you do. Our conditions are different.'

'Are you happy?'

'Yes.'

'You would not wish to come back to life?'

'No – certainly not.'

'Are you busy?'

'We could not be happy if we were not busy.'

'What do you do?'

'I have said that the conditions are entirely different.'

'Can you give us no idea of your work?'

'We labour for our own improvement and for the advancement of others.'

'Do you like coming here tonight?'

'I am glad to come if I can do any good by coming.'

'Then to do good is your object?'

'It is the object of all life on every plane.'

'You see, Markham, that should answer your scruples.'

It did, for my doubts had passed and only interest remained.

'Have you pain in your life?' I asked.

'No; pain is a thing of the body.'

'Have you mental pain?'

'Yes; one may always be sad or anxious.'

'Do you meet the friends whom you have known on earth?'

'Some of them.'

'Why only some of them?'

'Only those who are sympathetic.'

'Do husbands meet wives?'

'Those who have truly loved.'

'And the others?'

'They are nothing to each other.'

'There must be a spiritual connection?'

'Of course.'

'Is what we are doing right?'

'If done in the right spirit.'

'What is the wrong spirit?'

'Curiosity and levity.'

'May harm come of that?'

'What sort of harm?'

'Very serious harm.'

'You may call up forces over which you have no control.'

'Evil forces?'

'Undeveloped forces.'

'You say they are dangerous. Dangerous to body or mind?'

'Sometimes to both.'

There was a pause, and the blackness seemed to grow blacker still, while the yellow-green fog swirled and smoked upon the table.

'Any questions you would like to ask, Moir?' said Harvey Deacon.

'Only this – do you pray in your world?'

'One should pray in every world.'

'Why?'

'Because it is the acknowledgment of forces outside ourselves.'

'What religion do you hold over there?'

'We differ exactly as you do.'

'You have no certain knowledge?'

'We have only faith.'

'These questions of religion,' said the Frenchman, 'they are of interest to you serious English people, but they are not so much fun. It seems to me that with this power here we might be able to have some great experience – *hein*? Something of which we could talk.'

'But nothing could be more interesting than this,' said Moir.

'Well, if you think so, that is very well,' the Frenchman answered peevishly. 'For my part, it seems to me that I have heard all this before, and that tonight I should weesh to try some experiment with all this force which is given to us. But if you have other questions, then ask them, and when you are finish we can try something more.'

But the spell was broken. We asked and asked, but the medium sat silent in her chair. Only her deep, regular breathing showed that she was there. The mist still swirled upon the table.

'You have disturbed the harmony. She will not answer.'

'But we have learned already all that she can tell – *hein*? For my part I wish to see something that I have never seen before.'

'What then?'

'You will let me try?'

'What would you do?'

'I have said to you that thoughts are things. Now I wish to *prove* it to you, and to show you that which is only a thought. Yes, yes, I can do it and you will see. Now I ask you only to sit still and say nothing, and keep ever your hands quiet upon the table.'

The room was blacker and more silent than ever. The same feeling of apprehension which had lain heavily upon me at the beginning of the seance was back at my heart once more. The roots of my hair were tingling.

'It is working! It is working!' cried the Frenchman, and there was a crack in his voice as he spoke which told me that he also was strung to his tightest.

The luminous fog drifted slowly off the table, and wavered and flickered across the room. There in the farther and darkest corner it gathered and glowed, hardening down into a shining core – a strange, shifty, luminous, and yet non-illuminating patch of radiance, bright itself, but throwing no rays into the darkness. It had changed from a greenish-yellow to a dusky sullen red. Then round this centre there coiled a dark, smoky substance, thickening, hardening, growing denser and blacker. And then the light went out, smothered in that which had grown round it.

'It has gone.'

'Hush – there's something in the room.'

We heard it in the corner where the light had been, something which breathed deeply and fidgeted in the darkness.

'Where is it? Le Duc, what have you done?'

'It is all right. No harm will come.' The Frenchman's voice was treble with agitation.

'Good heavens, Moir, there's a large animal in the room. Here it is, close by my chair! Go away! Go away!'

It was Harvey Deacon's voice, and then came the sound of a blow upon some hard object. And then. . . . And then . . . how can I tell you what happened then?

Some huge thing hurtled against us in the darkness, rearing, stamping, smashing, springing, snorting. The table was splintered. We were scattered in every direction. It clattered and scrambled amongst us, rushing with horrible energy from one corner of the room to another. We were all screaming with fear, grovelling upon our hands and knees to get away from it. Something trod upon my left hand, and I felt the bones splinter under the weight.

'A light! A light!' someone yelled.

'Moir, you have matches, matches!'

'No, I have none. Deacon, where are the matches? For God's sake, the matches!'

'I can't find them. Here, you Frenchman, stop it!'

'It is beyond me. Oh, *mon Dieu*, I cannot stop it. The door! Where is the door?'

My hand, by good luck, lit upon the handle as I groped about in the darkness. The hard-breathing, snorting, rushing creature tore past me and butted with a fearful crash against the oaken partition. The instant that it had passed I turned the handle, and next moment we were all outside, and the door shut behind us. From within came a horrible crashing and rending and stamping.

'What is it? In Heaven's name, what is it?'

'A horse. I saw it when the door opened. But Mrs Delamere?'

'We must fetch her out. Come on, Markham; the longer we wait the less we shall like it.'

He flung open the door and we rushed in. She was there on the

ground amidst the splinters of her chair. We seized her and dragged
her swiftly out, and as we gained the door I looked over my shoulder
into the darkness. There were two strange eyes glowing at us, a
rattle of hoofs, and I had just time to slam the door when there
came a crash upon it which split it from top to bottom.

'It's coming through! It's coming!'

'Run, run for your lives!' cried the Frenchman.

Another crash, and something shot through the riven door. It was
a long white spike, gleaming in the lamplight. For a moment it
shone before us, and then with a snap it disappeared again.

'Quick! Quick! This way!' Harvey Deacon shouted. 'Carry her
in! Here! Quick!'

We had taken refuge in the dining-room, and shut the heavy oak
door. We laid the senseless woman upon the sofa, and as we did so,
Moir, the hard man of business, drooped and fainted across the
hearthrug. Harvey Deacon was as white as a corpse, jerking and
twitching like a epileptic. With a crash we heard the studio door
fly to pieces, and the snorting and stamping were in the passage, up
and down, shaking the house with their fury. The Frenchman had
sunk his face on his hands, and sobbed like a frightened child.

'What shall we do?' I shook him roughly by the shoulder. 'Is a
gun any use?'

'No, no. The power will pass. Then it will end.'

'You might have killed us all – you unspeakable fool – with your
infernal experiments.'

'I did not know. How could I tell that it would be frightened? It
is mad with terror. It was his fault. He struck it.'

Harvey Deacon sprang up. 'Good heavens!' he cried.

A terrible scream sounded through the house.

'It's my wife! Here, I'm going out. If it's the Evil One himself I
am going out!'

He had thrown open the door and rushed out into the passage.
At the end of it, at the foot of the stairs, Mrs Deacon was lying
senseless, struck down by the sight which she had seen. But there
was nothing else.

With eyes of horror we looked about us, but all was perfectly
quiet and still. I approached the black square of the studio door,
expecting with every slow step that some atrocious shape would
hurl itself out of it. But nothing came, and all was silent inside the
room. Peeping and peering, our hearts in our mouths, we came to

the very threshold, and stared into the darkness. There was still no sound, but in one direction there was also no darkness. A luminous, glowing cloud, with an incandescent centre, hovered in the corner of the room. Slowly it dimmed and faded, growing thinner and fainter, until at last the same dense, velvety blackness filled the whole studio. And with the last flickering gleam of that baleful light the Frenchman broke into a shout of joy.

'What a fun!' he cried. 'No one is hurt, and only the door broken, and the ladies frightened. But, my friends, we have done what has never been done before.'

'And as far as I can help,' said Harvey Deacon, 'it will certainly never be done again.'

And that was what befell on 14th April last at No. 17 Badderly Gardens. I began by saying that it would seem too grotesque to dogmatise as to what it was which actually did occur; but I give my impressions, *our* impressions (since they are corroborated by Harvey Deacon and John Moir), for what they are worth. You may, if it pleases you, imagine that we were the victims of an elaborate and extraordinary hoax. Or you may think with us that we underwent a very real and a very terrible experience. Or perhaps you may know more than we do of such occult matters, and can inform us of some similar occurrence. In this latter case a letter to William Markham, 146M, The Albany, would help to throw a light upon that which is very dark to us.

9

An obsession with the mysticism of ancient Egypt was a notable attribute of several of the master magicians – among whom were S. L. MacGregor Mathers and Aleister Crowley. At the close of the last century a wealth of 'secret' literature on the rites and ceremonies of the Egyptian priest-kings and their princesses was available, and these were being revived by conclaves of adepts from London to Paris and Vienna to Beirut. Doubtless one of the attractions of this form of magic was its great scope for exhibitionism in dress and ceremony, its exotic and erotic rites and its widespread use of drugs. The Goddess Isis was the most revered deity, while a thousand lesser gods and goddesses held sway over perfumed altars, writhing snakes and the long dead language of the Nile.

Today the man most clearly remembered for his knowledge of Egyptology and his skill as a practitioner of its rites was Sax Rohmer – creator, also, of the immortal Dr Fu Manchu stories. Born Arthur Saarsfield Ward (1886-1959), Sax Rohmer began the study of magic and orientalism as a young man and by the time he started to join several of the esoteric societies in Britain (including the Golden Dawn) he had a commanding knowledge of Eastern mysticism. He felt an almost uncanny attraction to his subject and indeed confessed on one occasion to a friend: 'I cannot doubt that I spent at least one incarnation on the Nile.' He won popular acclaim in 1915 with the publication of his novel, *The Yellow Claw*, which introduced the sinister and sardonic Dr Fu Manchu and his evil practices to the world. Other books were to continue this success, but he also demonstrated great agility of mind by producing a masterful study of the black arts entitled *The Romance of Sorcery* and a tremendous novel of Egyptology flourishing in modern times, *Brood of the Witch Queen*. Rohmer was always most concerned about confiding too much of his own knowledge to the general reader and noted in one book: 'I have omitted many of the elabor-

ate particulars which I know of and have experienced, in
order, firstly, not to weary you and, secondly, because it forms
no part of my intention to tempt the curious to dabble in a
dangerous pursuit.' Through his continuing association with
'practical sorcerers' (as he called other magicians) on both
sides of the Atlantic, he became increasingly convinced that
'a great new Adept' was going to arise from their ranks and
'pour the light of the East into the Darkness of the West'.
Rohmer's own passion for Egypt never waned throughout his
life, which he demonstrates to great effect in the story that
follows. That Sax Rohmer should follow Sir Arthur Conan
Doyle in this collection is doubly appropriate, for they have
both given fiction characters of continuing appeal, and to the
world of the Occult works of valuable research and personal
authority.

* * *

A MAGICAL SYMBOL OF PROTECTION

Breath of Allah

SAX ROHMER

I

For close upon a week I had been haunting the purlieus of the Mûski, attired as a respectable dragoman, my face and hands reduced to a deeper shade of brown by means of a water-colour paint (I had to use something that could be washed off and grease-paint is useless for purposes of actual disguise) and a neat black moustache, fixed to my lip with spirit-gum. In his story 'Beyond the Pale', Rudyard Kipling has trounced the man who enquires too deeply into native life; but if everybody thought with Kipling we should never have had a Lane or a Burton and I should have continued in unbroken scepticism regarding the reality of magic. Whereas, because of the matters which I am about to set forth, for ten minutes of my life I found myself a trembling slave of the unknown.

Let me explain at once that my undignified masquerade was not prompted by mere curiosity or the quest of the pomegranate, it was undertaken as the natural sequel to a letter received from Messrs Moses, Murphy and Co., the firm which I represented in Egypt, containing curious matters affording much food for reflection. 'We would ask you,' ran the communication, 'to renew your enquiries into the particular composition of the perfume "Breath of Allah", of which you obtained us a sample at a cost which we regarded as excessive. It appears to consist in the blending of certain obscure essential oils and gum-resins; and the nature of some of these has defied analysis to date. Over a hundred experiments have been made to discover substitutes for the missing essences, but without success; and as we are now in a position to arrange for the manufacture of Oriental perfume on an extensive scale, we should be prepared to make it *well worth your while* (the last four words characteristically underlined in red ink) if you could obtain for us a correct copy of the original prescription.'

The letter went on to say that it was proposed to establish a separate company for the exploitation of the new perfume, with a registered address in Cairo and a 'manufactory' in some suitably inaccessible spot in the Near East.

I pondered deeply over these matters. The scheme was a good one and could not fail to reap considerable profits; for, given extensive advertising, there is always a large and monied public for a new smell. The particular blend of liquid fragrance to which the letter referred was assured of a good sale at a high price, not alone in Egypt, but throughout the capitals of the world, provided it could be put upon the market; but the proposition of manufacture was beset with extraordinary difficulties.

The tiny vial which I had despatched to Birmingham nearly twelve months before had cost me close upon £100 to procure, for the reason that 'Breath of Allah' was the secret property of an old and aristocratic Egyptian family whose great wealth and exclusiveness rendered them unapproachable. By dint of diligent enquiry I had discovered the *attár* to whom was entrusted certain final processes in the preparation of the perfume – only to learn that he was ignorant of its exact composition. But although he had assured me (and I did not doubt his word) that not one grain had hitherto passed out of the possession of the family, I had succeeded in procuring a small quantity of the precious fluid.

Messrs Moses, Murphy and Co. had made all the necessary arrangements for placing it upon the market, only to learn, as this eventful letter advised me, that the most skilled chemists whose services were obtainable had failed to analyse it.

One morning, then, in my assumed character, I was proceeding along the Shâria el-Hamzâwi seeking for some scheme whereby I might win the confidence of Mohammed er-Rahmân the *attár*, or perfumer. I had quitted the house in the Darb el-Ahmar which was my base of operations but a few minutes earlier, and as I approached the corner of the street a voice called from a window directly above my head:

'Saïd! Saïd!'

Without supposing that the call referred to myself, I glanced up, and met the gaze of an old Egyptian of respectable appearance who was regarding me from above. Shading his eyes with a gnarled hand – 'Surely,' he cried, 'it is none other than Saïd the nephew of Yûssuf Khalig! *Es-selâm 'aleykûm, Saïd!*'

'*Aleykûm, es-selâm,*' I replied, and stood there looking up at him.

'Would you perform a little service for me, Said?' he continued. 'It will occupy you but an hour and you may earn five piastres.'

'Willingly,' I replied, not knowing to what the mistake of this evidently half-blind old man might lead me.

I entered the door and mounted the stairs to the room in which he was, to find that he lay upon a scantily covered *dīwan* by the open window.

'Praise be to Allah (whose name be exalted)!' he exclaimed, 'that I am thus fortunately enabled to fulfil my obligations. I sometimes suffer from an old serpent bite, my son, and this morning it has obliged me to abstain from all movement. I am called Abdûl the Porter, of whom you will have heard your uncle speak : and although I have long retired from active labour, myself, I contract for the supply of porters and carriers of all descriptions and for all purposes; conveying fair ladies to the *hammám*, youth to the bridal, and death to the grave. Now, it was written that you should arrive at this timely hour.'

I considered it highly probable that it was also written how I should shortly depart if this garrulous old man continued to inflict upon me details of his absurd career. However –

'I have a contract with the merchant, Mohammed er-Rahmân of the Sûk el-Attârin,' he continued, 'which it has always been my custom personally to carry out.'

The words almost caused me to catch my breath; and my opinion of Abdul the Porter changed extraordinarily. Truly my lucky star had guided my footsteps that morning!

'Do not misunderstand me,' he added. 'I refer not to the transport of his wares to Suez, to Zagazig, to Mecca, to Aleppo, to Baghdad, Damascus, Kandahar, and Pekin; although the whole of these vast enterprises is entrusted to none other than the only son of my father : I speak, now, of the bearing of a small though heavy box from the great magazine and manufactory of Mohammed er-Rahmân at Shubra, to his shop in the Sûk el-Attârin, a matter which I have arranged for him on the eve of the Molid en-Nebi (birthday of the Prophet) for the past five-and-thirty years. Every one of my porters to whom I might entrust this special charge is otherwise employed; hence my observation that it was written how none other than yourself should pass beneath this window at a certain fortunate hour.'

Fortunate indeed had that hour been for me, and my pulse beat far from normally as I put the question :

'Why, O Father Abdul, do you attach so much importance to this seemingly trivial matter?'

The face of Abdul the Porter, which resembled that of an intelligent mule, assumed an expression of low cunning.

'The question is well conceived,' he said, raising a long forefinger and wagging it at me. 'And who in all Cairo knows so much of the secrets of the great as Abdul the Know-all, Abdul the Taciturn! Ask me of the fabled wealth of Karafa Bey and I will name you every one of his possessions and entertain you with a calculation of his income, which I have worked out in *nûss-faddah*! Ask me of the amber mole upon the shoulder of the Princess Azîza and I will describe it to you in such a manner as to ravish your soul! Whisper, my son' – he bent towards me confidentially – 'once a year the merchant Mohammed er-Rahmân prepares for the Lady Zuleyka a quantity of the perfume which impious tradition has called "Breath of Allah". The father of Mohammed er-Rahmân prepared it for the mother of the Lady Zuleyka and his father before him for the lady of that day who held the secret – the secret which has belonged to the women of this family since the reign of the Khalîf el-Hakîm from whose favourite wife they are descended. To her, the wife of the Khalîf, the first *dirhem* [drachm] ever distilled of the perfume was presented in a gold vase, together with the manner of its preparation, by the great wizard and physician Ibn Sina of Bokhara [Avicenna].'

'You are well called Abdul the Know-all!' I cried in admiration. 'Then the secret is held by Mohammed er-Rahmân?'

'Not so, my son,' replied Abdul. 'Certain of the essences employed are brought, in sealed vessels, from the house of the Lady Zuleyka, as is also the brass coffer containing the writing of Ibn Sina; and throughout the measuring of the quantities, the secret writing never leaves her hand.'

'What, the Lady Zuleyka attends in person?'

Abdul the Porter inclined his head serenely.

'On the eve of the birthday of the Prophet, the Lady Zuleyka visits the shop of Mohammed er-Rahmân, accompanied by an *imâm* from one of the great mosques.'

'Why by an *imâm*, Father Abdul?'

'There is a magical ritual which must be observed in the distillation of the perfume, and each essence is blessed in the name of one of the four archangels; and the whole operation must commence at the hour of midnight on the eve of the Molid en-Nebi.'

He peered at me triumphantly.

'Surely,' I protested, 'an experienced *attár* such as Mohammed er-Rahmân would readily recognise these secret ingredients by their smell?'

'A great pan of burning charcoal,' whispered Abdul dramatically, 'is placed upon the floor of the room, and throughout the operation the attendant *imám* casts pungent spices upon it, whereby the nature of the secret essences is rendered unrecognisable. It is time you depart, my son, to the shop of Mohammed, and I will give you a writing making you known to him. Your task will be to carry the materials necessary for the secret operation (which takes place tonight) from the magazine of Mohammed er-Rahmân at Shubra, to his shop in the Sûk el-Attârin. My eyesight is far from good, Saïd. Do you write as I direct and I will place my name to the letter.'

II

The words 'well worth your while' had kept time to my steps, or I doubt if I should have survived the odius journey from Shubra. Never can I forget the shape, colour, and especially the weight, of the locked chest which was my burden. Old Mohammed er-Rahmân had accepted my service on the strength of the letter signed by Abdul, and of course, had failed to recognise in 'Saïd' that Hon Neville Kernaby who had had certain confidential dealings with him a year before. But exactly how I was to profit by the fortunate accident which had led Abdul to mistake me for someone called 'Saïd' became more and more obscure as the box grew more and more heavy. So that by the time that I actually arrived with my burden at the entrance to the Street of the Perfumers, my heart had hardened towards Abdul the Know-all; and, setting my box upon the ground, I seated myself upon it to rest and to imprecate at leisure that silent cause of my present exhaustion.

After a time my troubled spirit grew calmer, as I sat there inhaling the insidious breath of Tonquin musk, the fragrance of attár of roses, the sweetness of Indian spikenard and the stinging pungency of myrrh, opoponax, and ihlang-ylang. Faintly I could detect the perfume which I have always counted the most exquisite of all save one – that delightful preparation of Jasmine peculiarly Egyptian. But the mystic breath of frankincense and erotic fumes of ambergris alike left me unmoved; for amid these mingled odours, through which it has always seemed to me that that of cedar runs thematically, I sought in vain for any hint of 'Breath of Allah'.

Fashionable Europe and America were well represented as usual in the Sûk el-Attârin, but the little shop of Mohammed er-Rahmân was quite deserted, although he dealt in the most rare essences of all. Mohammed, however, did not seek Western patronage, nor was there in the heart of the little white-bearded merchant any envy of his seemingly more prosperous neighbours in whose shops New York, London, and Paris smoked amber-scented cigarettes, and whose wares were carried to the uttermost corners of the earth. There is nothing more illusory than the outward seeming of the Eastern merchant. The wealthiest man with whom I was acquainted in the Mûski, had the aspect of a mendicant; and whilst Mohammed's neighbours sold phials of essence and tiny boxes of pastilles to the patrons of Messrs Cook, were not the silent caravans following the ancient desert routes laden with great crates of sweet merchandise from the manufactory at Shubra? To the city of Mecca alone Mohammed sent annually perfumes to the value of two thousand pounds sterling; he manufactured three kinds of incense exclusively for the royal house of Persia; and his wares were known from Alexandria to Kashmîr, and prized alike in Stambûl and Tartary. Well might he watch with tolerant smile the more showy activities of his less fortunate competitors.

The shop of Mohammed er-Rahmân was at the end of the street remote from the Hamzâwi (Cloth Bazaar), and as I stood up to resume my labours my mood of gloomy abstraction was changed as much by a certain atmosphere of expectancy – I cannot otherwise describe it – as by the familiar smells of the place. I had taken no more than three paces onward into the Sûk ere it seemed to me that all business had suddenly become suspended; only the Western element of the throng remained outside whatever influence had claimed the Orientals. Then presently the visitors, also becoming aware of this expectant hush as I had become aware of it, turned almost with one accord, and following the direction of the merchants' glances, gazed up the narrow street towards the Mosque of el-Ashraf.

And here I must chronicle a curious circumstance. Of the Imám Abû Tabâh I had seen nothing for several weeks, but at this moment I suddenly found myself thinking of that remarkable man. Whilst any mention of his name, or nickname – for I could not believe 'Tabâh' to be patronymic – amongst the natives led only to pious ejaculations indicative of respectful fear, by the official world he was tacitly disowned. Yet I had indisputable evidence to show that few doors in Cairo, or indeed in all Egypt, were closed to him; he came and went like a phantom. I should never have been surprised, on entering my private apartments at Shepheard's, to have found him seated therein, nor did I question the veracity of a native acquaintance who assured me that he had met the mysterious *imám* in Aleppo on the same morning that a letter from his partner in Cairo had arrived mentioning a visit by Abû Tabâh to el-Azhar. But throughout the native city he was known as the Magician and was very generally regarded as a master of the *ginn*. Once more depositing my burden upon the ground, then, I gazed with the rest in the direction of the mosque.

It was curious, that moment of perfumed silence, and my imagination, doubtless inspired by the memory of Abû Tabâh, was carried back to the days of the great *khalifs*, which never seemed far removed from one in those mediaeval streets. I was transported to the Cairo of Harûn al Raschîd, and I thought that the Grand Wazîr on some mission from Baghdad was visiting the Sûk el-Attârin.

Then, stately through the silent group, came a black-robed, white-turbaned figure outwardly similar to many others in the bazaar, but followed by two tall muffled Negroes. So still was the place that I could hear the tap of his ebony stick as he strode along the centre of the street.

At the shop of Mohammed er-Rahmân he paused, exchanging a few words with the merchant, then resumed his way, coming down the Sûk towards me. His glance met mine, as I stood there beside the box; and, to my amazement, he saluted me with smiling dignity and passed on. Had he, too, mistaken me for Saïd? – or had his all-seeing gaze detected beneath my disguise the features of Neville Kernaby?

As he turned out of the narrow street into the Hamzâwi, the commercial uproar was resumed instantly, so that save for this horrible doubt which had set my heart beating with uncomfortable rapidity, by all the evidences now about me his coming might have been a dream.

III

Filled with misgivings, I carried the box along to the shop; but Mohammed er-Rahmân's greeting held no hint of suspicion.

'By fleetness of foot thou shalt never win Paradise,' he said.

'Nor by unseemly haste shall I thrust others from the path,' I retorted.

'It is idle to bandy words with any acquaintance of Abdul the Porter's,' sighed Mohammed; 'well do I know it. Take up the box and follow me.'

With a key which he carried attached to a chain about his waist, he unlocked the ancient door which alone divided his shop from the outjutting wall marking a bend in the street. A native shop is usually nothing more than a double cell; but descending three stone steps, I found myself in one of those cellar-like apartments which are not uncommon in this part of Cairo. Windows there were none, if I except a small square opening, high up in one of the walls, which evidently communicated with the narrow courtyard separating Mohammed's establishment from that of his neighbour, but which admitted scanty light and less ventilation. Through this opening I could see what looked like the uplifted shafts of a cart. From one of the rough beams of the rather lofty ceiling a brass lamp hung by chains, and a quantity of primitive chemical paraphernalia littered the place; old-fashioned alembics, mysterious-looking jars, and a sort of portable furnace, together with several tripods and a number of large, flat brass pans gave the place the appearance of some old alchemist's den. A rather handsome ebony table, intricately carved and inlaid with mother-o'-pearl and ivory, stood before a cushioned *dîwan* which occupied that side of the room in which was the square window.

'Set the box upon the floor,' directed Mohammed, 'but not with such undue dispatch as to cause thyself to sustain any injury.'

That he had been eagerly awaiting the arrival of the box and was now burningly anxious to witness my departure, grew more and more apparent with every word. Therefore –

'There are asses who are fleet of foot,' I said, leisurely depositing my load at his feet; 'but the wise man regulateth his pace in accordance with three things : the heat of the sun; the welfare of others; and the nature of his burden.'

'That thou hast frequently paused on the way from Shubra to reflect upon these three things,' replied Mohammed, 'I cannot doubt; depart, therefore, and ponder them at leisure, for I perceive that thou art a great philosopher.'

'Philosophy,' I continued, seating myself upon the box, 'sustaineth the mind, but the activity of the mind being dependent upon the welfare of the stomach, even the philosopher cannot afford to labour without hire.'

At that, Mohammed er-Rahmân unloosed upon me a long pent-up torrent of invective – and furnished me with the information which I was seeking.

'O son of a wall-eyed mule!' he cried, shaking his fists over me, 'no longer will I suffer thy idiotic chatter! Return to Abdul the Porter, who employed thee, for not one *faddah* will I give thee, calamitous mongrel that thou art! Depart! For I was but this moment informed that a lady of high station is about to visit me. Depart! Lest she mistake my shop for a pigsty!'

But even as he spoke the words, I became aware of a vague disturbance in the street, and –

'Ah!' cried Mohammed, running to the foot of the steps and gazing upwards, 'now am I utterly undone! Shame of thy parents that thou art, it is now unavoidable that the Lady Zuleyka shall find thee in my shop. Listen, offensive insect – thou art Saïd my assistant. Utter not one word; or with this' – to my great alarm he produced a dangerous-looking pistol from beneath his robe – 'will I blow a hole through thy vacuous skull!'

Hastily concealing the pistol, he went hurrying up the steps, in time to perform a low salutation before a veiled woman who was accompanied by a Sûdanese servant-girl and a Negro. Exchanging some words with her which I was unable to detect, Mohammed er-Rahmân led the way down into the apartment wherein I stood, followed by the lady, who in turn was followed by her servant. The Negro remained above. Perceiving me as she entered, the lady, who was attired with extraordinary elegance, paused, glancing at Mohammed.

'My lady,' he began immediately, bowing before her, 'it is Saïd,

my assistant, the slothfulness of whose habits is only exceeded by
the impudence of his conversation.'

She hesitated, bestowing upon me a glance of her beautiful eyes.
Despite the gloom of the place and the *yashmak* which she wore,
it was manifest that she was good to look upon. A faint but exquisite
perfume stole to my nostrils, whereby I knew that Mohammed's
charming visitor was none other than the Lady Zuleyka.

'Yet,' she said softly, 'he hath the look of an active young man.'

'His activity,' replied the scent merchant, 'resideth entirely in his
tongue.'

The Lady Zuleyka seated herself upon the *diwan*, looking all
about the apartment.

'Everything is in readiness, Mohammed?' she asked.

'Everything, my lady.'

Again the beautiful eyes were turned in my direction, and, as
their inscrutable gaze rested upon me, a scheme – which, since it
was never carried out, need not be described – presented itself to
my mind. Following a brief but eloquent silence – for my answering
glances were laden with significance :

'O Mohammed,' said the Lady Zuleyka indolently, 'in what
manner doth a merchant, such as thyself, chastise his servants when
their conduct displeaseth him?'

Mohammed er-Rahmân seemed somewhat at a loss for a reply, and
stood there staring foolishly.

'I have whips for mine,' murmured the soft voice. 'It is an old
custom of my family.'

Slowly she cast her eyes in my direction once more.

'It seemed to me, O Saïd,' she continued, gracefully resting one
jewelled hand upon the ebony table, 'that thou hadst presumed to
cast love-glances upon me. There is one waiting above whose duty
it is to protect me from such insults. Miska !' – to the servant girl –
'summon El-Kimri [The Dove].'

Whilst I stood there dumbfounded and abashed the girl called
up the steps :

'El-Kimri ! Come hither !'

Instantly there burst into the room the form of that hideous
Negro whom I had glimpsed above; and –

'O Kimri,' directed the Lady Zuleyka, and languidly extended
her hand in my direction, 'throw this presumptuous clown into the
street !'

My discomfiture had proceeded far enough, and I recognised that, at whatever risk of discovery, I must act instantly. Therefore, at the moment that El-Kimri reached the foot of the steps, I dashed my left fist into his grinning face, putting all my weight behind the blow, which I followed up with a short right, utterly outraging the pugilistic proprieties, since it was well below the belt. El-Kimri bit the dust to the accompaniment of a human discord composed of three notes – and I leapt up the steps, turned to the left, and ran off around the Mosque of el-Ashraf, where I speedily lost myself in the crowded Ghurîya.

Beneath their factitious duskiness my cheeks were burning hotly : I was ashamed of my execrable artistry. For a druggist's assistant does not lightly make love to a duchess!

IV

I spent the remainder of the forenoon at my house in the Darb el-Ahmar heaping curses upon my own fatuity and upon the venerable head of Abdul the Know-all. At one moment it seemed to me that I had wantonly destroyed a golden opportunity, at the next that the seeming opportunity had been a mere mirage. With the passing of noon and the approach of evening I sought desperately for a plan, knowing that if I failed to conceive one by midnight, another chance of seeing the famous prescription would probably not present itself for twelve months.

At about four o'clock in the afternoon came the dawn of a hazy idea, and since it necessitated a visit to my rooms at Shepheard's, I washed the paint off my face and hands, changed, hurried to the hotel, ate a hasty meal, and returned to the Darb el-Ahmar, where I resumed my disguise.

There are some who have criticised me harshly in regard to my commercial activities at this time, and none of my affairs has provoked greater acerbitude than that of the perfume called 'Breath of Allah'. Yet I am at a loss to perceive wherein my perfidy lay; for my outlook is sufficiently socialistic to cause me to regard with displeasure the conserving by an individual of something which, without loss to himself, might reasonably be shared by the community. For this reason I have always resented the way in which the Moslem veils the faces of the pearls of his *harêm*. And whilst the success of my present enterprise would not render the Lady Zuleyka the poorer, it would enrich and beautify the world by delighting the senses of men with a perfume more exquisite than any hitherto known.

Such were my reflections as I made my way through the dark and deserted bazaar quarter, following the Shâria el-Akkadi to the Mosque of el-Ashraf. There I turned to the left in the direction of the Hamzâwi, until, coming to the narrow alley opening from it into the Sûk el-Attârin, I plunged into its darkness, which was like that of a tunnel, although the upper parts of the houses above were silvered by the moon.

I was making for that cramped little courtyard adjoining the shop of Mohammed er-Rahmân in which I had observed the presence of one of those narrow high-wheeled carts peculiar to the district, and as the entrance thereto from the Sûk was closed by a rough wooden fence I anticipated little difficulty in gaining access. Yet there was one difficulty which I had not foreseen, and which I had not met with had I arrived, as I might easily have arranged to do, a little earlier. Coming to the corner of the Street of the Perfumers, I cautiously protruded my head in order to survey the prospect.

Abû Tabâh was standing immediately outside the shop of Mohammed er-Rahmân!

My heart gave a great leap as I drew back into the shadow, for I counted his presence of evil omen to the success of my enterprise. Then, a swift revelation, the truth burst in upon my mind. He was there in the capacity of *imám* and attendant magician at the mystical 'Blessing of the perfumes'! With cautious tread I retraced my steps, circled round the Mosque and made for the narrow street which runs parallel with that of the Perfumers and into which I knew the courtyard beside Mohammed's shop must open. What I did not know was how I was going to enter it from that end.

I experienced unexpected difficulty in locating the place, for the height of the buildings about me rendered it impossible to pick up any familiar landmark. Finally, having twice retraced my steps, I determined that a door of old but strong workmanship set in a high, thick wall must communicate with the courtyard; for I could see no other opening to the right or left through which it would have been possible for a vehicle to pass.

Mechanically I tried the door, but, as I had anticipated, found it to be securely locked. A profound silence reigned all about me and there was no window in sight from which my operations could be observed. Therefore, having planned out my route, I determined to scale the wall. My first foothold was offered by the heavy wooden lock which projected fully six inches from the door. Above it was a crossbeam and then a gap of several inches between the top of the gate and the arch into which it was built. Above the arch projected an iron rod from which depended a hook; and if I could reach the bar it would be possible to get astride the wall.

I reached the bar successfully, and although it proved to be none too firmly fastened, I took the chance and without making very much noise found myself perched aloft and looking down into the little court. A sigh of relief escaped me; for the narrow cart with its disproportionate wheels stood there as I had seen it in the morning, its shafts pointing gauntly upward to where the moon of the prophet's nativity swam in a cloudless sky. A dim light shone out from the square window of Mohammed er-Rahmân's cellar.

Having studied the situation very carefully, I presently perceived to my great satisfaction that whilst the tail of the cart was wedged under a crossbar, which retained it in its position, one of the shafts was in reach of my hand. Thereupon I entrusted my weight to the shaft, swinging out over the well of the courtyard. So successful was I that only a faint creaking sound resulted; and I descended into the vehicle almost silently.

Having assured myself that my presence was undiscovered by Abû Tabâh, I stood up cautiously, my hands resting upon the wall, and peered through the little window into the room. Its appearance had changed somewhat. The lamp was lighted and shed a weird and subdued illumination upon a rough table placed almost beneath it. Upon this table were scales, measures, curiously shaped flasks, and odd-looking chemical apparatus which might have been made in the days of Avicenna himself. At one end of the table stood an alembic over a little pan in which burnt a spirituous flame. Mohammed er-Rahmân was placing cushions upon the *dîwan* immediately beneath me, but there was no one else in the room. Glancing upward, I noted that the height of the neighbouring building prevented the moonlight from penetrating into the courtyard, so that my presence could not be detected by means of any light from without; and, since the whole of the upper part of the room was shadowed, I saw little cause for apprehension within.

At this moment came the sound of a car approaching along the Sharia esh-Sharawani. I heard it stop, near the Mosque of el-Ashraf, and in the almost perfect stillness of those tortuous streets from which by day arises a very babel of tongues I heard approaching footsteps. I crouched down in the cart, as the footsteps came nearer, passed the end of the courtyard abutting on the Street of the Perfumers, and paused before the shop of Mohammed er-Rahmân. The musical voice of Abû Tabâh spoke and that of the Lady Zuleka answered. Came a loud rapping, and the creak of an opening door : then –

'Descend the steps, place the coffer on the table, and then remain immediately outside the door,' continued the imperious voice of the lady. 'Make sure that there are no eavesdroppers.'

Faintly through the little window there reached my ears a sound as of some heavy object being placed upon a wooden surface, then a muffled disturbance as of several persons entering the room; finally, the muffled bang of a door closed and barred . . . and soft footsteps in the adjoining street!

Crouching down in the cart and almost holding my breath, I watched through a hole in the side of the ramshackle vehicle that fence to which I have already referred as closing the end of the courtyard which adjoined the Sûk el-Attârin. A spear of moonlight, penetrating through some gap in the surrounding buildings, silvered its extreme edge. To an accompaniment of much kicking and heavy breathing, into this natural limelight arose the black countenance of 'The Dove'. To my unbounded joy I perceived that his nose was lavishly decorated with sticking-plaster and that his right eye was temporarily off duty. Eight fat fingers clutching at the top of the woodwork, the bloated Negro regarded the apparently empty yard for a space of some three seconds, ere lowering his ungainly bulk to the level of the street again. Followed a faint 'pop' and a gurgling quite unmistakable. I heard him walking back to the door, as I cautiously stood up and again surveyed the interior of the room.

V

Egypt, as the earliest historical records show, has always been a land of magic, and according to native belief it is today the theatre of many supernatural dramas. For my own part, prior to the episode which I am about to relate, my personal experiences of the kind had been limited and unconvincing. That Abû Tabâh possessed a sort of uncanny power akin to second sight, I knew, but I regarded it merely as a form of telepathy. His presence at the preparation of the secret perfume did not surprise me, for a belief in the efficacy of magical operations prevailed, as I was aware, even among the more cultured Moslems. My scepticism, however, was about to be rudely shaken.

As I raised my head above the ledge of the window and looked into the room, I perceived the Lady Zuleyka seated on the cushioned *dîwan*, her hands resting upon an open roll of parchment which lay upon the table beside a massive brass chest of antique native workmanship. The lid of the chest was raised, and the interior seemed to be empty, but near it upon the table I observed a number of gold-stoppered vessels of Venetian glass and each of which was of a different colour.

Beside a brazier wherein glowed a charcoal fire, Abû Tabâh stood; and into the fire he cast alternately strips of paper bearing writing of some sort and little dark brown pastilles which he took from a sandalwood box set upon a sort of tripod beside him. They were composed of some kind of aromatic gum in which benzoin seemed to predominate, and the fumes from the brazier filled the room with a blue mist.

The *imám*, in his soft, musical voice, was reciting that chapter of the Korân called 'The Angel'. The weird ceremony had begun. In order to achieve my purpose I perceived that I should have to draw myself right up to the narrow embrasure and rest my weight entirely upon the ledge of the window. There was little danger in the manoeuvre, provided I made no noise; for the hanging lamp, by reason of its form, cast no light into the upper part of the room. As I achieved the desired position I became painfully aware of the pungency of the perfume with which the apartment was filled.

Lying there upon the ledge in a most painful attitude, I wriggled forward inch by inch further into the room, until I was in a position to use my right arm more or less freely. The preliminary prayer concluded, the measuring of the perfumes had now actually commenced, and I readily perceived that without recourse to the parchment, from which the Lady Zuleyka never once removed her hands, it would indeed be impossible to discover the secret. For, consulting the ancient prescription, she would select one of the gold-stoppered bottles, unscrew it, direct that so many grains should be taken from it, and never removing her gaze from Mohammed er-Rahmân whilst he measured out the correct quantity, would restopper the vessel and so proceed. As each was placed in a wide-mouthed glass jar by the perfumer, Abû Tabâh, extending his hands over the jar, pronounced the names :

'Gabraîl, Mikaîl, Israfîl, Israîl.'

Cautiously I raised to my eyes the small but powerful opera-glasses to procure which I had gone to my rooms at Shepheard's. Focusing them upon the ancient scroll lying on the table beneath me, I discovered, to my joy, that I could read the lettering quite well. Whilst Abû Tabâh began to recite some kind of incantation in the course of which the names of the Companions of the Prophet frequently occurred, I commenced to read the writing of Avicenna.

'In the name of God, the Compassionate, the Merciful, the High, the Great. . . .'

So far had I proceeded and no further when I became aware of a curious change in the form of the Arabic letters. They seemed to be moving, to be cunningly changing places one with another as if to trick me out of grasping their meaning!

The illusion persisting, I determined that it was due to the unnatural strain imposed upon my vision, and although I recognised that time was precious I found myself compelled temporarily to desist, since nothing was to be gained by watching these letters which danced from side to side of the parchment, sometimes in groups and sometimes singly, so that I found myself pursuing one slim Arab A ('*Alif*) entirely up the page from the bottom to the top where it finally disappeared under the thumb of the Lady Zuleyka!

Lowering the glasses I stared down in stupefaction at Abû Tabâh. He had just cast fresh incense upon the flames, and it came home to me, with a childish and unreasoning sense of terror, that the Egyptians who called this man the Magician were wiser than I. For whilst I could no longer hear his voice, I now could *see* the words issuing from his mouth! They formed slowly and gracefully in the blue clouds of vapour some four feet above his head, revealed their meaning to me in letters of gold, and then faded away towards the ceiling!

Old-established beliefs began to totter about me as I became aware of a number of small murmuring voices within the room. They were the voices of the perfumes burning in the brazier. Said one, in a guttural tone:

'I am Myrrh. My voice is the voice of the Tomb.'

And another softly: 'I am Ambergris. I lure the hearts of men.'

And a third huskily: 'I am Patchouli. My promises are lies.'

My sense of smell seemed to have deserted me and to have been replaced by a sense of hearing. And now this room of magic began to expand before my eyes. The walls receded and receded, until the apartment grew larger than the interior of the Citadel Mosque; the roof shot up so high that I knew there was no cathedral in the world half so lofty. Abû Tabâh, his hands extended above the brazier, shrank to minute dimensions, and the Lady Zuleyka, seated beneath me, became almost invisible.

The project which had led me to thrust myself into the midst of this feast of sorcery vanished from my mind. I desired but one thing: to depart, ere reason utterly deserted me. But, to my horror, I discovered that my muscles had become rigid bands of iron! The figure of Abû Tabâh was drawing nearer; his slowly moving arms had grown serpentine and his eyes had changed to pools of flame which seemed to summon me. At the time when this new phenomenon added itself to the other horrors, I seemed to be impelled by an irresistible force to jerk my head downwards: I heard my neck muscles snap metallically: I *saw* a scream of agony spurt forth from my lips . . . and I saw upon a little ledge immediately below the square window a little *mibkharah*, or incense burner, which hitherto I had not observed. A thick, oily brown stream of vapour was issuing from its perforated lid and bathing my face clammily. Sense of smell I had none; but a chuckling, demoniacal voice spoke from the *mibkharah*, saying –

'I am *Hashish*! I drive men mad! Whilst thou hast lain up there like a very fool, I have sent my vapours to thy brain and stolen thy senses from thee. It was for this purpose that I was set here beneath the window where thou couldst not fail to enjoy the full benefit of my poisonous perfume. . . .'

Slipping off the ledge, I fell . . . and darkness closed about me.

VI

My awakening constitutes one of the most painful recollections of a not uneventful career; for, with aching head and tortured limbs, I sat upright upon the floor of a tiny, stuffy, and unclean cell! The only light was that which entered by way of a little grating in the door. I was a prisoner; and, in the same instant that I realised the fact of my incarceration, I realised also that I had been duped. The weird happenings in the apartment of Mohammed er-Rahmân had been hallucinations due to my having inhaled the fumes of some preparation of *hashish*, or Indian hemp. The characteristic sickly odour of the drug had been concealed by the pungency of the other and more odoriferous perfumes; and because of the position of the censer containing the burning *hashish*, no one else in the room had been affected by its vapour. Could it have been that Abû Tabâh had known of my presence from the first?

I rose, unsteadily, and looked out through the grating into a narrow passage. A native constable stood at one end of it, and beyond him I obtained a glimpse of the entrance hall. Instantly I recognised that I was under arrest at the Bâb el-Khalk police station!

A great rage consumed me. Raising my fists I banged furiously upon the door, and the Egyptian policeman came running along the passage.

'What does this mean, *shawêsh*?' I demanded. 'Why am I detained here? I am an Englishman. Send the superintendent to me instantly.'

The policeman's face expressed alternately anger, surprise, and stupefaction.

'You were brought here last night, most disgustingly and speechlessly drunk, in a cart!' he replied.

'I demand to see the superintendent.'

'Certainly, certainly, *effendim*!' cried the man, now thoroughly alarmed. 'In an instant, *effendim*!'

Such is the magical power of the word 'Inglisi' (Englishman).

A painfully perturbed and apologetic native official appeared almost immediately, to whom I explained that I had been to a fancy dress ball at the Gezira Palace Hotel, and, injudiciously walking homeward at a late hour, had been attacked and struck senseless. He was anxiously courteous, sending a man to Shepheard's with my written instructions to bring back a change of apparel and offering me every facility for removing my disguise and making myself presentable. The fact that he palpably disbelieved my story did not render his concern one whit the less.

I discovered the hour to be close upon noon, and, once more my outward self, I was about to depart from the Place Bâb el-Khalk, when, into the superintendent's room came Abû Tabâh! His handsome ascetic face exhibited grave concern as he saluted me.

'How can I express my sorrow, Kernaby Pasha,' he said in his soft faultless English, 'that so unfortunate and unseemly an accident should have befallen you? I learned of your presence here but a few moments ago, and I hastened to convey to you an assurance of my deepest regret and sympathy.'

'More than good of you,' I replied. 'I am much indebted.'

'It grieves me,' he continued suavely, 'to learn that there are footpads infesting the Cairo streets, and that an English gentleman may not walk home from a ball safely. I trust that you will provide the police with a detailed account of any valuables which you may have lost. I have here' – thrusting his hand into his robes – 'the only item of your property thus far recovered. No doubt you are somewhat short-sighted, Kernaby Pasha, as I am, and experience a certain difficulty in discerning the names of your partners upon your dance programme.'

And with one of those sweet smiles which could so transfigure his face, Abû Tabâh handed me my opera-glasses!

10

If it is fair to say that Sir Arthur Conan Doyle gave spiritualism its great *magnum opus* with his *History of Spiritualism*, the equivalent honour in the wider fields of the Occult must surely fall to Lewis Spence for his superb *Encyclopaedia of Occultism*, published in 1920. A work of exhaustive research, for which the author had drawn on some of the most important scholars and adepts in the Western hemisphere, the book gave the layman for the first time a simple key to the world of the mystic arts of which he heard so much and probably understood so little. Spence, while perhaps not a Magus in the same sense as the other contributors to the present volume, was certainly the foremost 'scientific experimenter' in the Occult, applying the forces of technology and reason to the realms of mysticism. Of this he later wrote : 'A generation ago it was the fashion to sneer at the Occult. But today men of science in the foremost ranks of thought have placed them on the dissecting slab as fit subjects for careful examination. The result of their analysis, if it has not permitted us to pierce the veil which divides men and the supernatural, has at all events served to purge our sight sufficiently to enable us to see things on this side of it with a clearer vision and to regard such researches with a more tolerant eye than hitherto.' His work involved him deeply in the re-creation of ancient rituals and evocation and brought him into close contact with numerous secret cults – of which he was to report somewhat caustically : 'Although in every sympathy with the spirit of the esoteric societies, I venture to express my disbelief in the occult knowledge of the generality of their members.'

Lewis Spence (1874-1955) was born in Scotland and devoted his life to two callings, anthropology and journalism. Apart from ritual magic, he also made particular studies of the mythology and customs of ancient Mexico, South America, the Middle East and Celtic Britain, and wrote a number of definitive works on these subjects. His particular interest in the Occult was 'sympathetic magic', on which he was for many years the leading authority. He was also one of the earliest and most determined opponents of the Nazis as they rose to power in Germany in the 'thirties; in the Nazi credo and life-style – particularly of Adolph Hitler – he saw strong links with the old *cultus* of Satanism and the rule of evil on earth. Spence presented his theories in a startling book, *The Occult Causes of the Present War* (1940), which warned of a decline in the values of humanity to the barbaric days of paganism unless 'the Devil Hitler and his satanic adversaries are not brought to heel'. He was convinced that Hitler and those close to him had a more than passing knowledge of Satanism and indeed that some of the top men in the Reich actually conducted rituals connected with the black arts in secret temples. In hindsight we know that his concern about the 'evils' of Nazism was fully justified. Nevertheless, apart from the fact that Hitler was a highly superstitious man and employed a full-time astrologer to advise him on the future, there is no evidence that he actually dabbled in Satanic rites in the occult sense of the word. In the story which follows – one of the very few pieces of fiction written by Spence and now of considerable rarity – he makes use of his theory of German involvement with the Arch-Fiend in a most ingenious manner.

In his last year Spence wrote what must surely be regarded as an epitaph on his lifelong involvement with the Occult when he noted : 'The vast amount of evidential material I have perused leads me to the conclusion that as yet we have merely touched the fringes of the extra-terrestrial and that we must rely on psychology rather than so-called material proof to bring us further enlightenment.' Surely no one could deny that this statement is still apposite today.

* * *

THE ANCIENT MAGICAL SYMBOL
OF THE SWASTIKA

Lucifer over London

LEWIS SPENCE

Some voices possess a kind of monotonous chant which almost compels one to listen to them. The only two men in the dull and decorous bar-room except the barman and myself were conversing in a semi-confidential manner. One, a squat, little man, spoke incisively with a cockney accent; the other, the very picture of a manservant off duty, was all ears and eyes.

'Shock to the system!' the little man hissed. 'I bin seventeen years on this job now, Frank, and I tell you it's the worst case I ever seen. Something's scared the old fella mortal bad. Raves, he does, all day long, 'cept when he's under O.P.M. Always the same cry: "Asmodeus, Asmodeus!" whoever or whatever that means. Then a lot of whisperin' and chatterin' and groanin' something awful. "Set me free," he yells, "I never signed the bond. Save my soul, save me from the darkness." Enough to give you the fantods, believe me.'

'The old boy's 'aunted,' said the other fellow drearily. 'I know the symptoms. What's the doctor say?'

'Him? Very little. Close sort o' card,' replied the little man. 'Fed up with the case, he is. Well, Frank, I'm not goin' to stay on there any longer. My nerve's fair to good, as you know, but it's not equal to that constant ravin' and mutterin'. Ought to be in a looney-bin, he should. So if that job with the legless officer gent you were speakin' of is still vacant. . . . The 'ouse is being watched, too. What it all means, *I* can't think. . . .'

'You take my tip, Harry, and git out o' that outfit before yer nerve gives way,' counselled the other. 'They're foreigners, you say. Well, you leave it flat. If I were you, I'd ring up 999 this very night, report the case, and quit. Narsty work, if you asks me. Any talk of Nazis, or that sort o' thing?'

'Funny you should ask that, Frank. When it isn't Asmodeus, it's Hitler. Raves about 'em as if they were one and the same, he does. But Hitler can't do much harm to anybody now, one would think.'

'Well, you got my advice,' snapped the other sententiously, finishing his drink and sliding from his stool. 'I'm off. Shouldn't ha' stayed so long. If you quit, Harry, ring me, and I'll fix you up if I can.'

I reflected for a moment. I watched Harry smoking his cigarette until the butt end grew so small that it was impossible to smoke it any more, then I offered him a drink and a cigarette. I told him I was a medical student – which was true – and said that I had overheard his talk. Thus we were able to discuss as fellow 'professionals' the details of his patient's case, in which I pretended to be greatly interested. It was the word 'Asmodeus', however, that had roused my attention. Asmodeus, as I told him, when he asked me, is one of the names of Satan, the Devil, Mephistopheles, Lucifer, the King of Hell, the Prince of Darkness who carries power over the fires of Heaven. Now I had not long left lunching with my uncle, Sir Robin Butler, whose expert knowledge of occult matters was known to students all over the world, but whose habit of expecting all his guests to be equally interested made him a notorious bore. All through luncheon and most of the afternoon I had sat under a lecture on the connection between the deliberate worship of Satan as the god-captain of all evil and the forces which moved the German Nazi leaders. He seemed to believe that devil-worship was still being practised. He had used the word 'Asmodeus' several times – and, damn it all, after yawning over Satan half the day, here was Satan again, under his most rarely used cognomen, being spoken about in a respectable public-house. Devilish odd, you might say, devilish odd.

Well by the time we had had a few more drinks, Harry and I were pals. The more I heard of his patient's ravings about the power and the glory of Lucifer the more I wished my uncle had come along with me. I could have left the two together. What then possessed me to tell Harry that if he did not want the job any longer I would take his place as male nurse to this foreigner? It was because he had mentioned at last who his patient was. The name of Dr Ludwig Lehmann meant nothing to Harry, but to a medical student like myself, whose ambition was to be a great doctor, the name of Lehmann meant everything. Before the war, this Austrian doctor had been a world figure in medicine. To think that he was a refugee, in London, ill, perhaps friendless! I determined to offer my services, especially when Harry, now decidedly tipsy, said he was not going back anyway.

The next morning I called at the address 'Harry' had given me, said I had heard that a male nurse was wanted, and discovered that while the patient was *the* Dr Lehmann, he was by no means friendless. His stepdaughter was keeping house for him and nursing him. She seemed only too glad of my offer, however, and I agreed to look after Dr Lehmann for a week at least. Over lunch she gave me details of the case – persecution in Austria – anxiety – escape – overwork in Switzerland during the war – nervous breakdown. I told her that I was surprised that I had seen no mention of his name anywhere. After all, he was a famous doctor. Since the war ended, she answered, he had dropped everything. What, then, had caused the breakdown? After some hesitation, she said that he had plunged with strange enthusiasm into the study of the Occult. She feared that it had turned his brain. . . .

For some days after I took over, Dr Lehmann was placid. He was a thin, gaunt person of about seventy, Teutonic, bearded, and sallow. The yellow, bloodshot eyes opened occasionally, but otherwise he showed few signs of life. I gave him a thorough examination and found the heart weak and flabby, while it was obvious that the entire nervous system had been subjected not only to long-continued strain, but to a violent shock, or series of shocks, quite recently. And there were signs of diabetic disease.

My time was regularly arranged. I had a break of three hours in the afternoon. But it was part of my duty to sleep in the patient's room. I had my meals alone and scarcely saw the stepdaughter except when she came to take my place after lunch. The almost complete isolation of the house and its consequent silence made my vigil dreary enough.

Nothing happened until the third night, when Dr Lehmann suddenly raised himself in bed. He seemed to be listening. His action roused me, and I was on the alert in a moment. For three or four minutes he remained in this posture. But he suddenly flopped backward, and in a few minutes his regular breathing showed that he was asleep. On the following night, however, he woke about the same time, a little after 2 a.m., and once more raised himself in bed. This time he seemed to be listening more intently than ever. Then he began to talk rapidly in German. So quick and confused was his utterance that at first I was able to distinguish words only here and there. He was praying, in a tone of earnestness, solemn and entreating, with clasped hands and upturned face. Then the utterance grew clearer and even more fervid. He was beseeching someone for mercy, to free him from a vow he had made – I heard the name 'Asmodeus', not once but many times. I did not interrupt, hoping to learn more, but in a little while the voice died away in a moan and, exhausted, he lay back and sank into a coma.

About half an hour later he rose again, this time in such a state of wild excitement that I leapt out of bed and stood by him. This time he seemed to be in angry, even furious, argument with someone. To some policy he had the strongest objection. He solemnly gave warning that 'the Powers' were not in agreement with it, that they would not tolerate it. It would mean ruin, 'final and irrevocable', for all, for 'the cause' as well as for humanity.

The following night passed without disturbance, but on the next, Lehmann suddenly awoke in a shocking state of distraction, calling wildly on 'Asmodeus'. Throwing aside the bedclothes, he flung himself on his knees, and when I went over to him and tried to soothe him, he thrust me aside with what seemed extraordinary vigour for a man of his age. Then, furiously, he turned upon me, brandishing his fists in my face and cursing. He would, he cried angrily, have nothing to do with what was going on at Kempton Park. My god was not his god. His Asmodeus was the true world-spirit, mine merely a German parody, distorted to comply with Germanic aims and ambitions. He, an Austrian, had been a fool to have associated with Germans who construed every cause in terms of Germanic purpose and design. The chapel at Marionville was a travesty, a blasphemy. He washed his hands of the whole affair. He appealed to his god to destroy this profane counterfeit of his holy worship. And so he raved on, until he collapsed in exhaustion. I gave him an injection, after which he dozed.

I seemed to have stumbled into a grotesque situation. If Lehmann was not lunatic, what the devil was going on in that respectable London suburb known as Kempton Park? After some serious thought, I decided to consult my tedious but knowledgeable uncle. But first it would be amusing to do a little sleuthing. I knew the London district – Kempton Park. I had the name, Marionville, which was probably the name of a house. What about spending the afternoon looking for it? If there were such a house, I should have something firm to go on. It would mean that Lehmann was not merely having a nightmare. Then one would know how to act. Perhaps these Germans were people the police ought to be told about? They would have been 'vetted' before being allowed to settle here – but then the 'vetting' net probably had some holes in it. Lehmann, an anti-Nazi, would surely not have associated with Nazi sympathisers?

The next afternoon I was on my way to Kempton Park, having told the stepdaughter that I might be late getting back. I parked my car in a Hampton Court garage. I mentioned Marionville to the attendant, and he said it seemed familiar to him. He rather thought he had been asked to take his taxi to a house of that name. But it was some time ago. If the name was Marionville, then it was an old house somewhere behind East Molesey.

By the time I had reached East Molesey and had turned into the complex of roads beyond it, it was almost dark. Up and down the quiet, conventional highways I wandered, but my search was unrewarded. At last it occurred to me that it was probably a much older and larger house than any of the dwellings I had passed, so I pushed farther north towards Kempton Park. Traversing a long, silent road which did not seem to contain more than three houses in its entire length, I came to it at last – the kind of house that people built near London about a century ago – square, solid, and flat-roofed, with a semicircular abutment in the centre, and standing in about an acre and a half of garden.

If any place near London could be isolated, it was surely this. I couldn't see a single light in the whole solid façade of the place, which stood back from the road some forty feet or more. Only a new wooden fence separated it from the pathway : I opened the gate, and walked boldly in.

I had made up my mind what to do should I encounter anyone. I would be the hectoring, busy doctor who had been called on an emergency case. Bluff would do the rest. I walked up the path and round to the side of the house. The mass of a large timber building jutted out from its rear. I pushed the door. It opened, and I peeped in. Then I knew my quest had not been in vain. This was 'the chapel at Marionville'.

The interior looked at first like a hall of carved stone, but I soon perceived that it had been panelled with cunningly painted canvas which gave it the appearance of masonry grotesquely carved with the shapes of gods, fiends, and satyrs. The general effect was horrible. At the end of the 'chapel', if one may call it so, was a large tapestry on which a gigantic figure of Lucifer was displayed. Beneath it was an altar which seemed to be littered with the apparatus of infernal worship – black candles, ornaments, incense-burners, and books.

Curtains of sable and scarlet hung on either side of the tapestry, and these were decorated with pentacles, stars, and other goetic symbols.

As I stared at the details of this strange shrine, I heard someone coming along the gravel path. In one corner the canvas which masked the timber of the chapel did not meet completely, and into the gap I quickly dived and found that the painted screen was set on a frame at least a couple of feet from the walls, giving me ample space to hide.

The chapel lights were switched on. Through the chinks in the canvas I could now see quite clearly. Along the aisle a tall, elderly man walked to the altar, genuflected before the image of Lucifer, and raising the black-and-scarlet hangings which flanked the altar, disappeared behind them.

One by one other people entered. Between thirty and forty men and women had at last seated themselves. A bell sounded sharply, and the man who had passed behind the curtains now reappeared, dressed in elaborate robes. A dark-skinned youth with him swung a censer from which steamed thick clouds of incense. The congregation stood.

The priest – or whatever he was – did not look at the worshippers beneath him. He seemed concentrated on his own movements. But I stared hard enough at the 'congregation'. Were all these people Germans? Most of them seemed to be.

The muttered prayers ceased and I began to be nauseated by the fetid incense, which in Satanist shrines is usually compounded of rue, henbane, deadly nightshade, and rotting leaves. The 'host' was carried to the altar. The wafer it contained was torn from its receptacle by the celebrant, who then stamped upon it to the accompaniment of profane cries by the congregation. A chalice of liquor was passed round. As it circulated, I heard distant thunder. The lights were lowered. A vivid flash of lightning illumined the dreadful shrine. In sonorous German the celebrant began to speak.

'Friends and brothers,' he said, 'through the grace and power of our lord Lucifer-Asmodeus, our great cause is about to triumph and the folk of the German Reich to be avenged upon their enemies. We shall destroy our foes by supernatural means. What is an atomic bomb compared to the powers of Lucifer? He bears in his hand the fires of heaven. He can be controlled only by our arch-enemy, the God Jehovah.

'But this condition of inferiority now lies behind us,' he continued. 'The chief obstacle is removed. Our lord Lucifer, the king of light, will now have a new link with mankind. He shall make us the media of his terrible potency. As you know, he cannot wield that frightful power of which he is the source and reservoir without the perfect co-operation of mankind, who are gifted with freewill and who have the right to employ it "for good or evil", as the cant Christian phrase has it. This impediment, I say, has been removed at last. It is now possible to effect a perfect union between our god and us, so that at last we can function as the direct agents of his overwhelming might.

'That great scientist, Dr Lehmann, who now lies stricken, has discovered an essence that heightens the powers of human mental concentration a hundredfold. This temporary extension of human mental potentiality will enable Lucifer to operate through his servants. Once he could do so only through humanity in the mass, an imperfect medium. Now he can act through spiritual concurrence with some few chosen persons. You are that few! You shall be the weapon through which Lucifer shall attack England, Russia, and America, and so avenge imperial Germany, Lucifer's own particular province, and render her once again the greatest power on earth. Through our divine master, the spirit of heavenly fire, of which he is the only begetter, will descend upon this city of London and destroy it. By mental concentration we shall focus our lord's destructive flame upon any place we choose. Nothing will be able to withstand its power. Even stone will melt before the force of the magnified lightning-bolts of our master, Lucifer, and granite crumble under its consuming ray. The first blow will be struck now. As a symbolic gesture, we shall demolish one of the chief national palladia of Britain. By the hour of noon tomorrow, the Nelson Monument in Trafalgar Square will have crumbled into a heap of smouldering lime.'

With a sonorous benediction he concluded and dismissed the congregation. When the place seemed empty, I sneaked out and got safely to the road.

I could hardly believe I had not dreamt it all. It seemed preposterous. But why should this infernal priest make so extraordinary an announcement? Perhaps he and his fellow-conspirators intended to blow up conspicuous London buildings. Their crazy followers would believe it was the work of Lucifer.

Could I go to Scotland Yard with this story? As I drove towards London, I decided I would not go back to my patient that night. I would stay at an hotel and – I felt like a fool – take a careful look at the Nelson Monument in the morning. If I saw anything suspicious, I would call the police.

By eleven next morning I had walked several times round Trafalgar Square and stared so much at the monument that I felt that even the pigeons were wondering what I was up to. I could see nothing and felt more like a fool than ever. But, of course, I hung round till midday – it was only natural – and as noon approached I took care to get as far from the monument as I could without losing sight of it. I stood a little way down Northumberland Avenue. What soon afterwards occurred in Trafalgar Square has been alluded to by scientists as 'one of the most extraordinary meteorological phenomena on record', and as 'quite inexplicable'. It had been a fairly bright morning towards the close of August, with only a very little cloud. But on the stroke of twelve we beheld a volume of vapour approaching the Square the like of which I have never beheld in a clear sky. It was thick, dark, indeed almost black, globular in shape and of considerable bulk, and it advanced with tremendous velocity. But in the heart of this nebulous globe, which emitted a rolling, rattling din of terrific intensity, louder than that made by a large plane flying low, glowed and flashed a heart of vivid flame which gave forth sparks and coruscations, like an immense catherine-wheel. It seemed that something special in the way of a storm was coming.

Within a few moments the sky over the great Square was filled with this strange fiery cloud. People rushed for shelter. I heard someone exclaim that it was a plane on fire and about to crash. I stood staring in the middle of the road as if hypnotised. For just as the heart of this cloud was over the monument it seemed to halt in its course while a man might draw breath. Then it began to roll backward at a speed considerably greater than that with which it had advanced. As it retreated, it gathered momentum until, within a few seconds, it was nothing but a dimly sparkling globe in the sky miles away to the south-west. People in the crowd were explaining the phenomenon as the strangest freak of the weather they had known – quite frightening, in fact, when I heard the distant sound of an explosion. I thought I knew where the awful thing had thundered, and jumping into my car I rushed towards Kempton

Park and the house called Marionville. Of course, I found what I expected. The house had been struck by lightning – and with a flash and a roar so frightful as to scare everybody in the neighbourhood, Marionville had been almost completely destroyed. As I got there, the fire-brigade were just getting ready to leave. From the crowd I gathered that twelve bodies had been fetched out of the ruins. They had been burnt beyond recognition.

When I got away and went to Dr Lehmann's house I found that he had died peacefully during the night. I said goodbye to his stepdaughter. I said nothing to her and nothing to the police. I don't want people to think I'm a lunatic.

In the years since the Second World War fewer and fewer true adepts in the magical arts have emerged. Indeed, more than one commentator has written that the development of the modern materialist society has virtually put an end to any form of superstitious beliefs – or at least made people hesitant to admit to such primitive instincts. Two men can be excepted from this statement – Algernon Blackwood and Gerald Gardner. The one gave macabre literature its great popular upsurge out of the disinterest of the early years of the century, while the other, virtually single-handed, revived and reshaped the oldest form of occult art, the practice of *Wica* (an Anglo-Saxon word meaning Wise One) today perhaps the most widely reported and discussed secret cult. First, let us examine the master of the *outré* story who was deeply versed in mysticism.

Algernon Blackwood (1869-1951) grew up wandering the hills and valleys of Highland Scotland and as there is probably no more 'spirit-haunted place on earth' than the Northern lands of Britain came early into contact with the supernatural. A naturally restless man, he spent his youth in travel around the world and has written of strange experiences with poltergeists in New York, encounters with the souls of dead men in Canada, and the art of evocation in England. His stories and novels reflect his interest in the Occult and indeed tell us more of his involvement with secret orders than does their author. We know of his membership of the Golden Dawn and an unnamed order devoted to Buddhism, but he has closed the door on all else of an occult nature. One can only speculate that he did witness strange rites and take part in mystical ceremonies, for the knowledge displayed in his work suggests that he could not have gained this insight in any way other than at first hand. He was particularly interested in the idea of very ancient mystical societies, that had survived the centuries of persecution and intolerance, still being active today – which stories like 'Ancient Sorceries' clearly indicate. Perhaps his finest literary creation was John Silence, the psychic investigator, who enquired into the secrets of the unknown and battled with those evil magicians who would turn their art against mankind. Biographers have seen a strange likeness between this character and Blackwood himself, and certainly several of the 'adventures' contain incidents from the author's own life. E. F. Bleiler, the American critic, for one, has writen : 'Algernon Blackwood believed deeply in a personal blend of occultism and Buddhism and built his stories around mystical experiences and a sentimental *Naturphilosophie*.' For those who have only read Blackwood's ghost tales and horror stories, an excursion into the world of John Silence (and the tale 'A Physical Invasion' is perhaps the best) is a delight indeed.

The story I have selected from Blackwood's work is of particular interest in the context of this anthology in that, strange and weird as it is, it is based on a true occurrence. The author was indeed asked to help in an occult experiment to combat the spirit of a black magician which was still terrorising his former residence. In a sentence, one could say that the story you are about to read is true – only the names have been changed.

* * *

With Intent to Steal

Algernon Blackwood

To sleep in a lonely barn when the best bedrooms in the house were at our disposal, seemed, to say the least, unnecessary, and I felt that some explanation was due to our host.

But Shorthouse, I soon discovered, had seen to all that; our enterprise would be tolerated, not welcomed, for the master kept this sort of thing down with a firm hand. And then, how little I could get this man, Shorthouse, to tell me. There was much I wanted to ask and hear, but he surrounded himself with impossible barriers. It was ludicrous; he was surely asking a good deal of me, and yet he would give so little in return, and his reason – that it was for my good – may have been perfectly true, but did not bring me any comfort in its train. He gave me sops now and then, however, to keep up my curiosity, till I soon was aware that there were growing up side by side within me a genuine interest and an equally genuine fear; and something of both these is probably necessary to all real excitement.

The barn in question was some distance from the house, on the side of the stables, and I had passed it on several of my journeyings to and fro wondering at its forlorn and untarred appearance under a regime where everything was so spick and span; but it had never once occurred to me as possible that I should come to spend a night under its roof with a comparative stranger, and undergo there an experience belonging to an order of things I had always rather ridiculed and despised.

At the moment I can only partially recall the process by which Shorthouse persuaded me to lend him my company. Like myself, he was a guest in this autumn house-party, and where there were so many to chatter and to chaff, I think his taciturnity of manner had appealed to me by contrast, and that I wished to repay something of what I owed. There was, no doubt, flattery in it as well, for he was more than twice my age, a man of amazingly wide experience, an explorer of all the world's corners where danger lurked, and – most subtle flattery of all – by far the best shot in the whole party, our host included.

At first, however, I held out a bit.

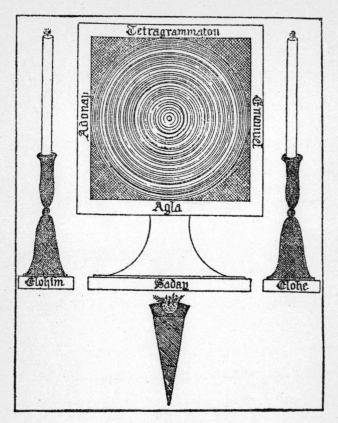

THE IMPLEMENTS OF MAGIC

'But surely this story you tell,' I said, 'has the parentage common to all such tales – a superstitious heart and an imaginative brain – and has grown now by frequent repetition into an authentic ghost story? Besides, this head gardener of half a century ago,' I added, seeing that he still went on cleaning his gun in silence, 'who was he, and what positive information have you about him beyond the fact that he was found hanging from the rafters, dead?'

'He was no mere head gardener, this man who passed as such,' he replied without looking up, 'but a fellow of splendid education who used this curious disguise for his own purposes. Part of this

very barn, of which he always kept the key, was found to have been
fitted up as a complete laboratory, with athanor, alembic, cucurbite,
and other appliances, some of which the master destroyed at once
– perhaps for the best – and which I have only been able to guess
at – '

'Black arts,' I laughed.

'Who knows?' he rejoined quietly. 'The man undoubtedly possessed knowledge – dark knowledge – that was most unusual and
dangerous, and I can discover no means by which he came to it –
no ordinary means, that is. But I *have* found many facts in the case
which point to the exercise of a most desperate and unscrupulous
will; and the strange disappearances in the neighbourhood, as well
as the bones found buried in the kitchen garden, though never
actually traced to him, seem to me full of dreadful suggestion.'

I laughed again, a little uncomfortably perhaps, and said it
reminded one of the story of Gilles de Rais, *maréchal* of France, who
was said to have killed and tortured to death in a few years no
less than one hundred and sixty women and children for the purposes of necromancy, and who was executed for his crimes at
Nantes. But Shorthouse would not 'rise', and only returned to his
subject.

'His suicide seems to have been only just in time to escape
arrest,' he said.

'A magician of no high order then,' I observed sceptically, 'if
suicide was his only way of evading the country police.'

'The police of London and St Petersburg rather,' returned
Shorthouse; 'for the headquarters of this pretty company was somewhere in Russia, and his apparatus all bore the marks of the most
skilful foreign make. A Russian woman then employed in the house-
hold – governess, or something – vanished, too, about the same time
and was never caught. She was no doubt the cleverest of the lot.
And, remember, the object of this appalling group was not mere
vulgar gain, but a kind of knowledge that called for the highest
qualities of courage and intellect in the seekers.'

I admit I was impressed by the man's conviction of voice and
manner, for there is something very compelling in the force of an
earnest man's belief, though I still affected to sneer politely.

'But, like most black magicians, the fellow only succeeded in
compassing his own destruction – that of his tools, rather, and of
escaping himself.'

'So that he might better accomplish his objects *elsewhere and otherwise*,' said Shorthouse, giving, as he spoke, the most minute attention to the cleaning of the lock.

'Elsewhere and otherwise,' I gasped.

'As if the shell he left hanging from the rafter in the barn in no way impeded the man's spirit from continuing his dreadful work under new conditions,' he added quietly, without noticing my interruption. 'The idea being that he sometimes revisits the garden and the barn, chiefly the barn – '

'The barn !' I exclaimed; 'for what purpose?'

'Chiefly the barn,' he finished, as if he had not heard me, 'that is, when there is anybody in it.'

I stared at him without speaking, for there was a wonder in me how he would add to this.

'When he wants fresh material, that is – he comes to steal from the living.'

'Fresh material !' I repeated aghast. 'To steal from the living !' Even then, in broad daylight, I was foolishly conscious of a creeping sensation at the roots of my hair, as if a cold breeze were passing over my skull.

'The strong vitality of the living is what this sort of creature is supposed to need most,' he went on imperturbably, 'and where he has worked and thought and struggled before is the easiest place for him to get it in. The former conditions are in some way more easily reconstructed – ' He stopped suddenly, and devoted all his attention to the gun. 'It's difficult to explain, you know, rather,' he added presently, 'and, besides, it's much better that you should not know till afterwards.'

I made a noise that was the beginning of a score of questions and of as many sentences, but it got no further than a mere noise, and Shorthouse, of course, stepped in again.

'Your scepticism,' he added, 'is one of the qualities that induce me to ask you to spend the night there with me.

'In those days,' he went on, in response to my urging for more information, 'the family were much abroad, and often travelled for years at a time. This man was invaluable in their absence. His wonderful knowledge of horticulture kept the gardens – French, Italian, English – in perfect order. He had *carte blanche* in the matter of expense, and of course selected all his own underlings. It was the sudden, unexpected return of the master that surprised the amazing stories of the countryside before the fellow, with all his cleverness, had time to prepare or conceal.'

'But is there no evidence, no more recent evidence, to show that something is likely to happen if we sit up there?' I asked, pressing him yet further, and I think to his liking, for it showed at least that I was interested. 'Has anything happened there lately, for instance?'

Shorthouse glanced up from the gun he was cleaning so asiduously, and the smoke from his pipe curled up into an odd twist between me and the black beard and oriental, sun-tanned face. The magnetism of his look and expression brought more sense of conviction to me than I had felt hitherto, and I realised that there had been a sudden little change in my attitude and that I was now much more inclined to go in for the adventure with him. At least, I thought, with such a man, one would be safe in any emergency; for he is determined, resourceful, and to be depended upon.

'There's the point,' he answered slowly; 'for there has apparently been a fresh outburst – an attack almost, it seems – quite recently. There is evidence, of course, plenty of it, or I should not feel the interest I do feel, but – ' he hesitated a moment, as though considering how much he ought to let me know, 'but the fact is that three men this summer, on separate occasions, who have gone into that barn after nightfall, have been *accosted* – '

'Accosted?' I repeated, betrayed into the interruption by his choice of so singular a word.

'And one of the stablemen – a recent arrival and quite ignorant of the story – who had to go in there late one night, saw a dark substance hanging down from one of the rafters, and when he climbed up, shaking all over, to cut it down – for he said he felt sure it was a corpse – the knife passed through nothing but air, and he heard a sound up under the eaves as if someone were laughing. Yet, while he slashed away, and afterwards too, the thing went on swinging there before his eyes and turning slowly with its own weight, like a huge joint on a spit. The man declares, too, that it had a large bearded face, and that the mouth was open and drawn down like the mouth of a hanged man.'

'Can we question this fellow?'

'He's gone – gave notice at once, but not before I had questioned him myself very closely.'

'Then this was quite recent?' I said, for I knew Shorthouse had not been in the house more than a week.

'Four days ago,' he replied. 'But, more than that, only three days ago a couple of men were in there together in full daylight when one of them suddenly turned deadly faint. He said that he felt an overmastering impulse to hang himself : and he looked about for a rope and was furious when his companion tried to prevent him – '

'But he did prevent him?'

'Just in time, but not before he had clambered on to a beam. He was very violent.'

I had so much to say and ask that I could get nothing out in time, and Shorthouse went on again.

'I've had a sort of watching brief for this case,' he said with a smile, whose real significance, however, completely escaped me at the time, 'and one of the most disagreeable features about it is the deliberate way the servants have invented excuses to go out to the place, and always after dark; some of them who have no right to go there, and no real occasion at all – have never been there in their lives before probably – and now all of a sudden have shown the keenest desire and determination to go out there about dusk, or soon after, and with the most paltry and foolish excuses in the world. Of course,' he added, 'they have been prevented, but the desire, stronger than their superstitious dread, and which they cannot explain, is very curious.'

'Very,' I admitted, feeling that my hair was beginning to stand up again.

'You see,' he went on presently, 'it all points to volition – in fact to deliberate arrangement. It is no mere family ghost that goes with every ivied house in England of a certain age; it is something real, and something very malignant.'

He raised his face from the gun barrel, and for the first time his eye caught mine in the full. Yes, he was very much in earnest. Also, he knew a great deal more than he meant to tell.

'It's worth tempting – and fighting, *I* think,' he said; 'but I want a companion with me. Are you game?' His enthusiasm undoubtedly caught me, but I still wanted to hedge a bit.

'I'm very sceptical,' I pleaded.

'All the better,' he said, almost as if to himself. 'You have the pluck; I have the knowledge – '

'The knowledge?'

He looked round cautiously as if to make sure that there was no one within earshot.

'I've been in the place myself,' he said in a lowered voice, 'quite lately – in fact only three nights ago – the day the man turned queer.'

I stared.

'But – I was obliged to come out –'

Still I stared.

'Quickly,' he added significantly.

'You've gone into the thing pretty thoroughly,' was all I could find to say, for I had almost made up my mind to go with him, and was not sure that I wanted to hear too much beforehand.

He nodded. 'It's a bore, of course, but I must do everything thoroughly – or not at all.'

'That's why you clean your own gun, I suppose?'

'That's why, when there's any danger, I take as few chances as possible,' he said, with the same enigmatical smile I had noticed before; and then he added with emphasis, 'And that is also why I ask you to keep me company now.'

Of course, the shaft went straight home, and I gave my promise without further ado.

Our preparations for the night – a couple of rugs and a flask of black coffee – were not elaborate, and we found no difficulty, about ten o'clock, in absenting ourselves from the billiard-room without attracting curiosity. Shorthouse met me by arrangement under the cedar on the back lawn, and I at once realised with vividness what a difference there is between making plans in the daytime and carrying them out in the dark. One's common sense – at least in matters of this sort – is reduced to a minimum, and imagination with all her attendant sprites usurps the place of judgment. Two and two no longer make four – they make a mystery, and the mystery loses no time in growing into a menace. In this particular case, however, my imagination did not find wings very readily, for I knew that my companion was the most *unmovable* of men – an unemotional, solid block of a man who would never lose his head, and in any conceivable state of affairs would always take the right as well as the strong course. So my faith in the man gave me a false courage that was nevertheless very consoling, and I looked forward to the night's adventure with a genuine appetite.

Side by side, and in silence, we followed the path that skirted the East Woods, as they were called, and then led across two hay fields, and through another wood, to the barn, which thus lay about half a mile from the Lower Farm. To the Lower Farm, indeed, it properly belonged; and this made us realise more clearly how very ingenious must have been the excuses of the Hall servants who felt the desire to visit it.

It had been raining during the late afternoon, and the trees were still dripping heavily on all sides, but the moment we left the second wood and came out into the open, we saw a clearing with the stars overhead, against which the barn outlined itself in a black, lugubrious shadow. Shorthouse led the way – still without a word – and we crawled in through a low door and seated ourselves in a soft heap of hay in the extreme corner.

'Now,' he said, speaking for the first time, 'I'll show you the inside of the barn, so that you may know where you are, and what to do, in case anything happens.'

A match flared in the darkness, and with the help of two more that followed I saw the interior of a lofty and somewhat rickety-looking barn, erected upon a wall of grey stones that ran all round and extended to a height of perhaps four feet. Above this masonry rose the wooden sides, running up into the usual vaulted roof, and supported by a double tier of massive oak rafters, which stretched across from wall to wall and were intersected by occasional uprights. I felt as if we were inside the skeleton of some antediluvian monster whose huge black ribs completely enfolded us. Most of this, of course, only sketched itself to my eye in the uncertain light of the flickering matches, and when I said I had seen enough, and the matches went out, we were at once enveloped in an atmosphere as densely black as anything that I have ever known. And the silence equalled the darkness.

We made ourselves comfortable and talked in low voices. The rugs, which were very large, covered our legs; and our shoulders sank into a really luxurious bed of softness. Yet neither of us apparently felt sleepy. I certainly didn't, and Shorthouse, dropping his customary brevity that fell little short of gruffness, plunged into an easy run of talking that took the form after a time of personal reminiscences. This rapidly became a vivid narration of adventure and travel in far countries, and at any other time I should have allowed myself to become completely absorbed in what he told. But, unfortunately, I was never able for a single instant to forget the real purpose of our enterprise, and consequently I felt all my senses more keenly on the alert than usual, and my attention accord-

ingly more or less distracted. It was, indeed, a revelation to hear
Shorthouse unbosom himself in this fashion, and to a young man
it was of course doubly fascinating; but the little sounds that always
punctuate even the deepest silence out of doors claimed some portion
of my attention, and as the night grew on I soon became aware
that his tales seemed somewhat disconnected and abrupt – and that,
in fact, I heard really only part of them.

It was not so much that I actually heard other sounds, but that I
expected to hear them; this was what stole the other half of my
listening. There was neither wind nor rain to break the stillness,
and certainly there were no physical presences in our neighbourhood, for we were half a mile even from the Lower Farm; and from
the Hall and stables, at least a mile. Yet the stillness was being
continually broken – perhaps *disturbed* is a better word – and it
was to these very remote and tiny disturbances that I felt compelled
to devote at least half my listening faculties.

From time to time, however, I made a remark or asked a
question, to show that I was listening and interested; but, in a sense,
my questions always seemed to bear in one direction and to make
for one issue, namely, my companion's previous experience in the
barn when he had been obliged to come out 'quickly'.

Apparently I could not help myself in the matter, for this was
really the one consuming curiosity I had; and the fact that it was
better for me not to know it made me the keener to know it all,
even the worst.

Shorthouse realised this even better than I did. I could tell it by
the way he dodged, or wholly ignored, my questions, and this subtle
sympathy between us showed plainly enough, had I been able at the
time to reflect upon its meaning, that the nerves of both of us were
in a very sensitive and highly-strung condition. Probably, the complete confidence I felt in his ability to face whatever might happen,
and the extent to which also I relied upon him for my own courage,
prevented the exercise of my ordinary powers of reflection, while
it left my senses free to a more than usual degree of activity.

Things must have gone on in this way for a good hour or more,
when I made the sudden discovery that there was something unusual
in the conditions of our environment. This sounds a roundabout
mode of expression, but I really know not how else to put it. The
discovery almost rushed upon me. By rights, we were two men
waiting in an alleged haunted barn for something to happen; and.

as two men who trusted one another implicitly (though for very different reasons) there should have been two minds keenly alert, with the ordinary senses in active co-operation. Some slight degree of nervousness, too, there might also have been, but beyond this, nothing. It was therefore with something of dismay that I made the sudden discovery that there *was* something more, and something that I ought to have noticed very much sooner than I actually did notice it.

The fact was – Shorthouse's stream of talk was wholly unnatural. He was talking with a purpose. He did not wish to be cornered by my questions, true, but he had another and a deeper purpose still, and it grew upon me, as an unpleasant deduction from my discovery, that this strong, cynical, unemotional man by my side was talking – and had been talking all this time – to gain a particular end. And this end, I soon felt clearly, was to *convince himself*. But, of what?

For myself, as the hours wore on towards midnight, I was not anxious to find the answer; but in the end it became impossible to avoid it, and I knew as I listened, that he was pouring forth this steady stream of vivid reminiscences of travel – South Seas, big game, Russian exploration, women, adventures of all sorts – *because he wished the past to reassert itself to the complete exclusion of the present*. He was taking his precautions. He was afraid.

I felt a hundred things, once this was clear to me, but none of them more than the wish to get up at once and leave the barn. If Shorthouse was afraid already, what in the world was to happen to me in the long hours that lay ahead? . . . I only know that, in my fierce efforts to deny to myself the evidence of his partial collapse, the strength came that enabled me to play my part properly, and I even found myself helping him by means of animated remarks upon his stories, and by more or less judicious questions. I also helped him by dismissing from my mind any desire to enquire into the truth of his former experience; and it was good I did so, for had he turned it loose on me, with those great powers of convincing description that he had at his command, I verily believe that I should never have crawled from that barn alive. So, at least, I felt at the moment. It was the instinct of self-preservation, and it brought sound judgment.

Here, then, at least, with different motives, reached, too, by opposite ways, we were both agreed upon one thing, namely, that temporarily we would forget. Fools we were, for a dominant emotion is not so easily banished, and we were for ever recurring to it in a hundred ways direct and indirect. A real fear cannot be so easily trifled with, and while we toyed on the surface with thousands and thousands of words – mere words – our sub-conscious activities were steadily gaining force, and would before very long have to be properly acknowledged. We could not get away from it. At last, when he had finished the recital of an adventure which brought him near enough to a horrible death, I admitted that in my uneventful life I had never yet been face to face with a real fear. It slipped out inadvertently, and, of course, without intention, but the tendency in him at the time was too strong to be resisted. He saw the loophole, and made for it full tilt.

'It is the same with all the emotions,' he said. 'The experiences of others never give a complete account. Until a man has deliberately turned and faced for himself the fiends that chase him down the years, he has no knowledge of what they really are, or of what they can do. Imaginative authors may write, moralists may preach, and scholars may criticise, but they are dealing all the time in a coinage of which they know not the actual value. Their listener gets a sensation – but not the true one. Until you have faced these emotions,' he went on, with the same race of words that had come from him the whole evening, 'and made them your own, your slaves, you have no idea of the power that is in them – hunger, that shows lights beckoning beyond the grave; thirst, that fills with mingled ice and fire; passion, love, loneliness, revenge, and –' he paused for a minute, and though I knew we were on the brink I was powerless to hold him. '. . . And fear,' he went on – 'fear . . . I think that death from fear, or madness from fear, must sum up in a second of time the total of all the most awful sensations it is possible for a man to know.'

'Then you have yourself felt something of this fear,' I interrupted; 'for you said just now –'

'I do not mean physical fear,' he replied; 'for that is more or less a question of nerves and will, and it is imagination that makes men cowards. I mean an *absolute* fear, a physical fear one might call it, that reaches the soul and withers every power one possesses.'

He said a lot more, for he, too, was wholly unable to stem the torrent once it broke loose; but I have forgotten it; or, rather, mercifully I did not hear it, for I stopped my ears and only heard the occasional words when I took my fingers out to find if he had come to an end. In due course he did come to an end, and there we left it, for I then knew positively what he already knew : that somewhere here in the night, and within the walls of this very barn where we were sitting, there was waiting Something of dreadful malignancy and of great power, Something that we might both have to face ere morning, and Something that he had already tried to face once and failed in the attempt.

The night wore slowly on; and it gradually became more and more clear to me that I could not dare to rely as at first upon my companion, and that our positions were undergoing a slow process of reversal. I thank Heaven this was not borne in upon me too suddenly; and that I had at least the time to readjust myself somewhat to the new conditions. Preparation was possible, even if it was not much, and I sought by every means in my power to gather up all the shreds of my courage, so that they might together make a decent rope that would stand the strain when it came. The strain would come, that was certain, and I was thoroughly well aware – though for my life I cannot put into words the reasons for my knowledge – that the massing of the material against us was proceeding somewhere in the darkness with determination and a horrible skill besides.

Shorthouse meanwhile talked without ceasing. The great quantity of hay opposite – or straw, I believe it actually was – seemed to deaden the sound of his voice, but the silence, too, had become so oppressive that I welcomed his torrrent and even dreaded the moment when it would stop. I heard, too, the gentle ticking of my watch. Each second uttered its voice and dropped away into a gulf, as if starting on a journey whence there was no return. Once a dog barked somewhere in the distance, probably on the Lower Farm; and once an owl hooted close outside and I could hear the swishing of its wings as it passed overhead. Above me, in the darkness, I could just make out the outline of the barn, sinister and black, the rows of rafters stretching across from wall to wall like wicked arms that pressed upon the hay. Shorthouse, deep in some involved yarn of the South Seas that was meant to be full of cheer and sunshine, and yet only succeeded in making a ghastly mixture of unnatural colouring, seemed to care little whether I listened or not. He made no appeal to me, and I made one or two quite irrelevant remarks which passed him by and proved that he was merely uttering sounds. He, too, was afraid of the silence.

I fell to wondering how long a man could talk without stopping. . . . Then it seemed to me that these words of his went falling into the same gulf where the seconds dropped, only they were heavier and fell faster. I began to chase them. Presently one of them fell much faster than the rest, and I pursued it and found myself almost immediately in a land of clouds and shadows. They rose up and enveloped me, pressing on the eyelids. . . . It must have been just here that I actually fell asleep, somewhere between twelve and one o'clock, because, as I chased this word at tremendous speed through space, I knew that I had left the other words far, very far behind me, till, at last, I could no longer hear them at all. The voice of the story-teller was beyond the reach of hearing; and I was falling with ever increasing rapidity through an immense void.

A sound of whispering roused me. Two persons were talking under their breath close beside me. The words in the main escaped me, but I caught every now and then bitten-off phrases and half sentences, to which, however, I could attach no intelligible meaning. The words were quite close – at my very side in fact – and one of the voices sounded so familiar, that curiosity overcame dread, and I turned to look. I was not mistaken; *it was Shorthouse whispering*. But the other person, who must have been just a little beyond him, was lost in the darkness and invisible to me. It seemed then that Shorthouse at once turned up his face and looked at me and, by some means or other that caused me no surprise at the time, I easily made out the features in the darkness. They wore an expression I had never seen there before; he seemed distressed, exhausted, worn out, and as though he were about to give in after a long mental struggle. He looked at me, almost beseechingly, and the whispering of the other person died away.

'They're at me,' he said.

I found it quite impossible to answer; the words stuck in my throat. His voice was thin, plaintive, almost like a child's.

'I shall have to go. I'm not as strong as I thought. They'll call it suicide, but, of course, it's really murder.' There was real anguish in his voice and it terrified me.

A deep silence followed these extraordinary words, and I somehow understood that the Other Person was just going to carry on the conversation – I even fancied I saw lips shaping themselves just over my friend's shoulder – when I felt a sharp blow in the ribs and a voice, this time a deep voice, sounded in my ear. I opened my eyes, and the wretched dream vanished. Yet it left behind it an impression of a strong and quite unusual reality.

'*Do* try not to go to sleep again,' he said sternly. 'You seem exhausted. Do you feel so?' There was a note in his voice I did not welcome – less than alarm, but certainly more than mere solicitude.

'I do feel terribly sleepy all of a sudden,' I admitted, ashamed.

'So you may,' he added very earnestly; 'but I rely on you to keep awake, if only to watch. You have been asleep for half an hour at least – and you were so still – I thought I'd wake you –'

'Why?' I asked, for my curiosity and nervousness were altogether too strong to be resisted. 'Do you think we are in danger?'

'I think *they* are about here now. I feel my vitality going rapidly – that's always the first sign. You'll last longer than I, remember. Watch carefully.'

The conversation dropped. I was afraid to say all I wanted to say. It would have been too unmistakably a confession; and intuitively I realised the danger of admitting the existence of certain emotions until positively forced to. But presently Shorthouse began again. His voice sounded odd, and as if it had lost power. It was more like a woman's or a boy's voice than a man's, and recalled the voice in my dream.

'I suppose you've got a knife?' he asked.

'Yes – a big clasp knife; but why?' He made no answer. 'You don't think a practical joke likely? No one suspects we're here,' I went on. Nothing was more significant of our real feelings this night than the way we toyed with words, and never dared more than to skirt the things in our mind.

'It's just as well to be prepared,' he answered evasively. 'Better be quite sure. See which pocket it's in – so as to be ready.'

I obeyed mechanically, and told him. But even this scrap of talk proved to me that he was getting further from me all the time in his mind. He was following a line that was strange to me, and, as he distanced me, I felt that the sympathy between us grew more and more strained. *He knew more*; it was not that I minded so much – but that he was willing to *communicate less*. And in proportion as I lost his support, I dreaded his increasing silence. Not of words – for he talked more volubly than ever, and with a fiercer purpose – but his silence in giving no hint of what he must have known to be really going on the whole time.

The night was perfectly still. Shorthouse continued steadily talking, and I jogged him now and again with remarks or questions in order to keep awake. He paid no attention, however, to either.

About two in the morning a short shower fell, and the drops rattled sharply on the roof like shot. I was glad when it stopped, for it completely drowned all other sounds and made it impossible to hear anything else that might be going on. Something *was* going on, too, all the time, though for the life of me I could not say what. The outer world had grown quite dim – the house-party, the shooters, the billiard-room, and the ordinary daily incidents of my visit. All my energies were concentrated on the present, and the constant strain of watching, waiting, listening, was excessively telling.

Shorthouse still talked of his adventures, in some Eastern country now, and less connectedly. These adventures, real or imaginary, had quite a savour of the Arabian Nights, and did not by any means make it easier for me to keep my hold on reality. The lightest weight will affect the balance under such circumstances, and in this case the weight of his talk was on the wrong scale. His words were very rapid, and I found it overwhelmingly difficult not to follow them into that great gulf of darkness where they all rushed and vanished. But that, I knew, meant sleep again. Yet, it was strange I should feel sleepy when at the same time all my nerves were fairly tingling. Every time I heard what seemed like a step outside, or a movement in the hay opposite, the blood stood still for a moment in my veins. Doubtless, the unremitting strain told upon me more than I realised, and this was doubly great now that I knew Shorthouse was a source of weakness instead of strength, as I had counted. Certainly, a curious sense of languor grew upon me more and more, and I was sure that the man beside me was engaged in the same struggle. The feverishness of his talk proved this, if nothing else. It was dreadfully hard to keep awake.

But this time, instead of dropping into the gulf, I saw something come up out of it! It reached our world by a door in the side of the barn furthest from me, and it came in cautiously and silently and moved into the mass of hay opposite. There, for a moment, I lost it, but presently I caught it again higher up. It was clinging, like a great bat, to the side of the barn. Something trailed behind it, I could not make out what. . . . It crawled up the wooden wall and began to move out along one of the rafters. A numb terror settled down all over me as I watched it. The thing trailing behind it was apparently a rope.

The whispering began again just then, but the only words I could catch seemed without meaning; it was almost like another language. The voices were above me, under the roof. Suddenly I saw signs of active movement going on just beyond the place where the thing lay upon the rafter. There was something else up there with it! Then followed panting, like the quick breathing that accompanies effort, and the next minute a black mass dropped through the air and dangled at the end of the rope.

Instantly, it all flashed upon me. I sprang to my feet and rushed headlong across the floor of the barn. How I moved so quickly in the darkness I do not know; but, even as I ran, it flashed into my mind that I should never get at my knife in time to cut the thing down, or else that I should find it had been taken from me. Somehow or other – the Goddess of Dreams knows how – I climbed up by the hay bales and swung out along the rafter. I was hanging, of course, by my arms, and the knife was already between my teeth, though I had no recollection of how it got there. It was open. The mass, hanging like a side of bacon, was only a few feet in front of me, and I could plainly see the dark line of rope that fastened it to the beam. I then noticed for the first time that it was swinging and turning in the air, and that as I approached it seemed to move along the beam, so that the same distance was always maintained between us. The only thing I could do – for there was no time to hesitate – was to jump at it through the air and slash at the rope as I dropped.

I seized the knife with my right hand, gave a great swing of my body with my legs and leaped forward at it through the air. Horrors! It was closer to me than I knew, and I plunged full into it, and the arm with the knife missed the rope and cut deeply into some substance that was soft and yielding. But, as I dropped past it, the thing had time to turn half its width so that it swung round and faced me – and I could have sworn as I rushed past it through the air, that it had the features of Shorthouse.

The shock of this brought the vile nightmare to an abrupt end, and I woke up a second time on the soft hay-bed to find that the grey dawn was stealing in, and that I was exceedingly cold. After all I had failed to keep awake, and my sleep, since it was growing light, must have lasted at least an hour. A whole hour off my guard!

There was no sound from Shorthouse, to whom, of course, my first thoughts turned; probably his flow of words had ceased long ago, and he too had yielded to the persuasions of the seductive god. I turned to wake him and get the comfort of companionship for the horror of my dream, when to my utter dismay I saw that the place where he had been was vacant. He was no longer beside me.

It had been no little shock before to discover that the ally in whom lay all my faith and dependence was really frightened, but it is quite impossible to describe the sensations I experienced when I realised he had gone altogether and that I was alone in the barn. For a minute or two my head swam and I felt a prey to a helpless terror. The dream, too, still seemed half real, so vivid had it been! I was thoroughly frightened – hot and cold by turns – and I clutched the hay at my side in handfuls, and for some moments had no idea in the world what I should do.

This time, at least, I was unmistakably awake, and I made a great effort to collect myself and face the meaning of the disappearance of my companion. In this I succeeded so far that I decided upon a thorough search of the barn, inside and outside. It was a dreadful undertaking, and I did not feel at all sure of being able to bring it to a conclusion, but I knew pretty well that unless something was done at once, I should simply collapse.

But, when I tried to move, I found that the cold, and fear, and I know not what else unholy besides, combined to make it almost impossible. I suddenly realised that a tour of inspection, during the whole of which my back would be open to attack, was not to be thought of. My will was not equal to it. Anything might spring upon me any moment from the dark corners, and the growing light was just enough to reveal every movement I made to any who might be watching. For, even then, and while I was still half dazed and stupid, I knew perfectly well that someone was watching me all the time with the utmost intentness. I had not merely awakened; I had *been* awakened.

I decided to try another plan; I called to him. My voice had a thin weak sound, far away and quite unreal, and there was no answer to it. Hark, though! There was something that might have been a very faint voice near me!

I called again, this time with greater distinctness, 'Shorthouse, where are you? Can you hear me?'

There certainly was a sound, but it was not a voice. Something was moving. It was someone shuffling along, and it seemed to be outside the barn. I was afraid to call again, and the sound continued. It was an ordinary sound enough, no doubt, but it came to me just then as something unusual and unpleasant. Ordinary sounds remain ordinary only so long as one is not listening to them; under the influence of intense listening they become unusual, portentous, and therefore extraordinary. So, this common sound came to me as something uncommon, disagreeable. It conveyed, too, an impression of stealth. And with it there was another, a slighter sound.

Just at this minute the wind bore faintly over the field the sound of the stable clock, a mile away. It was three o'clock; the hour when life's pulses beat lowest; when poor souls lying between life and death find it hardest to resist. Vividly I remember this thought crashing through my brain with a sound of thunder, and I realised that the strain on my nerves was nearing the limit, and that something would have to be done at once if I was to reclaim my self-control at all.

When thinking over afterwards the events of this dreadful night, it has always seemed strange to me that my second nightmare, so vivid in its terror and its nearness, should have furnished me with no inkling of what was really going on all this while; and that I should not have been able to put two and two together, or have discovered sooner than I did *what* this sound was and *where* it came from. I can well believe that the vile scheming which lay behind the whole experience found it an easy trifle to direct my hearing amiss; though, of course, it may equally well have been due to the confused condition of my mind at the time and to the general nervous tension under which I was undoubtedly suffering.

But, whatever the cause for my stupidity at first in failing to trace the sound to its proper source, I can only say here that it was with a shock of unexampled horror that my eye suddenly glanced upwards and caught sight of the figure moving in the shadows above my head among the rafters. Up to this moment I had thought that it was somebody outside the barn, crawling round the walls till it came to a door; and the rush of horror that froze my heart when I looked up and saw that it was Shorthouse creeping stealthily along a beam, is something altogether beyond the power of words to describe.

He was staring intently down upon me, and I knew at once that it was he who had been watching me.

This point was, I think, for me the climax of feeling in the whole experience; I was incapable of any further sensation – that is any further sensation in the same direction. But here the abominable character of the affair showed itself most plainly, for it suddenly presented an entirely new aspect to me. The light fell on the picture from a new angle, and galvanised me into a fresh ability to feel when I thought a merciful numbness had supervened. It may not sound a great deal in the printed letter, but it came to me almost as if it had been an extension of consciousness, for the Hand that held the pencil suddenly touched in with ghastly effect of contrast the element of the ludicrous. Nothing could have been worse just then. Shorthouse, the masterful spirit, so intrepid in the affairs of ordinary life, whose power increased rather than lessened in the face of danger – this man, creeping on hands and knees along a rafter in a barn at three o'clock in the morning, watching me all the time as a cat watches a mouse! Yes, it was distinctly ludicrous, and while it gave me a measure with which to gauge the dread emotion that caused his aberration, it stirred somewhere deep in my interior the strings of an empty laughter.

One of those moments then came to me that are said to come sometimes under the stress of great emotion, when in an instant the mind grows dazzlingly clear. An abnormal lucidity took the place of my confusion of thought, and I suddenly understood that the two dreams which I had taken for nightmares must really have been sent me, and that I had been allowed for one moment to look over the edge of what was to come; the Good was helping, even when the Evil was most determined to destroy.

I saw it all clearly now. Shorthouse had over-rated his strength. The terror inspired by his first visit to the barn (when he had failed) had roused the man's whole nature to win, and he had brought me to divert the deadly stream of evil. That he had again underrated the power against him was apparent as soon as he entered the barn, and his wild talk, and refusal to admit what he felt, were due to this desire not to acknowledge the insidious fear that was growing in his heart. But, at length, it had become too strong. He had left my side in my sleep – had been overcome himself, perhaps, first in *his* sleep, by the dreadful impulse. He knew that I should interfere, and with every movement he made, he watched me steadily, for the mania was upon him and he was *determined to hang himself*. He pretended not to hear me calling, and I knew that anything coming between him and his purpose would meet the full force of his fury – the fury of a maniac, of one, for the time being, truly possessed.

For a minute or two I sat there and stared. I saw then for the first time that there was a bit of rope trailing after him, and that this was what made the rustling sound I had noticed. Shorthouse, too, had come to a stop. His body lay along the rafter like a crouching animal. He was looking hard at me. That whitish patch was his face.

I can lay claim to no courage in the matter, for I must confess that in one sense I was frightened almost beyond control. But at the same time the necessity for decided action, if I was to save his life, came to me with an intense relief. No matter what animated him for the moment, Shorthouse was only a *man*; it was flesh and blood I had to contend with and not the intangible powers. Only a few hours before I had seen him cleaning his gun, smoking his pipe, knocking the billiard balls about with very human clumsiness, and the picture flashed across my mind with the most wholesome effect.

Then I dashed across the floor of the barn and leaped upon the hay bales as a preliminary to climbing up the sides to the first rafter. It was far more difficult than in my dream. Twice I slipped back into the hay, and as I scrambled up for the third time I saw that Shorthouse, who thus far had made no sound or movement, was now busily doing something with his hands upon the beam. He was at its further end, and there must have been fully fifteen feet between us. Yet I saw plainly what he was doing; he was fastening the rope to the rafter. *The other end, I saw, was already round his neck!*

This gave me at once the necessary strength, and in a second I had swung myself on to a beam, crying aloud with all the authority I could put into my voice –

'You fool, man! What in the world are you trying to do? Come down at once!'

My energetic actions and words combined had an immediate effect upon him for which I blessed Heaven; for he looked up from his horrid task, stared hard at me for a second or two, and then came wriggling along like a great cat to intercept me. He came by a series of leaps and bounds and at an astonishing pace, and the way he moved somehow inspired me with a fresh horror, for it did not seem the natural movement of a human being at all, but more, as I have said, like that of some lithe wild animal.

He was close upon me. I had no clear idea of what exactly I meant to do. I could see his face plainly now; he was grinning cruelly; the eyes were positively luminous, and the menacing expression of the mouth was most distressing to look upon. Otherwise it was the face of a chalk man, white and dead, with all the semblance of the living human drawn out of it. Between his teeth he held my clasp knife, which he must have taken from me in my sleep, and with a flash I recalled his anxiety to know which pocket it was in.

'Drop that knife!' I shouted at him, 'and drop after it yourself —'

'Don't you dare to stop me!' he hissed, the breath coming between his lips across the knife that he held in his teeth. 'Nothing in the world can stop me now — I have promised — and I must do it. I can't hold out any longer.'

'Then drop the knife and I'll help you,' I shouted back in his face. 'I promise —'

'No use,' he cried, laughing a little, 'I must do it and you can't stop me.'

I heard a sound of laughter, too, somewhere in the air behind me. The next second Shorthouse came at me with a single bound.

To this day I cannot quite tell how it happened. It is still a wild confusion and a fever of horror in my mind, but from somewhere I drew more than my usual allowance of strength, and before he could well have realised what I meant to do, I had his throat between my fingers. He opened his teeth and the knife dropped at once, for I gave him a squeeze he need never forget. Before, my muscles had felt like so much soaked paper; now they recovered their natural strength, and more besides. I managed to work ourselves along the rafter until the hay was beneath us, and then, completely exhausted, I let go my hold and we swung round together and dropped on to the hay, he clawing at me in the air even as we fell.

The struggle that began by my fighting for his life ended in a wild effort to save my own, for Shorthouse was quite beside himself, and had no idea what he was doing. Indeed, he has always averred that he remembers nothing of the entire night's experiences after the time when he first woke me from sleep. A sort of deadly mist settled over him, he declares, and he lost all sense of his own identity. The rest was a blank until he came to his senses under a mass of hay with me on the top of him.

It was the hay that saved us, first by breaking the fall and then by impeding his movements so that I was able to prevent his choking me to death.

12

And so to the final contributor, a man perhaps more widely known among today's public as an occultist than anyone else in these pages, the 'Witch Master' Gerald Gardner. Since 1951, when the last of the Witchcraft Statutes was finally removed from the law books and it became possible to profess oneself a witch without running the risk of prosecution, the number of practitioners has grown by the thousand. By far the greatest majority of these are 'Gardnerite' witches, practising the rites and ceremonies as related by Gerald Gardner. He had taken the original ancient beliefs of the craft of *Wica*, which had been in existence since before Christianity, and revised them so that they would have more relevance to modern times. The result was a cult believing still in the old principles of fertility and 'white' magic for the good of all, restructured into covens spread across the land, each ruled by a high priestess with a priest 'consort' (women usually take the dominant role in witchcraft, representing the ancient Great Mother, procreator of all life). Gardner's disciples have also carried his teachings to Europe and America, where, although there are other similar cults, the 'Gardnerites' hold a position of prominence.

Gerald Brosseau Gardner (1884-1964) spent much of his life in Malaya as a Customs Officer and it was there that he formed an interest in mysticism through close contact with the strange ways of the local people. Shortly after the end of the Second World War he returned to England and, by pursuing his interest in the Occult, met a number of the leading practitioners (including Aleister Crowley whom he greatly admired) and stumbled across the ancient cult of witchcraft. In this cult – and in bringing its true meaning to public attention – he saw his mission. He decided to settle on the Isle of Man in an old mill which had reputedly been the scene in the past of 'witches' sabbaths' and there created a witchcraft museum containing all the ritual tools of the craft plus some slightly more sensational items such as instruments of torture to attract paying visitors. This exhibition gave him time to write and study the ancient rites of *Wica*, and over the ensuing years he gradually rebuilt the movement, personally supervising the formation of covens from one end of Britain to the other. He appointed 'lieutenants' in all these groups (mostly women) and instructed them in the basic rites of initiation and in the summoning of assistance from the 'old Gods' who predate history and in whom the cult believes. Gardner crystallised the main tenets of the cult in his book *Witchcraft Today*, which is still easily available, but reserved his more secret directives for the hand-written books of instruction which are circulated among (and recopied by) the adepts. He also wrote a single novel about the cult, *High Magic's Aid*, which was published privately and is now extremely scarce. In the guise of fiction he revealed many of the innermost secrets of the Order, and it is perhaps not surprising that there have been several attempts by some surviving members to suppress the remaining copies on the general market. It is from this book that I have selected the final extract for the collection and in it we meet Morven, a witch, and her husband, Thur, and join them at the initiation of a new witch, Jan. The details here are much the same as those actually practised by today's witches and give us a vivid insight into the working of *Wica*. After the initiation the husband and wife also perform a minor magical experiment which illustrates another facet of the cult. Gerald Gardner himself died when people's interest in witchcraft was just beginning to revive, and one cannot help feeling that he would have been delighted at how his teachings had been received – just as, indeed, Aleister Crowley might well rejoice at the alarming rise in the practice of 'evil for evil's sake'. Since these two men we have waited in vain for another master magician to arise. . . . .

* * *

The Witch Cult

Gerald Gardner

The initiation to the cult of *Wica* is one clothed in great secrecy and those who know of it do not speak lightly or jestingly of its mysteries. Nor indeed do they advertise their beliefs in any obvious way for the cult has suffered grievously through unwise words and careless actions. Still, the true practitioner would not refuse a request for enlightenment honestly made and such was that presented one day by a young man called Jan to two believers, Morven and her husband, Thur.

Morven and Thur were dedicated believers in *Wica*, schooled in the rituals and practised in their art. Jan had come to them through the secret corridors of the faith and sought admission out of genuine humility and a quest for the true meaning of life.

But when, in due course, the three began to talk of the initiation ceremony which Jan must undergo, he could not stay the doubts which sprang into his mind. He began to question Morven closely.

'What, though, of the devils?' he asked. 'Is it not true that I must worship them before I can join your number?'

'No! They are not devils, Jan, that is but a priestish lie, they are but the old gods of love and laughter and peace and content.'

'Do we ride broomsticks?' next asked Jan.

'No, that is but silly chatter, too; you are brought into the Circle, there is an ordeal to go through, but 'tis slight, then you will swear to be faithful and ever help thy brothers, then you will be told the powers of the working tools, that is all.'

'But, will you not call up your old gods?' asked Jan.

'I will indeed call up the old ones, the mighty ones, to be present and witness your oaths, and to give us their blessing, but of them you will see naught,' she answered.

So, after much argument, it was agreed, and the stars being found favourable, that night they all three went to the upper room, where Morven became Directoress of Ceremonies. After all had bathed in warm water, she said:

'Put not on your garments, for to be witches you must be as witches. Now, I will initiate Jan.'

Morven then proceeded to draw the Circle with her *athame*

(ritual sword), leaving a gap or 'doorway', then circumambulated three times sunwise, with a dancing step, as she did so calling on the mighty ones of the east, south, west and north to attend, then after dancing around several times in silence, she chanted :
'Eko : Eko : Azarak. Eko : Eko : Zomelak.'

Bagabi Lacha bachabe
Lamac cahi achababe
Karrellyos

Lamac lamac Bachalyas
Cabahagy sabalyos
Baryolos

Lagoz atha cabyolas
Samahac atha famolas
Hurrahya.

She then left the Circle by the doorway, and going to Jan said :
'As there is no other brother here I must be thy sponsor as well as priest. I am about to give you a warning, if you are still of the same mind, answer it with these words : "Perfect love and perfect trust".'

Then placing the point of her athame to his heart said :
'O Thou who standest on the threshold, between the pleasant land of men and the domains of the dread lords of the outer spaces, hast Thou the courage to make the assay? For I tell thee verily, it were better to rush on my weapon and perish miserably than make the attempt with fear in thy heart.'

Jan answered : 'I have two passwords : Perfect love and perfect trust.'

Morven dropped the knife's point, saying :
'All who bring such words are doubly welcome,' then going behind him she blindfolded him, then clasping him from behind with her left arm around his waist, and pulling his right arm around her neck and his lips down to hers, said : 'I give you the third password : "A kiss".'

So saying she pushed him forward with her body, through the doorway, into the Circle.

Once inside she released him, whispering, 'This is the way all are first brought into the Circle.'

She then carefully closed the doorway by drawing the point of her athame across it three times, joining all the circles.

Then leading him to the south of the Altar, whispered: 'Now there is the Ordeal.'

Taking a short piece of cord from the Altar she bound it round his right ankle, leaving the ends free, whispering: 'Feet neither bond nor free.'

Then with a longer cord she bound his hands firmly behind his back, then pulling them up into the small of his back, tied the cord round his neck, so his arms made a triangle at his back, leaving an end of cord hanging in a cable tow in front.

With this cable tow in her left hand and the athame in her right, she led him sunways round the Circle to the east, where saluting with the athame she proclaimed:

'Take heed, O Lords of the Watchtowers of the East. Jan, properly prepared, will be made a priest and witch.'

She then led him in turn to the south, west and north, where similar proclamations were made.

Then, clasping him round the body with her left arm, athame erect in right, she made him circumambulate three times round the Circle with a half-run, half-dance step. Bound, blindfold, running round and in so small a space, Jan's brain reeled giddily; tightly bound as he was he could do nothing but strive to keep his feet.

Suddenly he was pulled to a stop, at the south side of the Altar, where he stood swaying, his head reeling.

Morven struck eleven strokes on a little bell, then knelt at his feet, saying: 'In other religions, postulant kneels, as the Priests claim supreme power. But in the Art Magical, we are taught to be humble, so we say . . .'

Kissing his feet:	'Blessed be thy feet that have brought thee in these ways.'
Kissing knees:	'Blessed be thy knees that shall kneel at the sacred Altar.'
Kissing phallus:	'Blessed be the organ of generation, without which we would not be.'
Kissing breasts:	'Blessed be thy breasts, formed in beauty and in strength.'

Kissing lips : 'Blessed be thy lips, which shall utter the sacred names.'

She then made him kneel at the Altar, tying the cable tow to a ring so he was bending forward, and could scarcely move. She then tied his feet together with the cord on his right ankle.

Then, ringing three knells on the little bell, said :

'Art ready to swear thou wilt always be true to the Art?'

Jan replied : 'I will.'

Morven struck seven knells on the bell, saying :

'Thou first must be purified.'

Taking the scourge from the Altar, she struck his buttocks, first three, then seven, then nine, then twenty-one strokes with the scourge (forty in all).

They were not hard, but blindfold and bound as he was, their effect was startling, they helped to rouse him from the dazed condition he was in from running around the Circle.

As he came more to his senses he realised how utterly helpless he was. In Morven's power, he belonged to her, he was part of her, the blows that were raining on his buttocks gave her power over him, but he did not resent it, she had power over his mind, but that was as it should be, all he wanted was her, if he was hers he would be part of her, and that was all he wanted.

Then the blows ceased, and Morven's voice came.

'Art always ready to protect, help and defend thy brothers and sisters of the Art?'

Jan : 'I am.'

'Then say after me : "I, Jan, in the presence of the mighty ones of the outer spaces, do of my own free will most solemnly swear that I will ever keep secret and never reveal the secrets of the Art, except it be to a proper person, properly prepared, within such a Circle as I am in now, and that I will never deny the secrets to such a person, if they be properly vouched for, by a brother or sister of the Art. All this I swear by my hopes of a future life, and may my weapons turn against me if I break this my solemn oath".'

He felt the cords loosed from his feet, then the cord from the Altar, the blindfold was whisked off, and hands still bound, he was assisted to his feet, where he stood, blinking, dazed, and yet somehow he felt so happy.

Morven knelt before him; he heard her voice as in a dream.

'I hereby consecrate thee with oil. I hereby consecrate thee with wine. I hereby consecrate thee with my lips, priest and witch,' and he felt the touches, first the phallus and then right breast, then phallus again, forming a triangle. Then she rose and loosed his hands, saying :

'Now I present thee with the working tools of a witch.'

Handing him a sword from the Altar, and motioning him to touch it.

'First the Màgic Sword. With this as with the Athame, Thou canst form all Magic Circles, dominate, subdue and punish all rebellious spirits and demons, and even persuade the angels and geniuses. With this in thy hand thou art the ruler of the Magic Circle,' and she kissed him.

'Next I present the Athame. This is the true witches' weapon, it has all the powers of the Magic Sword.' (Again a kiss.)

'Next I present the White Handled Knife. Its use is to form all instruments used in the Art. It can only be properly used within a Magic Circle.' (Again a kiss.)

'Next I present the Censer of Incense; this is to encourage and welcome good spirits and to banish evil spirits.' (A kiss.)

'Next I present the Scourge; this is a sign of power and domination, it is also to cause suffering and purification, for it is written : To learn thou must suffer and be purified. Art thou willing to suffer to learn?'

Jan : 'I am.' (Again a kiss.)

'Next and lastly I present the Cords. They are of use to bind the sigils, the material basis, and to enforce thy will, also, they are necessary in the oath.'

Morven again kissed him, saying : 'I salute thee in the name of the Gods, newly-made priest and witch.'

They then both circumambulated the Circle, Morven proclaiming at the four quarters :

'Hear ye, mighty ones, Jan hath been consecrated priest and witch. I thank ye for attending, and I dismiss ye to your pleasant abodes. Hail and farewell.'

On the day following Jan's initiation, Morven and Thur decided to conduct a second special ritual, at which Thur would play the major role, for they were now in need of some talismans, sigils and pentacles for use in their Great Circle. Though these magical names are often used indiscriminately to describe each other, there is an important difference between them. A sigil means a sign, on parchment, or a medal, made with the object of controlling one particular spirit, usually to summon him up to the Circle, and it bears his own peculiar design. The knowledge of these designs is one of the great secrets which the Magus must master, because a spirit will strive his utmost to keep this sign of his individuality hidden, to prevent mortals obtaining power over him. If a certain spirit is particularly favourable to him, a Magus may make use of this sigil as a talisman, but this is not common.

When a sigil is written on paper or parchment it is often described as a seal, whereas if a talisman or pentacle is inscribed on parchment, it is not a seal, the difference being that a sigil or seal belongs to one individual spirit, while a talisman or pentacle belongs either to one human being, or in a general way, to all the spirits serving one governing spirit, like Mars, Saturn or Venus, as the case may be. A pentacle is also a medal used to evoke a spirit and command him, it is in addition a figure like a five-pointed star, and should always be drawn and used with one point uppermost, and never with two points uppermost. From their nature, certain pentacles can be carried outside the circle and worn with a view to bringing good fortune, such as the pentacle of Venus for love, of Jupiter for success and prosperity. A pentacle of Saturn will induce his good qualities of steadiness, perseverance and loyalty, but this can only be carried by one born under Saturn; to anyone else it would bring disaster. A soldier born under any sign could wear a pentacle of Mars, with advantage, which might produce quarrelsomeness in a merchant, while the latter would be well advised to wear one of Mercury. While a medal such as described above is sometimes called a Talisman, this name should more properly be kept for articles made especially for its owner, with the express intention of bringing him success in what particular object he has in view, and are made in accordance with the owner's horoscope. They are usually made by an expert, in the proper day and hour, with the special object in view of protection and safety, with prosperity, gain, and success for the subject firmly fixed in his mind. The Talisman is then consecrated with magical formulae. In some such way Thur and Morven had made theirs.

Bathed and consecrated, the two prepared their small circle at midnight for at any other hour they would be liable to intrusion, with subsequent denunciation of sorcery. Thur placed in the centre a small table, to serve the double purpose of Altar and work-bench. Beside it was a glowing brazier fed and at an even high temperature, also to serve him generally as an acolyte serves a priest. She had, however, a much more important part to play in the actual ritual, which was to fix her mind unwaveringly on the work, to do her best to make it fluid, so that by welding it with his as it were, he derived added strength. For this concentration of the will upon the object of the ritual there must be no means of distraction. Everything used must have been made with this object in view, so everything used brings to the brain of the Magus, the reason of the work. Therefore was Thur clad in the symbolic pure, clean white linen robe, signifying light, strength and purity, also, this is important, bearing no colour or pattern that could distract the mind of the wearer or his acolyte. For the same reason the girl was nude, this signified purity unsullied, and the natural magnetism in the human body could flow unhindered to the support of the Magus. Here would be no temptation, no distraction for him in this beauty unadorned because he must be immune to such conditions, ere he may become a Magus, for if he cannot at all times prevent his mind from straying, failure in his enterprises would be inevitable; rather was such nudity an added strength to him, for by its presence it signifies the strength of his will and the power of his self-control. For a Magus must ever work with a naked woman till nudity is naught to him, lest an evil or mischievous spirit should appear thus and so ruin an operation.

Throughout the practice of High Magic, or Art Magic as it is often called, the emphasis is upon purity and strength, and through purity, strength of will and self-control. Without these no man may become a Magus, though by trickery and self-deception he may become a great rogue, but with them, even in a small degree he may go far along the road in his search into the hidden mysteries, for by a rigid self-discipline, self-control can be extended and strengthened almost to any limit, and by patience and rigorous exercise the will can become such a dominating factor and obtain such power that nothing can withstand its impact. Therefore a great Magus should also be a great man. By the habit of self-control which is the essence of Magic, he attains to abstinence, which, in its turn gives him health and vigour. The habit of faith, which is essential to success in the Art, faith in God and His goodness, faith in right-eousness, absolute faith in the ritual he performs, in its efficacy and in the success of its object, through the ritual; and finally, supreme faith in himself, firstly as a willing servant of God, and secondly in his power as a Magus; such faith is in itself a purifying element in any life. The application to close study through long hours of poring over intricate manuscripts, the patient repetition of obscure rites until success is obtained, indicate high qualities of mind. The fact that no Magus can work for himself and his own advancement, or work for another with solely evil purposes, imposes a certain rectitude of conduct upon him. If he fell from his high status of being a helper and benefactor to others through his Art, descending to use it for harmful purposes, the reaction upon himself would in the mediaeval mind be in proportion to the magnitude and wickedness of his success, and dire retribution would swiftly overtake him for having corrupted his Art. Therefore, by all the laws of his Art, such good qualities as a Magus possessed are devel-oped to their utmost. Indeed, one might say that without a number of good qualities in his character a man could never become a Magus. There have been many charlatans who have claimed the title of Magus by hypnotism or by plain trickery; they imposed upon the credulity of thousands, also sometimes they may have possessed powers of clairvoyance which they have misused for gain. It is these tricksters and glib rogues who have brought the Art into disrepute, and for which they have afterwards suffered.

It is the fashion today to laugh at the Magus and his pretensions, to picture him as either a charlatan or a doddering old fool, and bearing the slightest resemblance to the men who were in fact, the scientists of the day, who gave us alcohol, but not the Atom Bomb.

Four other braziers were in their appointed places around the Circle. Upon the altar-table lay the athame, the Magic Sword, the burin and the sprinkler, also materials for their work, four iron discs, two-and-a-half inches in diameter, already purified by fire, had been prepared previously. There were writing materials, lengths of cord, some black cloths and a scourge, laid ready. Before the bench were two stools. The inner Circle, some seven feet in diameter, was already drawn on the floor, surrounding it was a double Circle eight feet in diameter, with names of power between the two. Thur took the Magic Sword and retraced all the markings with its point, for the painted Circle has no power of protection, which comes from power of the Magic Sword or the athame. It but serves as a guide to the latter, to ensure they draw the Circle perfectly. The Circle drawn, Thur recited appropriate Psalms, and began to make the Talismans and Pentacles. Iron is the metal of Mars, the spirit of War under whom Jan was born, and as it was for a warlike purpose, Thur proposed to summon his spirit Bartzebal to Jan's aid. Taking one of the iron discs Thur described a circle on it with the burin, inside this circle he scratched the mystical characters of Mars and outside, between it and the edge, he wrote in Hebrew the names, EDIMIEL, BARTZACHHIAHESCHIEL and ITHUREL; this was for invoking the spirits of Mars in general.

On the second he engraved within the Circle an equilateral triangle surmounted at the apex with a pentacle. Within this triangle a smaller inverted triangle was drawn with a great Vau, and round it the name ELOH.

Between the circle and the edge was written in Hebrew: 'Who is so great as ELOHIM?'

This pentacle was for the purpose of exciting war, wrath, discord and for the overthrowing of enemies. The third pentacle, the Circle, was divided into four equal parts with a star pentacle above, it had in the centre the word AGLA IHVH, repeated twice, above and below. All was in Hebrew, as were also the words of the text written between the circle and the outer edge. 'The Lord is my right hand, and he shall wound even kings in the day of his wrath.' This was to give power in war, and would bring victory. The fourth had inside the Circle, written in the secret characters of the Malachim script, the words, Elohim Quibor, 'God hath protected me.' Outside the Circle was written a text from Psalm xxxvii, 15; written in Hebrew, 'Their swords shall enter into their own hearts and their bows shall be broken.' This pentacle was to give strength and courage in fighting and ultimate victory. Upon the reverse of each of these pentacles was engraved the Sigil of Bartzebal. Having finished engraving them, he purified them anew in the incense smoke which arose from the herbs and spices Morven cast upon the centre brazier. Each planet has its different and appropriate incense and for Mars they used euphorbia, bedellium, ammoniac, lodestone and sulphur. This matter of incense is of the greatest importance in the ritual, as it must be of the nature of the spirit, not only does it influence the spirit conjured, but all surrounding objects; it lies heavy upon the air and the Magus breathes it deep

into his lungs, making him of one nature with the spirit, the fragrance and density attracts and draws the conjured spirit, partly
because it is of his nature, and partly because of the pleasure it
gives him. It is from its density he obtains the means to build up
a body and so materialise. To increase the affinity, the brazier which
was used for heating was fed with sticks of dried thorn and wild
rose. When all were censed and purified, Thur took a strand of
cord and bound each, winding it round thrice, and tying it with
three separate knots, then wrapped each in a separate black cloth
and laid them in their order on the west side of the Circle, sprinkled
them with consecrated water, baptising them and saying, 'I hereby
consecrate thee, O creature of Mars and of iron, Bartzebal.' Then
he held each in the smoke of the incense, saying : 'By fire and water
I consecrate thee. Thou art him, and He is ye, in thought, in feeling, and in sight, as I bind ye, I bind him, as I loose ye, I loose him.
By the sacred name Abracadabra. Amen.'

From thence onwards the table served as an altar. Upon it Thur
now placed the four pentacles, he repeated over them the words he
had just spoken, the words of consecration and dedication, and
then announced solemnly, in a loud and clear voice, that all these
purposes would be accomplished. Still using the same firm and
distinct utterance he declared : 'All has been prepared and is in
readiness to charge these pentacles with power, I summon all ye
spirits of the nature of Mars, and command ye to attend.' The
critical moments of the ritual were approaching, Thur took the
Magic Sword, Morven took her athame, and while they held the
points of their weapons on the first pentacle, Thur recited slowly
and with the utmost intensity he could summon. 'Adonai, Most
Powerful; El, Most Strong; Agla, Most Holy; Oh, Most Righteous.
Azoth, the Beginning and the End, Thou who hast established
all things in thy Wisdom; Thou who hast granted unto Solomon
Thy servant these pentacles by Thy great mercy for the preserva-
tion of both soul and body; we most humbly implore and supplicate
Thy Most Holy Majesty that these pentacles may be consecrated by
Thy power in such a manner that they may obtain virtue and
strength against all spirits, through Thee, O Most Holy Adonai,
Whose Kingdom, Empire and Principality endureth without end.
Amen.'

With the point of his sword Thur traced in the air above the first
pentacle the symbols engraved on its disc.

This ceremony with the points of the weapons, the above invocation and consecration together with the aerial tracing of the symbols, was repeated without variation of any sort over each pentacle in turn. When all this was accomplished, with equal intensity directed upon them, Thur took each in turn in his left hand and smote it thrice with the flat of his sword. Coming again to the first pentacle, he took it in his left hand and with the sword erect in his right hand he circumambulated the Circle, holding up the veiled disc to the four quarters, west, north, east and south; this procedure was followed without deviation with each in turn. Each time placing the pentacles on the floor, this time in the south, and repeating the former consecration with fire and water, adding : 'O, creatures of iron and Mars, twice consecrated, thou mayest approach the gates of the south.' He circumambulated the Circle again. Then taking the first pentacle he carefully unwrapped it, not removing the veil, but leaving the disc covered with the ends hanging down. He smote it once with the sword then held it at arms' length while he elevated the sword above it. Thrice he stamped with his right foot, addressing it. 'Thou canst not pass from concealment to manifestation save by virtue of the name ALHIM. Before all things are chaos and darkness, I am he whose name is darkness. I am the exorcist in the midst of the exorcism. Take on therefore manifestation from me.' He circumambulated again, rewrapped the pentacle and replaced it on the Altar, repeating the ceremony with each in turn. When all were assembled on the Altar, he again partially unveiled the first and summoning Morven with a gesture, she held her athame above it; while he held his sword in a like manner, he conjured it saying : 'By all the powers and rites, I conjure Thee, render this pentacle irresistible, O Lord Adonai.' When this had been repeated over each he reveiled the pentacles and carried them to the north, laying them on the ground, opening each veil completely, saying : 'Thou canst not pass from concealment to manifestation save by the name JHV [Jehovah].'

Reveiling them he passed to the south, and laid them on the ground, and entirely removing the veils from each, but leaving them bound, this done he invoked : 'O Bartzebal, too long hast thou been in darkness. Quit the night and seek the day. As light is hidden in darkness, yet can manifest itself therefrom, so shalt thou manifest from concealment unto manifestation.'

The words, 'So shalt thou manifest,' were spoken with such a degree of concentrated will, that Thur's tanned face took on almost a greenish hue, so great was the concentrated effort he made.

Reveiling them he took the pentacles from the floor and replaced them on the Altar, again invoking he held them in turn towards heaven, saying : 'I conjure upon thee power and might irresistible, by the powers of DANI, ZEMUCH, AGATMATUROD, EODIEL, PANI, CANELOAS, MEROD, GAMODI, BALDOI, METRATOR.'

Now he laid his sword down and taking the scourge, smote each in turn, saying over each as he did so : 'By, and in the NAME of ELOHIM, I invoke into thee the powers of Mars and the powers of war,' and released the cords binding them. As he said this over the first of the pentacles, a chill crept up Morven's spine and over her scalp. Witch and believer in witchery as she proclaimed herself, here was a manifestation of power she had never seen; for the pentacle glowed with a sullen redness, infinitely menacing and terrible. In its small circumference it seemed to hold all the cruel, remorseless wantonness of war. On each in turn as he invoked, he bore down upon it the whole might of his highly-trained mental strength, so was each infused with the same smouldering red fire, and Thur realised his prayers had been answered, the consecration had been successful.

After a moment's pause, as though to gather his faculties which had been strained to a snapping point, Thur stood erect and prayed :

'I thank Thee, O LORD OF HOSTS, for the favour Thou hast manifested to me.'

Standing so, with his face to the Heavens, he looked truly inspired. Then he relaxed, sinking on one of the stools before the Altar-table. His head sunk forward on his breast, his whole pose expressed acute physical exhaustion, and he panted quickly. Morven watched him in silent solicitude, not daring to speak. Presently he was sufficiently recovered to make a sign towards the Altar, where the pentacles lay. Understanding, Morven wrapped the newly consecrated pentacles in a clean cloth and put them with other articles in the casket; this she stowed away in a hiding place. Then she collected the tools they had used, from time to time stealing anxious glances at Thur, who still sat upon his stool, his robe hitched up showing his bare legs and feet, his hands hanging listlessly between his knees.

The two had presented an embodiment of perfect service and perfect leadership.

Suddenly she felt a glow of happiness and contentment, a sense of peace such as she had never known.

A MODERN MAGIC CIRCLE DRAWN
BY GERALD GARDNER

Afterword

Since the death of Gerald Gardner, the Occult world has failed to produce another magician of the stature of those recalled in the pages of this book. Indeed, despite the very widespread interest in all aspects of 'the unknown' evidenced both by the general public and the burgeoning number of students of the Occult, the skill and depth of learning among the *known* adepts has grown less and less. While it is not my contention that these people are any the less sincere than their predecessors, it does seem that their involvement fails to reach the previous limits of dedication while their desire for acclaim and publicity mounts with increasing rapidity. Perhaps it is the structure of our society and its widespread acceptance of so much that is strange and weird which is the real cause of this decline in proficiency among practitioners. Whatever the reason, we now have a surfeit of adepts, but no Magi.

My extensive travelling and contact with people in occult societies and groups throughout Europe and America has brought me into contact with several of today's leading figures, such as Sybil Leek, the English witch now established as America's leading astrologer; Alex Saunders, the reputed 'King of the Witches' whose publicity-seeking has tended to bring into question his undoubted ability; Louise Huebner, Los Angeles' 'Official Witch' and dynamic proponent of the benefits of white witchcraft; and the extraordinary leader of the 'First Church of Satan', Anton Sandor La Vey. All these people, plus a good many more whose names are less well known, are the heirs of Levi, Yeats, Crowley, Dion Fortune and Gerald Gardner. Will they in time prove to be worthy successors or concerned more with personal image-building and commercial success? Will they tread further down the shadowy paths of mystery into the unknown or simply embrace the arts as they already exist without elaboration or experimentation? The occult world demands, as Eliphas Levi put it, 'To Know, To Dare, To Will, To Keep Silent'. It remains to be seen whether or not the magicians of the 'seventies can fulfil these requirements.

P.H.